THE LONE WOLF AND THE BEAR

Pitt Series in Russian
and East European Studies

Jonathan Harris, Editor

MOSHE GAMMER

The Lone Wolf and the Bear

Three Centuries of Chechen Defiance of Russian Rule

University of Pittsburgh Press

*To Ruthy and Bilie,
the Jachin and Boaz of my inspiration.*

Published by the University of Pittsburgh Press, Pittsburgh, PA 15260
Copyright © 2006, Moshe Gammer
Manufactured in India
Printed on acid-free paper
10 9 8 7 6 5 4 3 2 1
ISBN 0-8229-5898-8

We are wolves,
Compared to dogs, we are few.
To the sound of double-barrelled guns
We have declined over time.
As in an execution
We soundlessly fell to the ground
but we have survived,
Even though we are banned.
We are wolves.
We are few.
There are hardly any of us.
We, wolves and dogs, share one mother,
But we refused to surrender.
Your lot is bowls with food,
Ours is hunger on frozen ground
Animals' tracks,
Snowfall under silent stars.
In the January frosts
You are allowed inside,
While we are surrounded by
A tightening ring of red lights.
You peep out through a crack in the door,
We roam in the woods.
You are really wolves
But you had not the guts for it.
You were grey,
Once you were brave,
But you were handed scraps
And became slaves.
You are glad to serve and flatter
For a crust of bread,
But the leash and chain
Are your prize—and well deserved!
Tremble in your cages
When we are out hunting!
Because, more than any bear,
We wolves hate
Dogs.

Anonymous poem widely
known and memorised by
Chechen youth during the
late Soviet period

CONTENTS

MAPS

PREFACE AND ACKNOWLEDGEMENTS

Chechnya's declaration of independence in 1991, Moscow's failure to prevent it, the first Russo-Chechen war (1994–6) which ended in Russian military defeat, followed by the second war (1999–) which at the moment of writing seems far from over, have generated a great deal of interest in, and consequently a growing number of publications about, the events themselves and the small people confronting a major World Power. However, to Chechen nationalists the events of the recent dozen-or-so years have not been isolated episodes. To them (and to the Islamists) they are simply the latest rounds in what they call their 'three hundred year long war' with Russia. This book is a study of this 'war', or rather, of Russo-Chechen relations since Russia first tried to expand into the Caucasus, in the sixteenth century. As relations with Russia have been crucial in the Chechens' lives, it is also a study in modern Chechen history.

A study of Chechen history has to tackle three sets of problems: the general ones, common to all studies of history; those related to the histories of ex-colonies; and problems specific to Russian and Soviet sources. On the general level each study depends on the quantity and quality of sources whose credibility and bias have to be taken into account. Sources, whether primary or secondary, do not necessarily report events accurately and therefore have to be approached with extreme caution. This is especially true of military and intelligence reports. The former, despite best intentions to 'stick to the facts', are written in the emotional turmoil following a battle and tend to exaggerate. The latter on many occasions intend purposefully to disperse disinformation.

In the case of ex-colonies the problem is the lack of interest on the part of the colonial power to study its colonies' histories. Only those parts related to 'pacification' and colonial rule are dealt with. The result is a lack of local sources, not because they do not exist, but because no one has been interested in uncovering them. Hence the histories of many ex-colonies have until fairly recently resembled maps of unknown continents, with only vague outlines of their shores and almost all the territory remaining blank.

Any study of Chechen history also suffers from a severe shortage of sources. The local ones have not only been disregarded, but in many cases destroyed. In some cases this happened during fighting, in others—especially during the Stalin years—it was done on purpose. The accessibility of Russian and Soviet sources—especially archives—has been limited, even after the dissolution of the Soviet Union. Moreover the available sources are affected by the Russian—and to a much greater extent Soviet—tradition to 'improve on the truth' in reports on all levels. The results are particularly problematic in the case of Soviet secret police sources, where it is impossible to be sure whether reported plots were real or invented by the reports' authors.

Furthermore, Chechen history resembles not only an ex-colonial blank map, but also a Soviet map of public consumption for which geographical data have been intentionally falsified. In other words, the little that is known of Chechen history has been severely distorted to fit Soviet policies and formulae. Even after the dissolution of the Soviet Union bias has remained. Most of the reports of events in Chechnya come from or via Moscow and thus reflect Russian biases. And many publications on Chechnya in the West tend to take sides for reasons alien to the Russo-Chechen conflict. Consequently too many of those siding with the Chechens do so because of Russophobia, while too many of those siding with Russia do so out of Islamophobia—having heard that the Chechens are Muslims.

It is true that in an age when even science has renounced any claims to 'objectivity', one cannot assert impartiality. Nevertheless, one has to admit one's biases and prejudices and attempt to remain distant from them. However, trying to do this does not mean being indifferent on moral issues. In this case, the author firmly believes in Lenin's words (which Lenin himself seems never to have meant seriously):

If any nation whatsoever is retained as part of a given State by force, if despite its expressed desire—whether expressed in the press, in popular assemblies, in the decisions of political parties, or by *rebellions and insurrections against national oppression*—it has not the right of choosing freely—the troops of the annexing or, generally, the more powerful nation being completely withdrawn and without any pressure being brought to bear—the constitutional forms of its national existence, then its incorporation is an annexation, that is, seizure and coercion.[1]

Finally, this book aims at presenting a concise introductory history of the Chechen defiance of Russian power since the sixteenth century. It is not a definitive study because by definition no study of history—indeed in the humanities as a whole—can be. Rather, its aim is to raise interest in the subject and promote further study.

Acknowledgements

Part of the expense for this study was covered by a grant from the Research Authority of Tel Aviv University. An important part of it was done during my stay at the Institute for Advanced Studies of the Hebrew University in Jerusalem. I am grateful to Professor Reuven Amitai and Dr Michal Biran for inviting me to the Institute and to both the Institute and its staff—Liba Maimon, Shani Feldman, Smadar Danziger, Dalia Avieli, Anette Orelle and Avi Aleharar—for their efficient and instant help on any matter.

I was assisted by too many individuals to be able to mention them all here. Among them were Mayrbek Vachagayev, Julietta Meskhidze, Marius Labentowicz and Oktay F. Tanrisever, who provided information, insights and references at crucial moments, and Anatoly Khazanov, Michael Reynolds and Yagil Henkin, who also read the draft and made useful comments. Needless to say, all mistakes are my own.

Finally, this study would not have been completed without the support, encouragement, endless patience and inspiration of my family. I am grateful to them all.

July 2005 M.G.

---

[1] 'Declaration of Rights of the Peoples of Russia', quoted in Robert Conquest, *The Nation Killers: The Soviet Deportation of Nationalities* (London: Macmillan, 1970), pp. 31–2. Emphasis by Conquest.

TRANSLITERATION AND THE CALENDAR

Transliteration from Russian is used as a rule in direct quotations, in Russian terms and in quoted works. Russified Chechen names as well as many Russian ones are rendered in their phonetic value rather than in transliteration. For example, Yeltsin and Yermolov, not Eltsin and Ermolov. Transliteration from Arabic and Chechen is a rather simplified one, without diacritics. Only the *'ayn* ('), the *hamza* (') and the guttural k (q) are retained.

As a rule only the Gregorian ('New Style') calendar is used throughout the book. In the few cases in which either the Julian ('Old Style') or the Hijri (Muslim) calendar is used this fact is stated.

This book is aimed at an English-reading audience. Therefore, all quotations are translated into English. While the sources are in various languages, references for further reading are kept as far as possible to English-language publications; only when English books or articles are missing is a recommendation made to publications in other languages.

ABBREVIATIONS

AO	Autonomous *Oblast*
ASSR	Autonomous Soviet Socialist Republic
AUMNC	Alliance of the United Mountaineers of the Northern Caucasus
CC	Central Committee
CheKa (ChK)	*Chrezvychainaia Komissiia po bor'be s kontr-revoliutsiei i sabotazhem* (Extraordinarry Commission for Combating Counter-Revolution and Sabotage)
ChINFSP	*Checheno-Ingushskii Narodnyi Front Sodeistviia Perestroike* (Chechen–Ingush Popular Front in Support of Perestroika)
CPSU	Communist Party of the Soviet Union
Dobrarmia	*Dobrovol'cheskaia Armiia* (Volunteer Army)
EC	Executive Committee
FSB	*Federal'naia Sluzhba Bezobzsnosti* (Federal Security Service)
FSU	*Former Soviet Union*
Gorkom	*Gorodskoi Kommitet* (City Committee)
GPU	*see* OGPU
GULag	*Glavnoe Upravlenie Lagerei* (Chief Administration of [detention] Camps)
KGB	*Kommitet Gosudarstrvennoi Bezopastnosti* (Committee for State Security)
Kolkhoz	*Kollektivnoe Khoziaistvo* (collective farm)
Komsomol	*Kommunisticheskii Soiuz Molodezhi* (Communist Youth League)
Kraikom	*Kraevoi Komitet* (Krai Committee)
KUTVa	*Kommunisticheskii Universitet Trudiashchikhsia Vostoka* (Communist University of the Toilers of the East)
OGPU	*Ob'edinennoe Gosudarstvennoe Politicheskoe Upravlenie* (United State Political Directorate)
NKGB	*Narodnyi Kommisariat Gosudastvennoi Bezopastnosti* (People's Commissariat for State Security)

NKVD	*Narodnyi Kommissariat Vnutrennikh Del* (People's Commissariat for Internal Affairs)
NSKPB	*Narodnaia Severo-Kavkazskaia Partiia Brat'ev* (People's Northern Caucasus Party of Brothers)
Obkom	*Oblastnoi Kommitet* (Oblast Committee)
OKChN	*Obshchenatsional'nyi Kongress Chechnskogo Naroda* (All-National Congress of the Chechen People)
OPKB	*Osvoboditel'naia Partiia Kavkazskikh Brat'ev* (Liberation party of the Caucasian Brothers)
OSCE	Organization of Security and Cooperation in Europe
Politruk	*Politicheskii Rukovoditel* (Political Guide)
Raiispolkom	*Raionnyi Ispolnitel'nyi Kommitet* (Regional [Sub-District] EC)
Raikom	*Raionnyi Kommitet* (Regional Committee)
Revkom	*Revoliutsionnyi Komitet* (Revolutionary Committee)
RSFSR	Russian Soviet Federated Socialist Republic
Selsovet'	*Sel'skoi Sovet* (Village Council)
SMERSH	Smert' Shpionam (Death to Spies)
Sovkhoz	*Sovetskoe Khoziaistvo* (Soviet [state] farm)
Spetskomendatura	*spetsial'naia komendatura* (Special Headquarters)
Spetsnaselentsy	*Spetsial'nye Nasselentsy* (Special Settlers)
SSR	Soviet Socialist Republic
TOZ	*tovarishchestvo obrabotki zemli* (Association of Land Cultivation)
TsIK	*Tsentral'nyii Ispolnitel'nyi Kommitet* (Central Executive Committee)
Venkommissar	*Voennyi Kommissar* (Military Commissar)
VUZ	*Vysshee Uchebnoe Zavedenie* (Institution of Higher Education)

GLOSSARY

abrek	bandit of honour
'adat	customary law
'alim (pl. *'ulama*)	learned man in Islam; doctor of Islamic law
amanat	hostage
aqsaqal	chief
aul	mountain village
borz	wolf
boyeviki	fighters (contemporary Chechen fighters are referred to in this way in the Russian sources)
chekist	member of the Soviet secret police
dhikr (*zikr*)	the main Sufi ceremony, in which members might attain a mystical experience
dözal	extended family
gar	clan
gazavat	holy war
glasnost'	'openness' (the policy carried out by Gorbachev in 1985-91)
guberniia	Province (in imperial Russia)
gyavur	infidel
haj	pilgrimage to Mecca
imam	leader
inogorodtsy	landless Slavic peasants renting land from the Cossacks
jigit	brave man, master of horsemanship excelling in martial skills
jihad	holy war
kafirun	infidels
kanly	blood feud
khutor	isolated farm, hamlet
kinjal	dagger
krai	province
kulak	Soviet term to designate 'rich' peasant

madrasa	Islamic institution of higher learning where *'ulama* are trained
majlis	council
maktab	Islamic institution of elementary education
marsho	freedom
Mavlud (Mawlid)	festival celebrating the birthday of the Prophet Muhammad or of
'saints',	usually Sufi sheikhs
mazar	place of pilgrimage
Mehq-Qel	'Council of the Land' deciding matters common to some or all tuqums
militsia	official Soviet name for the police
Miuridism	usual Russian name for the Naqshbandi brotherhood in the Cuacasus
munafiq (pl. munafiqun)	'hypocrite', i.e. collaborator with the Russians
murid	Sufi disciple
murshid	Sufi master
mut'a	marriage for a limited period after the elapse of which it is annulled automatically (practised by Shi'ites)
na'ib	deputy; administrative (and military) post under the Imams and the Russian empire
naibstvo (na'ibdom)	adminstrative unit headed by a na'ib
namaz	prayer
neq'i	clan
nokhchalla	norms and code of honour obligatory for all Chechens
nomenklatura	Soviet political elite
oblast	district
okrug	administrative unit; sub-district
partokratiia	nickname of the ex-Soviet elite in the post-Soviet space
perestroika	'reconstruction'. Gorbachev's policy in 1985-91
pristav	police officer in imperial Russia (also title given to various administrative posts)
qadi	judge according to the *shari'a*
Qurban Bayram (*'Id al-Adha*)	one of the two major Islamic festivals, celebrated in memory of Ishmael's deliverance from sacrifice by Abraham
raion	administrative unit, sub-district
shari'a	Islamic law
sheikh	Sufi master

shura	council
sovet	council
stanitsa	Cossack settlement
Sufism	the mystical current in Islam
ta'ifa	Sufi brotherhood
tariqa	the mystical way followed by a *ta'ifa*, also designating a Sufi brotherhood
Tawhli	'highlander', traditional Chechen name for a Daghestani
te'ip	tribe
terskii konnyi polk	Terek [Irregular] Cavalry Regiment
tsa'	extended family
tuqum	tribal confederation
'ulama	*see 'alim*
umma	the (Sunni) Muslim community
Uraz Bayram ('Id al-Fitr)	one of the two Islamic festivals, celebrates the end of the month of Ramadan
uzden	free man
Vaynakh	joint name of Chechens, Ingush and other kindred groups
vekil	deputy of a Sufi sheikh
vird	sub-order
Yezhovshchina	familiar name for the 1937 purges in the USSR
zakat	alms
Zikrizm	usual Russian name for the Qadiri brotherhood in the Caucasus
ziyart	place of pilgrimage

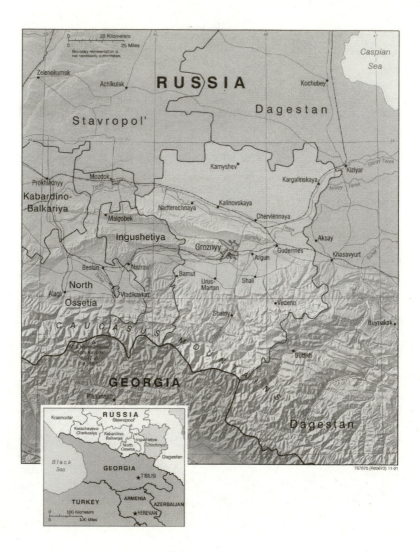

The topography of Chechnya.

Part I. BACKGROUND

The earth will dry on my grave,
Mother, my Mother!
And thou wilt forget me!
And over me rank grasses wave,
Father, my Father!
Nor wilt thou regret me!
When tears come thy dark eyes to lave,
Sister, dear Sister!
No more will grief fret thee!
But thou, my Brother the Elder, wilt never forget,
With vengeance denied me!
And thou, my Brother the Younger, wilt ever regret
Till thou liest beside me!
Hotly thou comest, oh death-bearing ball that I spurned,
For thou wast my Slave!
And thou, black earth, that my battle-steed tramples and churned,
Wilt cover my grave!
Cold art Thou, oh Death, yet I was thy Lord and Master!
My body sinks fast to earth; my Soul to Heaven flies faster![1]

---

[1] Chechen death song translated by John F. Baddeley, *The Russian Conquest of the Caucasus* (London: Longmans, Green, 1908), pp. 488–9.

1

THE PEOPLE AND THE LAND

The ethnic and linguistic composition of its population probably makes the 1,100-kilometres-long and 32 to 180-kilometres-wide range of the Caucasus the most varied area in the world. It is home to more than seventy native ethnic groups, the largest of which consists of the Chechens who in 1989, in the last Soviet census, numbered about a million people.

Chechnya, the Chechens' land, is a quadrilateral located in the north-eastern part of the Caucasus, demarcated by the Terek and Sunja rivers in the west and the north, the 'Andi range in the east which separates it from Daghestan, and the snow-covered twin range of the Caucasus in the south which separates it from Georgia. Like the rest of the Northern Caucasus, Chechnya is divided by parallel, gradually decreasing ranges running north-west to south-east. The northernmost and lowest of these are the Terek (Terekskii) and Sunja (Sundzhenskii) ranges located between the rivers after which they are named. The heartland of Chechnya—the low-land—lies between the Sunja range and river and the 'black mountains' (*chernye gory*).[2] It is in fact the widest of the valleys running between the different ranges. It is crossed by the Sunja's numerous tributaries, which cut through the mountain ranges in deep ravines and canyons. Their high water occurs, as all over the Caucasus, in the summer, when snow and ice melt in the higher altitudes.

Most of Chechnya is situated within the forest zone of the Caucasus. Before the Russian conquest it formed one dense primeval forest and even at the beginning of the 21st century the country still

---

[2] So called because being covered by dense forests they look dark against the background of the snow-covered main range.

had a great number of wooded areas, especially in the mountains. Thus it imposes a combination of two of the most difficult and complicated modes of war on any regular army used to pitched battle: mountain and forest warfare. In all the battles with the imperial Russian and Soviet armies the Chechens displayed great mastery in using these features to their advantage. In the 1990s they also proved their ability to adjust to modern conditions by imposing urban warfare on the Russian Federal forces and transforming the cities—first and foremost the capital Groznyi—into latter-day forests.

The Chechens derive their by now international name from the village of Chechen Aul, where the Russians first encountered them. Their self-appellation is Nokhchi, meaning 'people' or 'our people'. They are closely related to the Ingush living to the west and to the Kists who live south of the main range in Georgia.[3] Both groups are considered by the Chechens to be Chechen tribes, although the Ingush regard themselves as a separate people.[4] The languages they speak are mutually intelligible and belong to the Nakh sub-group of the north-eastern group of the Caucasian linguistic family. Accordingly, all three—Chechens, Ingush and Kists—are also referred to as Vaynakhs.

The Nakh languages are related to the language of the Hurrians, the founders of the ancient kingdoms of Mittani and Urartu. This gave rise to the claim of Chechen nationalist historiography that the Chechens are the descendants of these peoples, states and cultures and as such were the bearers of civilisation when in the fourth century BCE they moved north to their present habitat.[5] Some Russian ethnographers too hold that the high moral demands of the *nokhchalla*—the norms and code of honour obligatory on each Chechen—are signs that these people are the remnants of a highly

---

[3] The Chechens and Ingush are Sunni Muslims of the Hanafi school. The Kists are Orthodox Christians.

[4] See Alexandre Bennigsen and S. Enders Wimbush, *The Muslims of the Soviet Empire: A Guide* (London: Hurst, 1985), p. 189.

[5] L. O. Bubakhin and D[olkhan] A.-A. Khozhayev, 'Potomki Nefertiti', *Komsomol'skoe plemia* (Groznyi), 11 February 1989, p. 10; Lema Usmanov, *Nepokorennaia Chechnia* (Moscow: Izdatel'skii dom Parus, 1997), pp. 32–4; and cf. Yakub Vagapov, *Vainakhi i Sarmaty. Nakhskii plast v Sarmatskoi onomastike* (Groznyi: Kniga, 1990).

developed ancient civilisation.[6] However, very little is known of the Chechens' history before their encounter with Russia, since both imperial Russia and the Soviet Union discouraged its study. In a typically colonialist attitude the Chechens, like almost all the other non-Slavic peoples of the Soviet Union, were described as a *geschichtslose Nation* to whom Russia brought the light and blessings of civilisation.[7]

When encountered by Russia, the Chechens shared with all the other ethnic groups of the Northern Caucasus a common culture. In spite of ethnic and linguistic differences all these groups defined themselves as 'Mountaineers' (*gortsy* in Russian) and regarded themselves as akin to each other. Within a certain range of variation they all led a similar way of life, wore similar clothes and had similar traditions and customs. Some anthropologists classified their culture as belonging to the nomadic-patriarchal type.[8] What they meant was:

1. Even though the Mountaineers were not nomads, and while farming was their main occupation, the basis of economic life was livestock. Consequently people kept their wealth in herds of horses, cattle and especially sheep and goats.

2. Society was divided along patrilineal lines into extended families (*dözal* or *tsa'* in Chechen), clans (*gar* or *neq'i*), tribes (*te'ip*) and tribal confederations (*tuqum*). These served, with a different emphasis at each level, as foci of identification and mutual responsibility and were at the basis of the political, social and economic structures. One result of this configuration was extreme vigilance over one's freedom and the strong rejection of any authority external to the kin group. Another, in the case of murder, was vendetta (*kanly*).

---

[6] For example, Ian Veniaminovich Chesnov, 'Civilization and the Chechen', *Anthropology and Archaeology of Eurasia*, 34, 3 (winter 1995–6), pp. 28–40.

[7] Lowell R. Tillet, *The Great Friendship: Soviet Historians on the Non-Russian Nationalities* (Chapel Hill: University of North Carolina Press, 1969). For an example of this condescending attitude, see E.A. Varavina *et al.* (eds), *Ot vekovoi otstalosti-k sotsializmu. Osushchestvlenie leninskoi natsional'noi politiki v Checheno-Ingushetii (1917–1941gg.). Sbornik dokumentov i materialov* (Groznyi: Checheno-Ingushskoe Knizhnge Izdatelstvo, 1977). For the latest textbook of Chechen history, see Yavus Z. Ahmadov, *Istoriia Chechni s drevneiskikh vremen do kontsa XVIII veka* (Moscow: Mir Domu Tvoemu, 2001).

[8] Lewis J. Luzbetac, *Marriage and Family in Caucasia: A Contribution to the Study of*

3. They were a 'martial race', to use a nineteenth-century British term, raised to be warriors.[9] Frequent mutual raids were a manifestation of this spirit. People were seldom hurt in these raids, their object being almost exclusively the capture of cattle and/or horses without becoming entangled in a blood-feud. However, despite the economic importance of capturing the animals, such raids had greater significance: they were first and foremost an initiation test for young warriors in which they could prove their courage and prowess.

These basic values are reflected in the image of the wolf (*borz*), the centrality of which in Chechen self-perception is attested by its having been chosen as the emblem of the republic after independence. In 1997 the martial qualities of the wolf were emphasised by the Chechen author Lema Usmanov:

The lion and the eagle are both embodiments of strength, but they attack only the weak. The wolf is the only creature that dares to take on someone stronger than himself. The wolf's insufficient strength is compensated for with limitless audacity, courage and adroitness. If, however, he has lost the battle he dies silently, expressing neither fear nor pain. And he always dies facing his enemy.[10]

No less significant are its other qualities that the Chechens cherish: the wolf is loyal to its pack and is ready to sacrifice its life for them. Even more important, it loves freedom, cannot be tamed and would rather die resisting than surrender.[11] *Marsho*—freedom—is a central

---

North Caucasian Ethnology and Customary Law (Vienna-Mödling: St Gabriel's Mission Press, 1951). Of course the peoples of the North Caucasus were not nomads and differed in many spheres and respects from the Eurasian nomads roaming to their north.

[9] For a detailed description of Chechen and Daghestani society at the end of the eighteenth century, see Anna Zelkina, *In Quest of God and Freedom: The Sufi Response to the Russian Advances in the North Caucasus (Chechenya and Daghestan)* (London: Hurst, 2000), pp. 14–25.

[10] Usmanov (note 5), p. 42.

[11] The wolf has, however, one evident characteristic that the Chechens tend to keep silent about not to emphasise—it is a predator hunting, sometimes with extreme cruelty, any weaker, unprotected animal. With modernisation and Sovietisation destabilising the patriarchal, patrilineal structure of society and eroding the respect for the *nokhchalla*, incidence of such behaviour became more frequent. The wars of the 1990s, which ruined the social fabric and morality of

concept in both Chechen culture and the Chechen psyche. Although Chechen nationalists attach to it modern Western political connotations, traditionally its meaning went far beyond that of either the Western or the Islamic sense of the word. In the Chechen language the word also contained the connotation of 'peace' and 'well-being'. This is clearly demonstrated in daily greetings: welcoming a male guest Chechens say *'marsha woghiyla'* (*'yoghiyla'* to a woman; literally 'enter in freedom'). Good-bye is *'marsha ghoyla'* (go in freedom). Sending regards Chechens say *'marshalla doiytu'* (wish freedom to…) and proposing a toast they say *'Dala marshall doila'* (may God provide freedom).

To Chechens freedom also means equality. Traditional Vaynakh (and part of their Daghestani neighbours') society was not stratified. The Russians referred to the *tuqums* (and their Daghestani equivalents usually known as *jama'ats*)[12] as 'free societies' (*vol'nye obshchestva*). Land was owned communally and all men belonging to the *tuqum* were free—*uzdens*—and equal members of the community. Each *tuqum* was a sovereign polity. Matters common to some or all *tuqums* were decided in the *Mehq-Qel* (Council of the Land).[13] Consequently freedom, equality and non-acceptance of outside authority have been strongly embedded in the Chechen psyche. One can often hear young men and even teenagers asserting 'I am a free man and obey no one.' When confronted with the fact that they obey their seniors in their own family, the usual reply is: 'Yes, but I do it of my own free will.' Furthermore, these notions of freedom, equality and disobedience are strongly connected to the concepts of honour and manhood. Thus in the early 1990s one could often hear recently demobilised young men boasting how of in the Soviet army (known for its rigid discipline) they had not obeyed their sergeant or officer and had even beaten him up.

Chechen society, brought such behaviour to extremes, of which the 'slave trade' in hostages, mainly between the first and second Russo-Chechen wars, was the ultimate example.

[12] M. A. Aglarov, *Sel'skaia Obshchina v Nagornom Dagestane v XVII-Nachale XIX v.* (Moscow: Nauka, 1988).

[13] Naturally, contemporary Chechen historiography regards the *Mehq-Qel* as the full equivalent of a modern democratic parliament. Recent studies indicate that, contrary to what had been believed, the *Mehq-Qel* was not necessarily and not always a meeting of all the Chechen tribes, and that 'local' *Mehq-Qels* were also convened.

Grasping these concepts is crucial if one is to understand the long Chechen resistance to Russian rule. Generally Chechen society has retained these values throughout the intense changes it has undergone since its first contact with Russia: Islamisation, adherence to the Sufi brotherhoods, modernisation, urbanisation, Russification and Sovietisation.[14] The *nokhchalla* contained such demands on a man as 'chivalry, noble feelings, hospitality, honour, faithfulness in friendship, a spirit of self-sacrifice for the common good, courage in war, modesty in everyday life and yet vindictiveness bordering on inhumanity when fighting a treacherous enemy.'[15] These qualities were declared 'primitive and savage' by the Russian conquerors—who 'were endowed with many [but not all] of these qualities'—and banned by the Bolsheviks, who 'were absolutely devoid of them', as '"bourgeois-nationalist prejudice" and condemned to disappear for the sake of "communist re-education"'.[16] Consequently, accepting Russian rule was to the Chechens more than losing freedom in the Western sense of the word: it was losing one's manhood and—more important—one's soul.[17]

[14] If there has been any erosion, mainly since the 'deportation' (see chapter 13 below), it has been felt in a loosening of the adherence to the high moral standards of the *nokhchalla* among urbanised Chechens, especially among those living 'abroad', i.e. in other parts of the former Soviet Union. The collapse of social and moral values in the 1990s is mainly the result of the Russo-Chechen wars (see chapter 15, note 36).

[15] Abdurrakhman Avtorkhanov, 'The Chechens and the Ingush during the Soviet Period and its Antecedents' in Marie Bennigsen-Broxup (ed.), *The North Caucasus Barrier: The Russian Advance towards the Muslim World* (London: Hurst, 1992), p. 168.

[16] Ibid., p. 169.

[17] Still, like almost all human societies under similar circumstances in history, the overwhelming majority of Chechens had to carry on with their lives after the Russian occupation and to negotiate their own compromises with reality. As in all other cases in history, those who chose openly to defy, resist and confront the Russian authorities—and suffer the consequences—were a tiny minority, as were those who chose to cooperate with the authorities.

2

THE RUSSIAN ADVENT

Contacts between Russians and Chechens are the result of the Russian '*Drang nach Süden*', which brought Russians and Russia to the Caucasus. The Cossacks, who 'in the course of centuries added belt upon belt of fertile territory to their own possessions, and eventually to the Empire of the Tsars',[1] were the first to encounter the Chechens. These were the 'Greben Cossacks' (*grebenskie kozaki*, also known as '*Grebentsy*'). Tolstoy, who (apart from being one of the giants of world literature) should be regarded as an historical source due to his thorough research and accuracy down to the minutest detail, characterised them and summarised their history in the following words:

A long time ago, ancestors of the Old Believers fled from Russia and settled among the Chechens beyond the Terek, on the Greben range, the first range of the wooded mountains of Great Chechnya. Living among the Chechens, the Cossacks intermarried and adopted many of their customs, though they retained their Russian language in all its purity and their religion. There is still a legend among the Cossacks that Tsar Ivan the Terrible came to the Terek, summoned the Cossack elders from the Greben range, and granted them land on the north bank of the Terek. He is supposed to have exhorted them to remain friendly toward Russia and promised them not to force them against their will to become his subjects or to abandon their faith. To this day the Cossack families feel a kinship with the Chechens and share their predilection for freedom, idleness, looting, and war. Russian influence shows itself largely in its unattractive aspects: interference in elections, requisitioning of church bells, and the passage of Russian troops through the territory. The Cossack feels less natural hatred for a hostile Hillman who may have killed his brother than for the soldier who's

---

[1] J. F. Baddeley, *The Russian Conquest of the Caucasus*, London: Longmans, Green, 1908, p. 5.

been quartered with him to defend his village but who fills his house with tobacco smoke. For the enemy from the mountains he has respect, while he has nothing but scorn for the soldier he considers an oppressor. In a Cossack's eyes, a Russian *muzhik* is something alien, something wild and despicable, something of which he had a foretaste in the traders and settlers from the Ukraine, for whom he has scornful names. Standards of Cossack fashion in dress are set by Circassians. The best weapons are obtained from mountain tribesmen, and the fastest horses are bought or stolen from them. A young Cossack likes to show off his knowledge of the Tartar language and at times may even address another Cossack in Tartar. Nevertheless, this small Christian tribe, lost in one small corner of the world, surrounded by half-savage Mohammedans and by soldiers from the North, feels it's quite civilised, considers that only a Cossack is a human being, and professes deep contempt for all others.[2]

This legend about Ivan IV ('the Terrible') points to a couple of historical facts: one is that as early as his reign Moscow had already demonstrated an interest in the Caucasus, tried to become involved there and even attempted to expand into the region. This was a logical step following the completion of his conquest of the Volga basin—Kazan in 1552 and Astrakhan in 1556. Ivan himself married a Kabartay princess and thus justified his claim to sovereignty over Kabarda and the entire Northern Caucasus—a justification to which all his successors, including Romanovs and Bolsheviks, were to cling. Both of Ivan's immediate successors to the throne, his son Fedor (Theodore) and Boris Godunov, sent armies into Daghestan (in 1594 and 1604 respectively), but neither expedition was successful, being cut to pieces by the local rulers. Thus, while Moscow had the appetite, it could not satisfy it because on the whole it was weaker than the local powers in the Caucasus, not to mention their patrons—the Ottomans and the Safavids.

The other historical fact is that in the Caucasus, as in other areas, the Muscovite state followed the Cossacks, gradually incorporated them into its structure, and eventually submitted them to its own will and purpose. The move of the Grebentsy to the north (left) bank of the Terek was a landmark in this gradual process. However, this happened about a century after Ivan IV, in 1685 during the reign of Peter I ('the Great'). Here, together with the Terek Cos-

---

[2] Lev Nikolaevich Tolstoi, 'Kazaki', Chapter IV. Quotation from: Leo Tolstoy, *The Cossacks and the Raid*, tr. Andrew R. MacAndrew (New York: Signet Books, 1961, p/b), pp. 23–4.

sacks (*terskie kozaki*) who inhabited the delta of the Terek, and moved in 1712 to its left bank, they served as the beginning of what would gradually become 'the Caucasian Cordon Line'.[3] By 1717 the Grebentsy had become part of the Russian state, as was demonstrated by their contribution to Peter's ill-fated expedition against Khiva that year of 700 men, only two of whom survived.

Peter was the first after a long interval to attempt to intervene in the affairs of the Caucasus. In his Persian campaign of 1722 he conquered the Caspian littoral of the region. However, during the campaign a Russian regular cavalry detachment was defeated by the Chechens near Enderi, known in Russian sources as Andreevskii Aul. J. F. Baddeley wrote:

This was the first time that Russian regular troops had come into contact with that tribe in their native forests, and the result was ominous of what was to take place on numerous occasions during the ensuing 130 years.[4]

Peter's attempt and indeed the entire campaign ended in failure. The reason was as before: Russia was still too weak compared with both the local rulers and the major Muslim power patronising them—the Ottomans. However, he was successful in establishing the Terek as Russia's southern border and in building a defence line along it based on the two old Cossack armies (*voiska*) and a new one that had been brought over from the Don and settled on the Terek in 1722 to close the gap between them—the 'Terek family' (*tersko-semeinye*) Cossacks. In 1735, ten years after his death, Peter's work was concluded with the establishment of a fortress in Kyzliar, 'which up to 1863 was, so to speak, the Russian capital of the Caucasus'.[5]

Thus the Chechens had involuntarily become neighbours of the empire of the Tsars. A Chechen Soviet historian states that friendship and goodneighbourly relations existed

...between the Mountaineers and the Cossacks *during the erstwhile period of their settlement*, because they [the Cossacks ...] *had come not as conquerors but*

---

[3] For the development of the Caucasian Line, see Moshe Gammer, *Muslim Resistance to the Tsar: Shamil and the Conquest of Chechnia and Daghestan* (London: Frank Cass, 1994), pp. 1–4.

[4] Baddeley (note 1), p. 25.

[5] Adol'f Petrovich Berzhe, Introduction in A. P. Berzhe *et al.* (eds), *Akty Sobrannye Kavkazskoi Arkheograficheskoi Kommissiei*, Tbilisi: Tipografiia Kantselarii Glavno-nachal'stvuiushchedo Grazhdarshoi Chast'iuna Kavkaze, 1866–1904 (hereafter *AKAK*), vol. I, p. x.

as 'refugees' searching for a place where they could enjoy security and freedom. [...]
But these *peaceful and goodneighbourly relations continued only as long as the
Cossacks preserved their freedom* [of the Russian state; emphasis added].[6]

This is obviously an idyllic description deeply imbued with the
requirements of Soviet historiography. What should be said is that
the Chechens accepted their new neighbours as they had each new
nomadic tribe from time immemorial. A complex *modus vivendi*
soon developed between the Chechens and their new neighbours,
which entailed both co-operation and confrontation. All this changed once the Cossacks had become an instrument of Tsarist expan-
sionism. During the following centuries Russia—Tsarist, Soviet
and post-Soviet alike—would again and again supply the Chechens
with reasons to hate it and its people.[7]

The Chechens must have quickly come to the conclusion that
their new situation—proximity to the empire of the Tsars—was a
mixed curse. True, the presence of new settlers and forces, and the
market town of Kyzliar which had grown around the fortress, stim-
ulated some branches of the Chechen economy, especially in those
areas in direct proximity to the Russians. Indeed, in the second half
of the eighteenth century some groups of Chechens experienced
an economic 'boom'. This subject has been studied intensively by
Soviet historians, both Chechen and Russian, because it fitted
the Soviet historiographic formula of the 'eternal friendship of the
family of Soviet peoples under the guidance of the elder brother—
the Great Russian people'.[8] In particular it fitted two tenets of this
formula: first, that relations between the Russians and any other
nationality of the Soviet Union have been friendly since their first
contact—resistance to Russia was simply led by 'reactionary' upper

[6] Sharpudin Ahmadov, *Imam Mansur. Narodno-osvoboditel'noe dvizhenie v Chechne i
na Severnom Kavkaze v kontse XVIII v.* (Groznyi: Kniga, 1991), p. 67.

[7] Still, the Chechens have managed to separate between the personal and general
levels in their attitude to the Russians. Thus, an independent fact-finding mission
discovered in 1992 (to its surprise, perhaps) that most Chechens 'distinguish
between Russians in the abstract and the present Russian population of Chechnya,' and that 'relations between Russians and Chechens on a day-to-day basis
appear relatively unstrained.' (International Alert, Fact-Finding Mission to
Chechnia (24 September–3 October 1992), *Report* (London, n.d. [1993]), p. 32).

[8] For the development of this formula and its implications, see Lowel R. Tillet, *The
Great Friendship: Soviet Historians on the Non-Russian Nationalities*, Chapel Hill:
University of North Carolina Press, 1969.

classes—and second, that not only have the Russians brought to all the others the benefits of civilisation, but that everything good that has happened to these people originated in Russia. However, any benefits were far outweighed by

...the aggressive actions of the Tsarist authorities—the erection of fortresses on lands of the Mountaineers; the establishment of fortified points and Cossack settlements; the distribution among Tsarist officials of lands belonging to the Mountaineers; the forcible mobilisation of the local population to pave roads and build forts; and the extraction of heavy taxes and duties from the peasants—not to mention the actions of Tsarist generals who interfered in the internal life of the Mountaineers.

The Tsarist authorities, interested in establishing forts and fortresses on the lands of the Mountaineers, *aimed at pushing the people back into the mountains.* During the eighteenth century the [Russian] authorities answered the counter-actions of the Chechens with punitive expeditions connected with the burning of entire *auls* [mountain villages], the destruction of crops and food stores and the uprooting of gardens etc. [emphasis added][9]

Of course this description is one-sided, but one of its aims is to counterbalance official Soviet historiography, which asserted the opposite. The Chechens were certainly not innocent victims in the developing conflict. In particular their raids on the Russian line and settlements were a constant annoyance for the local Russian authorities and served as justification for punitive expeditions. They also strengthened the demand to 'pacify' the Chechens and to explain these punitive expeditions as a major means to this end.

However, in the overall balance the Chechens were indeed the victims. After all, the Tsars were uninvited guests who demanded to become masters. Many of the Chechen raids (though by no means all) were prompted by economic hardship resulting from the Russian seizure of their most fertile lands, denial of the use of their winter pasture, and trade boycotts that took advantage of the growing Chechen dependence on trade with the Russian-controlled territories. All these tactics were used within a wide range of means whose aim was Chechen submission to Russian rule. Other raids were in retaliation for Cossack raids, which the Russian authorities did little, if anything, to stop. (Not that the Russian authorities

[9] Ahmadov (note 6), pp. 71–2. Here and elsewhere 'fort' is a translation of '*ukreplenie*' and 'fortress' of '*krepost*'.

would necessarily have been strong enough to stop them had they tried.)

Ultimately Chechen (as well as other mountaineer) and Cossack raids, whatever their cause and aim, were to a great extent a kind of sport, an opportunity for men to demonstrate their courage, horsemanship and martial skills. As such they were never aimed at causing human casualties and almost never did. Nor did they as a rule cause material damage other than the stealing of animals. Conversely, Russian punitive expeditions were aimed at causing the greatest possible human and material damage. Furthermore, as in so many similar cases in history, those who actually received 'punishment' had not up till then been involved in the conflict, and were only now being dragged into it.

Thus, such expeditions served only to expand the circle of conflict—or, in the language of nineteenth-century Russian sources, 'to exasperate the Chechens'—and intensify it. Indeed, the expeditions, which at first had 'an episodic nature', had acquired by the second half of the eighteenth century 'a systematic character'.[10] No less important, the more the Chechens clashed with Russian regular forces, the more they learned how to fight them successfully and to use the Russians' shortcomings and the terrain to their own advantage. This would be demonstrated time and again throughout the nineteenth and twentieth centuries.

The Russian advance to the south in general, and into the Caucasus in particular, resumed in force under Catherine II ('the Great'). In 1763, within a year of her accession to the throne, Catherine asserted the Russian claim to Kabarda by erecting the fortress of Mozdok, which led to the Russo-Ottoman war of 1768–74 and a fourteen-year-long struggle (1765–79) with the Kabartay. During these years and beyond Prince Potemkin, Catherine's main aide and partner (and for a certain period her lover too), extended the existing defence line on the Terek westward up to the Black Sea and thus established the famous 'Caucasian Line'. The purpose of this line, wrote Potemkin to his Empress, was to

..bar the mountain peoples of different names ... from those areas to be exploited by our subjects; [those areas] which by their conditions facilitate

---

[10] Ibid., p. 74.

the establishment of wine vats, silk and paper mills, sheep, goat and horse husbandry, fruit gardening and cereal farming. [...] It also opens up a way to penetrate into those mountains ... and in due course exploit their deposits and minerals.[11]

The completion of the Caucasian Line laid 'a solid foundation for future successes against the tribes inhabiting the country between the Terek and the Black Sea coast'.[12] The concluding act in the establishment of the Caucasian Line was the 'merciless slaughter' of the Nogays by Suvorov, Catherine's most celebrated general. Suvorov summoned the Nogays to Eisk, on the shores of the Sea of Azov, where he read to them the proclamation made by the last Crimean khan of his abdication in favour of Catherine. The Nogay nomads, for centuries subjects of the Crimean khans, took an oath of allegiance to the Empress of all the Russias. Only then were they told that the Russian authorities planned to move them away from their home steppes and resettle them between the Volga and the Ural mountains (an area seriously depopulated because of a series of revolts culminating in the Pugachev rebellion of 1773–4 and by the flight of the Kalmyks to Xin-Jang in 1771). The Nogays tried to resist, but found the Russian forces ready and waiting. Driven into marshy ground and finding all escape routes blocked, they chose to kill their wives and children and die fighting rather then surrender into slavery. This scene would be repeated frequently during the Russian conquest of the Caucasus. Of the survivors 'an irreconcilable minority settled among the Circassians; the remainder made their submission and were transferred to the Crimea.'[13]

Under Catherine's rule this deed was not an exception, at least not a significant one. The treatment of her own subjects was not much better, so one should not have expected a 'softer' treatment of 'Asiatics'. After all, the overwhelming majority of Russia's officials and generals believed that the Tartars, Muslims and Turks were only able to understand the language of brute force. A product of this frame of mind is the Russian expression 'to speak Turkish' (*govorit' po turetskii*), meaning to beat someone up.

---

[11] Potemkin to Catherine II, printed in *Kubanskii Sbornik*, III (Ekaterinodar, 1898), p. 83 as quoted in ibid., p. 66.
[12] Baddeley (note 1), pp. 38–9.
[13] Ibid., p. 45.

However, the massacre had practical aims as well, and one of them must have been to shock the mountain people of the Caucasus into submission. There could be little doubt that the Mountaineers were in a state of deep shock, but the massacre seems to have had an effect opposite to that which the Russians desired. As the climax of their brutally offensive activities and measures, it strengthened the Mountaineers' resolve to resist the armies of the Tsar. It is perhaps no coincidence that in 1785, two years after the massacre of the Nogays, Sheikh Mansur, the first Imam (leader) of resistance, began his activity.

Part II. THE RUSSIAN CONQUEST

'It is impossible to subdue the Chechens unless to exterminate them completely.' (Pavel Sergeevich Potemkin)[1]

> *Never coveting*
> *The lands of someone else*
> *We've always found room enough*
> *Within our native land...*
> *And when*
> *The Tsarist crowds*
> *Forced on us their unjust war.*
> *That rock-hard*
> *Nature of ours*
> *Forbade us our heads to bow*
> *(Nurdin Murzayev.)*[2]

---

[1] V. A. Potto, *Dva veka terskogo kazachestva* (Vladikavkaz, 1912), vol. II, p. 146 as quoted in Mayrbek Vachagaev, 'Chechnia v kavkazskoi voine, 1816–1859' (Moscow, 1995), p. 54. Pavel Sergeevich Potemkin was a cousin of his famous namesake. In the 1780s he was commander-in-chief of the Caucasian Line.

[2] Nurdin Murzayev, 'Primechaniia k Istorii' in *Prodolzhenie Pesni*, Russian transl. Anisim Krongauz (Moscow, 1967), pp. 52–3.

3

THE FIRST GAZAVAT

Al-Imam al-Mansur al-Mutawakil 'ala Allah (the Victorious Leader who puts his trust in God) was the title assumed by Ushurum Sheikh (Ushurma, or Ucherman according to other sources) when he started to call his compatriots to repent and mend their ways in view of the Russian encroachment. He is known to the Chechens and other Mountaineers by this Arabic name. In Russian and subsequent Western sources and historiography he is usually called Sheikh Mansur.[3]

Evidence regarding Ushurum's early life is quite scanty and contradictory. Most historians believe he must have been born circa 1759/60, since in Russian captivity he stated he was over thirty years of age. That means he started his activity in his mid-twenties. A more plausible version, provided by someone claiming to be Mansur's descendent, states that he was born in 1732.[4] Whatever his year of birth, Ushurum clearly possessed

...even in the words of Tsarist historians, an outstanding personality and stood out sharply among his co-villagers. 'Generously endowed by nature with a supple and penetrating mind' and 'a strong will', he was an excellent psychologist and had the ability 'to steal his way into the confidence' of all those who surrounded him.[5]

---

[3] For descriptions of Mansur in Russian-Imperial, Soviet and Western historiography see Moshe Gammer, 'A Preliminary to the Decolonization of Shaykh Mansur', *Middle Eastern Studies*, 32, 1 (January 1996), pp. 191–202.

[4] Nart (pseud.), 'The Life of Mansur: Great Independence Fighter of the Caucasian Mountain People', *Central Asian Survey*, 10, 1–2 (March–June 1991), p. 83.

[5] Sharpudin Ahmadov, *Imam Mansur. Narodno-osvobitel'noe dvizhenie v Chechne i na Severnom Kavkaze v kontse XVIIIv.* (Groznyi: Kniga, 1991), p. 62. His quotations are from N. F. Dubrovin, *Istoriia voiny i vladychestva russkikh na Kavkaze* (St Peters-

According to a Chechen historian writing within the Soviet par-
adigm,[6] Ushurum was born into a poor family in the village of Aldy
on the outskirts of modern-day Groznyi; he passed his childhood as
a shepherd and remained illiterate throughout his life. This version,
first used for propaganda purposes by the Empress' deputies in the
Caucasus, became entrenched in Russian and Soviet historiography.
Its use by Chechen authors was meant to add to Mansur's qualities,
according to Soviet values, by showing he was 'a son of the people'.
In reality, Ushurum received a religious education both at home
and in Daghestan and became a mullah. Being an outstanding scholar he was given the title Sheikh by his fellow *'ulama*.[7] Some sources
claim that Ushurum had at one time or another become a Naqshbandi sheikh (thus explaining his title) and was the first to introduce
the Naqshbandiyya into the Caucasus.[8]

The Naqshbandiyya is one of the most widespread Sufi *tariqas* in
Islam.[9] 'Strictly orthodox'[10] from its inception, it spread from its area
of origin in Central Asia to India, where in the sixteenth century it
was transformed into 'the vanguard of renascent Islamic orthodoxy'.[11]
From India its 'militant revivalism'[12] spread to other parts of the Muslim world and influenced both resistance to foreign encroachment
and conquest and so-called 'fundamentalist' Islamic movements.

---

burg: Tipografiia Departmenta Udelov, 1886) and A. Tereshchenko, 'Lzheprorok Mansur', *Syn Otechestva*, 1856, nos 15–16.

[6] Ahmadov (note 5), p. 93.

[7] Julietta Meskhidze, 'Imam Shaykh Mansur: A Few Stanzas to a Familiar Portrait',
Central Asian Survey, 21, 3 (September 2002), p. 304.

[8] Alexandre Bennigsen, 'Un mouvement populaire au Caucase du XVIIIe siécle:
la "guerre Sainte" de Sheikh Mansur (1785–1794). Page mal connue et contro-
verseé des relations russo-turques', *Cahiers du Monde Russe et Soviétique*, V,
2 (April–June 1964), pp. 175–9.

[9] Sufism is Muslim mysticism; *tariqa*, or *tarikat* as it is pronounced in the Caucasus,
is in popular usage a Sufi order. For the Naqshbandiyya, its history and significance, see Hamid Algar, 'A Brief History of the Naqshbandi Order' in Marc
Gaborieu, Alexandre Popovic and Thierry Zarcone (eds), *Naqshbandis. Cheminements et situation actuelle d'un ordre mystique musulman* (Istanbul and Paris: Isis Press,
1990), pp. 3–44.

[10] Hamid Algar, 'The Naqshbandi Order: a Preliminary Survey of its History and
Significance', *Studia Islamica*, 44 (1970), p. 124.

[11] Bernard Lewis, *The Middle East and the West* (New York: Harper and Row,
1966), p. 66.

[12] Ibid., p. 97.

The revivalist, post-sixteenth-century Naqshbandiyya believed that the crisis the Muslim world underwent in the seventeenth and eighteenth centuries had arisen because the Muslim community—the *umma*—had gone astray. Furthermore, it considered restoring the *umma* to the right path—strict observance of the Muslim religious law, the *shari'a*, and the effort to imitate as fully as possible the behaviour of the Prophet in daily life—to be its duty. Only once the *shari'a* had been re-established and Muslims had returned to the right path would they become virtuous and strong again and able to wage *jihad*—holy war—in order to liberate themselves from foreign threat or occupation.

Whether a Naqshbandi or not, Mansur preached from the very beginning of his activity in mid-March 1785 similar ideas to the Naqshbandiyya, namely that the Muslims should repent of their sins and return to true Islam; or, in other words, abandon the '*adat* (local tribal custom) and live only according to the *shari'a*. Furthermore, and like Naqshbandis in other cases, he gave this task precedence over *jihad* against the infidel rule, and even explicitly instructed

...those who are subjects of the Russians [to] be true to them and avoid the smallest mischief until I enter into negotiation with Russia ... and if any of you causes them mischief, I shall deal with him with God's Grace.[13]

If Mansur believed he could arrive at a *modus vivendi* with the Russians, he was soon disappointed. The Russian authorities, suspicious of any religious (or other) movement or activity outside their control, and traditionally identifying Islam as the enemy, were alarmed by the lightning speed with which Mansur's fame, leadership and message spread among the Chechens and their neighbours. Soon they started to counteract Mansur's activity, issuing manifestos that 'ordered' the Chechens and other Mountaineers 'not to believe the false prophethood of this cheat', this 'tramp', stating that he

...has appeared among the Chechens and is disturbing the tranquillity of the people with false attractions. Calling himself a Prophet, which no sen-

---

[13] Mansur's appeal to the Kabartay, as quoted in Ahmadov (note 5), pp. 98–9. For similar behaviour of the Naqshbandis in Daghestan in the 1820s, see M. Gammer, *Muslim Resistance to the Tsar: Shamil and the Conquest of Chechnia and Daghestan*, London: Frank Cass, 1994, pp. 43–6.

sible person could—or should—believe, he attracts blinded superstitious men and deceives them.[14]

Using terms such as 'false prophet', 'cheat', 'tramp', 'rebel', 'savage' and 'wild beast', the Russian propaganda effort painted a highly negative picture of Mansur. This picture would endure in Russian and—with two or three exceptions—in Soviet historiography: a fact that perhaps suggests that successive regimes in St Petersburg and Moscow considered Mansur—or rather what he stood for—no less dangerous after his death than when was alive.[15]

Without much delay the Russian authorities moved from words to action. Colonel Pieri was commanded to march under cover of night to Aldy and capture Mansur alive. He did so on 15–17 July 1785 with a force of at least 4–5,000 infantry, a 'hundred' Cossacks and at least two artillery pieces. This force was observed on the first leg of its journey by the Chechens who, in accordance with the tactics they had developed facing the Russian army, offered little resistance. Thus, wrote a Russian historian,

Mansur's native *aul*, set on fire from its four corners, was taken and plundered by the Russian troops. Its unsuspecting residents had fled into the mountains. Mansur lost everything; his hut was razed to the ground, and he and his family barely succeeded in saving their souls. Any friendly disposition towards the Russians had disappeared and the Sheikh swore in the Prophet's name to take revenge. Meanwhile the Russian force was making its way by sword and fire. All Chechnya was shaken on hearing of the disaster that had befallen the Sheikh. *Mansur [then] stood at the head of the Mountaineers and declared holy war—gazavat* [emphasis added].[16]

Once on its way back through the forests, the Russian force was surrounded and attacked on all sides by the Chechens. Pieri, his deputy, nine of his senior officers and 300 men were killed and a huge number wounded. Left without their officers the men 'literally ran for their lives, because the Mountaineers hacked at them unarmed and captured them as they were blundering through the forest.'[17]

---

[14] Lt.-Gen. Potemkin's Proclamation to the Chechens and other Mountain Peoples, 2 [13] April 1785, no. 21, as quoted in Ahmadov (note 5), p. 114.

[15] M. Gammer (note 1).

[16] M. Ia. Korol'kov, 'Sheikh Mansur anapskii. (Epizod iz pervykh let zavoevaniia Kavkaza)', *Russkaia Starina*, 5 (1914), p. 412.

[17] Lt.-Gen. Potemkin to Prince G. A. Potemkin, 9 [20] November 1785, as quoted in Ahmadov (note 5), p. 128.

The Chechens captured 200 men and two cannon. Having developed and used these tactics successfully against the Russian regular troops, the Chechens would perfect them in the following decades, repeatedly destroying ever larger Russian forces.

Two days later, on 19 July 1785, Colonel Apraksin with a force of some 2,500 or more infantry, at least 1,100 cavalry (mainly Cossacks) and several artillery pieces 'punished' the village of Alkhan Yurt (which he found deserted) by burning it, but 'in no way did I dare' to cross the Sunja and 'punish the residents of Aldy, where the newly-appeared Sheikh had been residing.'[18] Nevertheless, in his report Apraksin presented his action as a major battle and exaggerated the number of enemy casualties. 'One may suppose', he wrote, 'that up to 170 people were killed by the artillery and up to 100 by the fire of the infantry.'[19]

New students of history are (or at least should be) taught that official reports and communications—like other primary sources—should not be taken literally or regarded as more 'truthful' than other sources. This is especially true of military reports. Even with the best of intentions to report the 'truth', men having faced death, and still in the emotional turmoil of battle, naturally tend to dramatise, exaggerating some events while completely forgetting or disregarding others. Such things should be expected everywhere and in all times. However, there have always been commanding officers whose great mastery of the pen, rather than their achievements on the battlefield, was the vehicle for their promotion and decorations. Indeed, it seems that usually the former grows in proportion to the diminution of the latter, or in other words, to the increase in failures on the battlefield.

In Russia, at least in some periods of its history, mastery of the pen seems to have become the norm.[20] But Prince Potemkin appears to

---

[18] Col. Apraksin to Lt.-Gen. Leont'ev, 8 [19] July 1785 as quoted in ibid., p. 132.

[19] Ibid., *loc cit.*

[20] During the conquest of the Caucasus in the nineteenth century, for example, inflated numbers of enemy casualties were reported by nearly every Russian commanding officer. The anecdote about the officer rebuking his aide-de-camp for being 'too stingy' in his report with regard to enemy casualties appears in almost all the memoirs of veterans. In fact, if one sums up all the casualties reported by Russian generals, the number is at least three times the entire native population (including women and children).

Tolstoy, again, supplies a precise yet masterly description of the huge gap between events and the way they were reported:

> ... On the other side of the ravine, by the outskirts of a young forest, a few horsemen could be seen at a distance of a quarter of a mile. These were the Chechens. [...] One of them fired at the line. Several soldiers fired back. The Chechens retreated and the firing ceased.
>
> But when Poltorátsky and his company came up he nevertheless gave orders to fire, and scarcely had the word been passed than along the whole line of sharpshooters the incessant, merry, stirring rattle of our rifles began, accompanied by pretty dissolving cloudlets of smoke. The soldiers, pleased to have some distraction, hastened to load and fired shot after shot. The Chechens evidently caught the feeling of excitement, and leaping forward one after another fired a few shots at our men. One of these shots wounded a soldier [who later died of his wound] (Lev Nikolaevich Tolstoi, 'Khadzhi Murat', Chapter V. Quotation from Leo Tolstoy, *Short Novels: Stories of God, Sex and Death*, vol. II, selected and introduced by Ernest J. Simmons. Transl. of *Hadji Murád* by Louise and Aylmer Maude. [New York: The Modern Library, 1962], p. 397).

The report of this incident ran as follows:

> *23rd November* Two companies of the Kurín regiment advanced from the fort on a wood-felling expedition. At midday a considerable number of Mountaineers suddenly attacked the wood-fellers. The sharpshooters began to retreat, but the 2nd Company charged with the bayonet and overthrew the Mountaineers. In this affair two privates were slightly wounded and one killed. The Mountaineers lost about a hundred men killed and wounded (ibid., p. 408).

The 'creativity' of commanding officers did not stop at the number of enemy casualties, however. For example, this is how a Russian colonel (and later a famous general) described a battle of his in June 1841

> ...[The enemy,] taking advantage of the darkness, fled in the direction of Kumukh, in the citadel of which one company and the load of [my] force had been left [... His] flight was in such a rush that by 7 o'clock in the morning he appeared in front of Kumukh and suddenly attacked it: (Argutinskii-Dolgorukii to Golovin, 3 [15] June 1841, as quoted in Gammer, *Muslim Resistance to the Tsar: Shanil and the Conquest of Chechnia and Daghestan* [London: Frank Cass, 1994], p. 132).

Post-Soviet Russian military reporting about operations in Chechnya falls within this tradition. It is also part of the Soviet tradition according to which *all* reports, civilian and military alike, were—and, more important, were expected to be—inflated, as aptly demonstrated by Vladimir Voinovich: reacting to reports of the completion of the potato harvest in a *kolkhoz*, the district party secretary 'was disturbed and phoned' the chairman 'to say, Lie, all right, but don't overdo it.' (Vladimir Voinovich, *The Life and Extraordinary Adventures of Private Ivan Chonkin*, transl. Richard Lourie [New York: Farrar, Straus and Giroux, 1977], pp. 258–9). And cf. another inflated report of an operation in Chechnya in 1929 in Alexander Nekrich, *The Punished Peoples: The Deportation and Fate of Soviet Minorities at the end of the Second World War* (New York: W. W. Norton, 1978), pp. 44–5.

have been a rare exception in Russian history in that he did not tolerate inflated reports. Hence he rebuked his cousin the commander of the Caucasian Line:

> If the matter is only the hiding inhabitants of Alkhanov's village [Alkhan Yurt], then the victory over them by such an overwhelming force could be reported more briefly. It is worthwhile, however, to remark that to kill 170 people with several cannon balls—26 to be exact … and one of them killed half this crowd—is an extraordinary example of artillery marksmanship. […] I wish that your Excellency would impress upon all the commanding officers […] that they should use artillery fire [only] where artillery can cause real damage.[21]

Both as victim of the Russians' treachery and aggression and as their conqueror, Mansur's call for *gazavat* was now answered by many Chechens and others, who flocked to him at Aldy. Soon he moved on to the offensive. On 26 July 1785, at the head of 5,000 men (the Russian estimate), he attacked Kyzliar. Though the storming of the fortress failed, he took a small fort nearby where he captured four cannon.

Less than two weeks later, on 7 August, Mansur arrived at Lesser Kabarda and two days after that attacked Grigoripolis. Forewarned by their native allies, the Russian garrison was ready. The Mountaineers' fierce attack on the fortress itself was repelled by extensive artillery fire. However, they burned all the constructions outside the walls and in a hard-fought battle forced a Russian regiment to retreat into the protection of the fortress. After two days of intensive fighting Mansur retreated, burning the fields and haystacks as he went. On his way back into the mountains the Imam persuaded the majority of the population of Lesser Kabarda to follow him. The same manoeuvre would be used half a century later by another Imam.

On 30 August Mansur attacked Kyzliar again, this time at the head of 12,000 men (the Russian estimate), For three days the repeated fierce attacks of the Mountaineers were repelled by the Russian artillery. On 2 September Mansur withdrew into the mountains, without giving up the idea of further attacks on Russian centres of power. Lieutenant-General Potemkin, on his return from St Petersburg to the Caucasian Line, found that from the Caspian to the Black Sea 'circumstances are in extreme confusion. The false prophet has so far been engaged in preparations to attack Kyzliar and all

---

[21] Prince G. A. Potemkin to Lt.-Gen. Potemkin, 5 [17] August 1785, as quoted in Ahmadov (note 5), pp. 133–4.

our other settlements. All the Kumyks, Chechens and other Mountaineers—even some of the Daghestanis—flock to him in order to
invade our boundaries.'[22]

Indeed, within less than two weeks of this report Mansur once
again attempted to storm Kyzliar. On 23 October 1785 he arrived
at the Terek only to find a Russian force on the opposite bank. His
enterprise checked, he arrived on 2 November in Lesser Kabarda
and there encountered a force of about 2,500 infantry and a similar
number of cavalry under the command of Colonel Nagel. In two
battles, on 11 and 13 November, only the artillery saved Nagel's
force. Both battles ended inconclusively, and the fatigued parties
retreated. Naturally, Nagel reported that he had won. However,
General Potemkin was closer to the facts: 'The rebel has not been
broken of his impertinence' and 'has never been so strong.'[23]

In December 1785 Mansur moved his residence from Aldy to
Shali. This step symbolises the end of the first stage of his movement, which Bennigsen calls 'the Spread of the Gazavat'.[24] During
this stage 'Mansur wanted to carry the Holy War into the two rich-
est regions in the Caucasus: Kabarda and the land of the Kumyks.'[25]
The second stage, which lasted from the winter of 1785/6 to the
summer of 1787, did not witness such dramatic events. 'From his
Chechen refuge he continued to struggle, proceeding to mobilise the
Mountaineers and harassing the "Caucasian Line", but in the spring
of 1786 the movement started to be short of air.'[26]

However, during this period harassing the Russians was neither
Mansur's only activity nor his most important one. First, he tried to
organise his followers on a more regular basis. Thus at the beginning of 1786 he instructed that 'each mosque' (i.e. parish) should
furnish three warriors with their supplies. That summer he instructed that each village should provide his force with ten men and
one-ninth of their crops and two men from each *kup* [quarter] for
guard duties.[27] Second, he attempted to enforce the *shari'a* among

[22] Lt.-Gen. Potemkin to Prince G. A. Potemkin, 30 September [11 October] 1785,
as quoted in ibid., pp. 182–3.
[23] Lt.-Gen. Potemkin to Prince G. A. Potemkin, 8 [19] November 1785, as quoted in ibid., p. 183.
[24] Bennigsen (note 8), p. 188.
[25] Ibid., p. 190.
[26] Ibid., p. 191.
[27] Ahmadov (note 5), pp. 197–8.

all the Muslim Mountaineers—and even beyond—by word and, whenever he had to and could, by the sword. Third, he tried both by word and the sword to convert the non-Muslim Mountaineers—mainly the pagan Ingush, but also the superficially christianised Ossets. For this purpose he even carried out several campaigns against the Ingush.[28] Fourth, he sent again and again to the Ottomans asking for help. Contrary to the claims of Soviet historiography of the early 1950s that Mansur was a 'Turkish spy', Alexandre Bennigsen showed clearly that the Ottomans were more than suspicious of Mansur during the first two stages of his movement, and regarded his activities also as damaging to their interests.[29] Fifth, in October 1786, when the number of his supporters had already significantly dwindled, Mansur 'sent his brother-in-law, the Kumyk Etta Batyrmurzin, to General Potemkin with a proposal to cease hostilities. Potemkin rejected this advance and demanded [Mansur's] unconditional surrender.'[30] This rigidity on the part of the Russian authorities would continue (with very few exceptions) throughout the nineteenth and twentieth centuries.

In one field Catherine's generals proved more sophisticated than most of their successors. In an attempt to undermine Mansur they authored, translated into (Ottoman) Turkish and distributed throughout the Caucasus copies of a letter supposedly sent to Mansur by Lieutenant-General Potemkin. In this letter the General thanked the Imam for his efforts in getting the Muslims to submit to Russia and promised him generous rewards.[31] Whatever the contribution of this letter to the decline of Mansur's power and influence in the eastern part of the Caucasus, by the summer of 1787 the Imam had decided to move westward, and on 16 July crossed the Kuban. About a month later, on 12 August 1787, Sultan Selim III declared war on Russia, and on 20 September Catherine II responded with a declaration of war on the Ottomans.

Thus started the third stage of Mansur's Gazavat, lasting from 1787 to 1791, in which he co-operated with the Ottomans in their war against Russia. At the head of a force of Circassians, many of

[28] E.g. ibid., pp. 142–3, 148.
[29] Bennigsen (note 8), pp. 180–3.
[30] Ibid., p. 191.
[31] Text and Russian comments quoted in Ahmadov (note 5), pp. 207–8.

whom did not possess firearms, Mansur faced the campaigns of Potemkin (1–6 October 1787) and his successor Tekeli (24 October–16 November 1787 and 30 September–24 October 1788), but was pushed back into Ottoman territory. His 'role in military operations was negligible,' Bennigsen concluded, but 'his political and religious activity must not be under-estimated.'[32] He encouraged the Circassians to support the Ottomans and exhorted, quite successfully, the Kabartay, Chechens, Kumyks and Daghestanis to harass the Russians. In the summer and autumn of 1790 he returned to Chechnya,[33] perhaps to prepare and assist Battal Pasha's campaign against the Russian Line in Kabarda (8–10 October 1790).

Furthermore, in the autumn of 1789 Mansur entered into communication with the 'Kirgiz-Kaisak people living in the north-eastern part of the Caspian basin' (the Kazakhs). He called on them to return to 'true' Islam and to attack Astrakhan, possibly in co-ordination with a parallel move on his (or the Ottomans') part from the opposite direction.[34] By that time Russian rule had been too fresh to completely disrupt the ties between the Caucasian Mountaineers and the nomads of the huge steppe belt from the Black Sea to the Tien-Shan mountains, let alone erase their memories. In the 1830s and 1840s the struggles of the Mountaineers and the Kazakhs against Russian conquest would be conducted in almost complete isolation from each other.

In March 1791 Mansur returned to Anapa. There he was cornered during the final Russian offensive against that stronghold of Ottoman power in the north-eastern part of the Black Sea and the north-western part of the Caucasus (20 May–3 July 1791). Upon the fall of the city, on 3 July 1791, Mansur fortified himself in a cellar and resisted fiercely until warned that unless he gave in, the Russians would blow up the entire building and all its residents—men, women and children.

General Gudovich, the conqueror of Anapa, publicly declared that all the prisoners of war would be set free after its conclusion. In addition to this, he stated, Mansur, since he was to be presented in

---

[32] Bennigsen (note 8), p. 195.
[33] Ahmadov (note 5), p. 262.
[34] Ibid., pp. 256–7.

person to Catherine II, would be given expenses in accordance with his position during his stay in St Petersburg. Promises aside, reality proved to be completely different:

Cheated by 'Semiramis of the North', one of the most depraved immoral and lewd women ever to sit on the throne of the Tsars, who had promised him his life and freedom, Mansur was incarcerated in the fortress of Schlüsselburg and within literally two to three years was reduced by galloping consumption, powerless to endure his longing for his beloved homeland, for which he had fought so fiercely.[35]

Like a comet, Mansur appeared as if out of nowhere, shone brightly for a short while and then departed. But he left a lasting impression on the Caucasus. To the Chechens he is a national hero, a fact that was underlined when his image was one of three to appear on the first postage stamps issued by the newly-independent Chechen Republic. (The other two were of Shamil and Dudayev.) Chechens are particularly proud of the fact that it was one of their own who, in the words of Baddeley, was 'the first to preach and lead' the struggle against the 'Russians in the Caucasus', to 'endeavour to unite' all the Mountaineers and to teach them 'that in religious reform lay the one chance of preserving their cherished liberty and independence'.[36] Indeed, for Chechens Imam Mansur is 'the forefather and pre-founder' both of 'the main ideas of the [Chechen] National Liberation Movement'[37] and of the aspiration for a political unification of the North Caucasian people. He is also regarded as the initiator of the Chechens' long National-Liberation struggle which is still being waged.[38]

Another way in which Mansur contributed to future generations, of which the Chechens are also proud, was by 'formulating in practice the strategy and tactics of the armed struggle'.[39] Indeed, the

---

[35] Andarbek Yandarov, Foreword to Ahmadov (note 5), p. 9.

[36] J. F. Baddeley, *The Russian Conquest of the Caucasus* (London: Longmans, Green, 1908), p. 47.

[37] A. Yandarov, Foreword to Ahmadov (note 5), p. 7.

[38] Thus the Chechens' insistence on 'the conclusion of a peace agreement as the logical completion to the three-centuries-long confrontation' as one of the (pre)-conditions to signing an agreement with Russia. Cf. 'Doklad predsedatelia ispolkama obshchenatsional' nogo S'ezda chechenskogo naroda, generala Dzhokhara Dudaeva, g. Groznyi, 8 iiun' 1991 g.', *Bart* (Understanding) (Groznyi), 6 (010), June 1991, p. 3.

[39] A. Yandarov, Foreword to Ahmadov (note 5), p. 7.

nineteenth-century Imams would consciously follow Mansur's pre-
cedents and act according to lessons derived from many of his other
actions. Mansur, it seems, was the first to realise that on their own
the different mountain communities would have no chance of resisting a great power such as Russia. Hence his grand strategy (adopted
and developed by later leaders of resistance) of following two separate but parallel paths: one, to unite all the Mountaineers (and also
the steppe nomads) in armed resistance to Russia, and two, to obtain Ottoman assistance. While the realisation of both aims was the
final objective, each should be followed separately at its own pace.

To succeed in either objective, but especially in that of unifica-
tion, the means was the promotion of Islam—though no doubt to
Mansur and to later Imams this was the first in their list of priorities.
Hence the drive to spread 'true' Islam, which in the long run was
Mansur's greatest legacy. Not only did he prepare the ground for the
Imams who followed, but he played the crucial role in completing
the Islamisation process of the lowland Chechens (and the Circassians, a fact underlined by Bennigsen) and initiating it among the
Ingush. Furthermore, Mansur's attempt to negotiate with the Russians would legitimise both the attempts of the Imams in the nineteenth century to do the same and the development of a strategy
employing their 'nuisance value' *vis-à-vis* the Russians.

Finally, Mansur seems to have been the first to point out the
value of concentrated attacks on a massive scale directed against the
Russian Line, and followed up with swift movements covering large
enough distances to surprise the Russians.

The capture of Mansur and the end of the war with the Ottomans did not put an end to fighting in Chechnya, or indeed in the
Northern Caucasus as a whole. Raids and counter-raids on different scales continued, sometimes more intensively, sometimes less. In
one such raid, in 1802, Colonel del Pozzo (who would later be commander of the Caucasian Line) was taken prisoner (and ransomed in
1804). After that, the two outstanding events of the first decade of
the nineteenth century were punitive expeditions in 1805 and 1806,
led respectively by Generals Glazenap and Bulgakov. Both seem to
have been the initiatives of 'enterprising' officers rather than actions
determined by the circumstances. Between 24 February and 30 March

Bulgakov's force of 10,000 men was overpowered by a joint Chechen–Daghestani force. This disaster put an end to large-scale operations for about a decade.

But to Catherine and her immediate successors Paul and Alexander I the Northern Caucasus, including Chechnya, was a side-issue even during Mansur's Gazavat. Now it descended even lower in the Russian order of priorities. Where the Caucasus were concerned interest and attention were focused on the affairs of Georgia. During the 1768–74 war with the Ottomans a Russian force stayed there for the first time. In 1783 Catherine signed a protectorate agreement with Erekle II, the king of Kartlo-Kakheti (eastern Georgia). This led to a series of events that culminated in the final annexation of Kartlo-Kakheti to Russia in 1801 by Catherine's grandson, Alexander I.

To the new Tsar (this was among his very first acts after accession) the annexation was but a first step leading to further expansion in the Caucasus. Attempts to realise these ambitions soon brought Russia into conflict with both the Ottoman and Qajar empires, and that at the height of the Napoleonic wars. Nevertheless, the peace treaties of Bucharest (1812) and Gulistan (1813) left Russia in control of most of the territory of Georgia and Azerbaijan. Only then and following the end of the Napoleonic wars did Russia find the time, resources and attention to complete the conquest of the mountains, so vital for its communications with the new possessions to the south.

This enterprise was entrusted to one of Alexander's closest confidants—Aleksei Petrovich Yermolov, who would soon adopt the *sobriquet* 'Proconsul of the Caucasus'. In 1816 Alexander appointed Yermolov governor and chief administrator of Georgia and the Caucasus, commander-in-chief of the separate 'Georgian' Army Corps and Ambassador Extraordinary to the Court of Fath 'Ali Shah in Tehran. Pushkin, impressed by Yermolov, wrote:

> *Submit and bow your snowy head*
> *O Caucasus, Yermolov marches.*[40]

---

[40] Aleksandr Sergeevich Pushkin, 'Kavkazskii plennik', Epilogue, transl. Susan Layton in *Russian Literature and Empire: Conquest of the Caucasus from Pushkin to Tolstoy* (Cambridge University Press, 1994), p. 101.

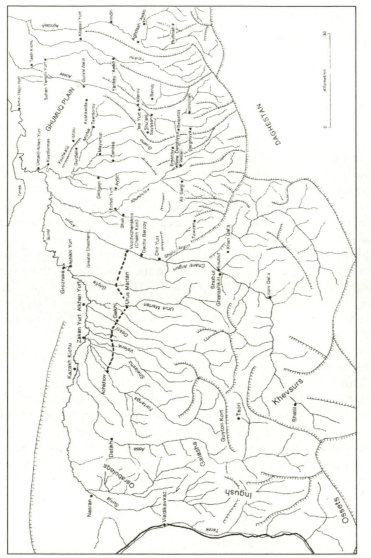

Chechnya in the 18th and 19th centuries.

4

THE BEGINNING OF THE
CAUCASIAN WAR

'Only forty years of age at the time of his Caucasian appointment, [Yer-molov] had already made a brilliant military career for himself. He had been decorated on the field by Suvorov while still in his teens; at twenty he was colonel. At the fall of Paris in 1814 he commanded both the Russian and Prussian Guards, and with the death of Kutuzov and Bagration he became the most illustrious and popular soldier in the Empire.[1]

In person no less than in character Yermolov impressed all who came near him as one born to command. Of gigantic stature and uncommon physical strength, with a round head set on mighty shoulders and framed in shaggy locks, there was something leonine in his whole appearance, which, coupled with unsurpassed courage, was well calculated to excite the admiration of his own men and strike terror into his semi-barbarous foes. Incorruptibly honest, simple, even rude in his habits, and of Spartan hardihood, his sword was ever absent from his side, and in city as in camp he slept wrapped only in his military cloak, and rose with the sun.

Careless of his life, a willing sharer in all privations, exacting to the utter-most at the call of duty, no commander was more sparing of his men when to spare them was consistent with success, none so thoughtful of their well-being, none so regardless of formality, none ever so unfeignedly friendly. […] To him the humblest, raggedest soldier who did his duty cheerfully … was a friend and brother. Habitually he addressed them as comrades; habit-ually he entered into their feelings, sympathized with them in their trou-bles and hardships, visited them by day and by night as they huddled round campfire and kettle, joked, laughed and chaffed with them.'[2]

---

[1] M. Whittock, 'Ermolov: Proconsul of the Caucasus', *The Russian Review*, XVIII, 1 (January 1959), p. 59.

[2] J. F. Baddeley, *The Russian Conquest of the Caucasus* (London: Longmans, Green, 1908), pp. 94–5.

It is not surprising, therefore, that Yermolov remained an admired hero in Russian Imperial historiography and to a lesser extent in its Soviet successor. Admiring, devoted, almost all those who served under him kept his myth alive, so that his period as 'Proconsul of the Caucasus' acquired the aura of a 'golden age' in the collective memory of Russia.

However, there was another side to Yermolov—his extreme xenophobia towards everything non-Russian. In this spirit he approached the Caucasus. His central idea, wrote Baddeley.

was that the whole of the Caucasus must, and should become an integral part of the Russian Empire; that the existence of independent or semi-independent states or communities of any description, whether Christian, Musulman, or Pagan, in the mountains or in the plains, was incompatible with the dignity and honour of his master, the safety and welfare of his subjects.[3]

Therefore, according to a Russian author, 'he set himself the aim of destroying any non-Russian nationality in the country.'[4]

Establishing his mission—the conquest of the mountains—Yermolov, in November 1817 and again in May 1818, unveiled detailed plans to the Emperor. First he suggested dealing with the Chechens, in his words 'the strongest and most dangerous people and on top of it fully assisted by their neighbours'.[5] The choice of Chechnya, argued a Russian historian, was not at all accidental:

This barely penetrable country lay first on the route for expansion of Russian rule. This was not only because of its proximity to Russia's possessions, with which it could not but clash continuously. Its [Chechnya's] main importance lay in the fact that this country, with its rich mountain pastures, its primeval forests dotted with oases of fertile fields and its plains watered by numerous rivers and covered by thick vegetation, was the breadbasket of rocky, barren Daghestan. Only after the conquest of Chechnya could the mountain peoples of the eastern strip of the Caucasus be forced into submission and a peaceful, civil way of life. But no task could be remotely as difficult as that of subjugating the semi-savage Chechen

---

[3] Ibid., p. 99.
[4] Semen Esadze, *Istoricheskaia zapiska ob upravlenii Kavkazom* (Tiflis: Tipografiia Gutenberg, 1907), p. 35.
[5] *AKAK*, vol. VI, pt. II, pp. 498–9, document no. 873, Yermolov to the Emperor, November 1817 (quotation from p. 498).

people and the even more savage nature of Chechnya in which the population found an impregnable shelter. The first attempts of the Russians to encroach on it and then penetrate deep into the country—the expedition of Pieri under Count Potemkin and Bulgakov's storming of the ravine of Khanqal'a [on 30 March 1807]—resulted in the bloodiest episodes and after Bulgakov were not repeated. Both nature and the people of Chechnya stood firmly guarding their independence.[6]

According to Yermolov himself, the Chechens were

…the basest of the bandits who attack the [Caucasian] Line. Their community is fairly small in numbers, although it has grown considerably during recent years because it has gladly welcomed the outlaws of all the other peoples who had left their native lands on account of one crime or another. Here [in Chechnya] they have found partners ready either to grant them shelter or to join their acts of banditry, and indeed they have become their [the Chechens'] guides into lands unknown to them. Chechnya may rightly be called the nest of all the bandits.[7]

Yermolov's plan was to establish a new Line along the (lower) Sunja, and settle Cossacks between that river and the Terek. Once the line was ready, Yermolov wrote to the Emperor:

I shall offer the villains dwelling between the Terek and the Sunja, called peaceful, rules [to regulate their ways] of life and a few duties, which will make clear to them that they are subject to Your Imperial Majesty, and not [your] allies, as they have hitherto deluded themselves. If they submit properly, I shall apportion them the necessary amount of land according to their numbers, dividing the rest among the cramped Cossacks and the Kara-Nogays; if not, I shall propose to them that they retire and join the other outlaws from whom they differ in name only, and in this case the whole of the land will be at our disposal.[8]

Thus 'the Chechens will be constrained within their mountains' and by losing 'agricultural land and pastures, in which they shelter their flocks in winter from the severe cold in the mountains', would have no choice but to submit.[9]

---

[6] V. A. Potto, *Kavkazskaia voina v ocherkakh epizodakh legendakh i biografiiakh*, vol. II (St Petersburg: Tipografiia R. Golike, 1885–7), pp. 65–6.

[7] Ibid., p. 83.

[8] *AKAK*, vol. VI, pt. II, pp. 447–8, document no. 798, Yermolov to the Emperor, 14 [26] May 1818.

[9] Ibid., p. 498.

Even before receiving the Tsar's final approval, Yermolov started work on the new Line. In 1817 the forts of Nazranovskoe (named after the place itself, later the capital of the Ingush Republic) and Prigradnyi Stan ('Blocking Camp') were erected. Immediately on receiving Alexander's approval Yermolov set out personally for Chechnya. On 22 June 1818 the fortress of Groznaia ('Menacing') was established and completed in October the same year. In 1870 the town that had grown around the fortress was given the status of a city—Groznyi. This city, in one of history's small ironies, was destined to become the capital city of the Chechen-Ingush ASSR under the Soviets, and thus of its successor—the Chechen Republic—and to be destroyed by the Russian army 177 years later.

Also in 1818 the Cossack *stanitsa* of Sholkovaia ('Silky') was founded. The following year Yermolov built a fortress opposite Enderi—Vnezapnaia ('Sudden')—and the fort of Goriachevodskoe ('Hot Water'). In 1820 gaps in the Line were filled by the forts of Neotstupnyi Stan ('Camp Unretreating'), Zlobnyi Okop ('Malicious Trench') and Gerzel Aul, as well as the small fortification of Urus Martan (both named after their locations). In 1821 the new Line was completed by the addition of its third cornerstone—the fortress of Burnaia ('Stormy') near Tarki in Daghestan not far from the city that became the capital of that republic, Makhachkala.

Facing the appearance of a Russian fortress 'in the very heart of Chechnya',[10] the Chechens, or at least some of them, first tried to stop its construction through negotiations. Failing that, they called on Nur Muhammad Khan of Avaristan (in Daghestan) for help. Reinforced by the Khan and about 1,000 Daghestanis, they tried in August 1818 to prevent the Russians from completing Groznaia, but were repelled mainly through the extensive use of grapeshot. While the general uprising and struggle in Daghestan in that and the following years are beyond the scope of this book, in Chechnya Yermolov responded to the resistance with a 'punitive expedition' before leaving to conduct operations in Daghestan.

In this expedition, in August–September 1819, as in all his dealings with the Chechens—indeed with all the natives who had refused to submit to Russian rule—Yermolov demonstrated extreme cruelty,

---

[10] Leonid Nikolaevich Kolosov, *Slavnyi Beibulat. Istoriko-biograficheskii ocherk* (Groznyi: Kniga, 1991) p. 35.

more than was suggested by a Russian author who wrote 'He was at least as cruel as the natives themselves.'[11] Furthermore, rebukes from both Alexander I and Nicholas I were to no avail. Yermolov conducted a systematic campaign of terror in which people were executed without trial on mere suspicion, and on some occasions entire families were wiped out simply because one of their members was considered anti-Russian. Also, captives of both sexes and all ages were sold into slavery (a fact which sheds a rather cynical light on the Russian argument that one of the aims of their pacification of the Caucasus was to stop the slave trade).[12]

However, on some occasions the captured men were pressed into military service and the women distributed among the Russian officers, so that in winter quarters 'for the officers, at least, the Commander-in-Chief setting the example, the time passed pleasantly enough in the company of native wives.'[13] Yermolov himself 'married' at least three native women and fathered at least five sons and one daughter. The shock and humiliation—both actual and symbolic—this behaviour caused to the Mountaineers was threefold: first, a Christian married a Muslim woman without having converted to Islam; second, these 'marriages' were made in accordance with the Shi'i custom of *mut'a*, that is marriage for a limited period of time after the elapse of which it is automatically annulled; and third, as if to add insult to injury, in one case at least, Yermolov forced a local Muslim—Iskander of Kaka-Yurt—to divorce his wife so 'the Proconsul' could marry her on the very same day.[14]

This behaviour alone should suffice to explain that for generations to come 'Yarmul' would remain a satanic figure in the memory of the Chechens. However, there was one deed, enacted during Yermolov's above-mentioned punitive expedition, that overshadowed everything else. Having already destroyed six major Chechen villages, he ordered General Sysoev to surround the village of Dadi Yurt with his troops and to slaughter all its inhabitants, men, women and children. On 27 September 1819 Sysoev did as ordered.

[11] Quoted in Baddeley (note 2), p. 97.
[12] M. Pogodin, *Aleksei Petrovich Ermolov. Materialy dlia ego biografii* (Moscow: Universitetskaia Tipografiia, 1863), p. 333.
[13] Baddeley (note 2), p. 145.
[14] Abuzar Aydamirov, *Khronologiia istorii Checheno-Ingushetii* (Groznyi: Kniga, 1991), p. 35.

Many Chechen folk traditions tell of the heroic defence of the village by its men, encouraged by the dancing and singing of the girls in the village square. Once all the men were killed, the women took their place, daggers in hands. To the Russians' astonishment the surviving young women preferred to cut their throats rather than become prisoners. The few women who were captured jumped from the ferry into the river, each of them taking the Russian officer she was assigned to.[15]

The slaughter of Dadi Yurt was one of the most influential events in shaping the Chechens' attitude toward Russia. Its impact has remained almost as strong as it was then. In 1990 a Chechen bard described this slaughter thus:

Arise, you slumbering braves,
Wake your children and your wives!
Hurry with your morning prayer—
Your village is hemmed in close.

Three rings of steel bayonets
And the daybreak is mixed with blood
It seems you'll have to tend your wounds in the morning fog.

The wholeness of this day will be shattered
By volleys into a thousand deaths—
Because the general, Yermolov, ordered
No child or woman be spared!

Open the Holy Book
And slowly recite your prayer of death.
Yes, brave men, today, the souls of many of you
Will part from their bodies.

But the infidels, whose rows of rifles
Are thicker than the number of your swords,
Won't see your backs—and God Almighty
Will take in His embrace your holy war [...]

Each blade of grass, each stone, each rock remembers
The pain and rage of our father's land
Generously share death with our enemies
Who've come uninvited, sword in hand [...]

You will never again hear,
The mu'adhdhin's sweet call to prayer,

[15] M. Vachagayev, 'Chechnia v Kavkazskoi voine, 1816–1859' (Moscow, 1995), pp. 72–3.

You brave men, not even one of you,
Your chests, full of bullets,
Will stand again. You are fortunate!

Not to see on top of your heap of cold bodies
Stabbed many times by our foe,
And have your heart broken at the sight
A weeping child Clinging to his mother's corpse![16]

Clearly the wound inflicted in 1819 is still open and bleeding. Furthermore, the poem testifies to another tragedy of the Chechens—the partial loss of their native language, as both the poet and so many of his audience find Russian a more convenient vehicle for art, culture and science.

But this fact has no direct bearing on Yermolov. The actions of the 'Proconsul' were normal in the empire of the Tsars where, according to an Austrian diplomat, 'the whole art of government is in the use of violence'.[17] Not least in the Caucasus where Russian rule was based on the claim: 'Fear and greed are the two mainsprings of everything that takes place here. [...] These people's only policy is force'[18]—a statement that reflected the theory of the consensus, the 'Suvorov school' as Baddeley called it, that 'Asiatics' could only understand force. Yermolov's opinion appeared no different:

Condescension in the eyes of the Asiatics is a sign of weakness, and out of pure humanity I am inexorably severe. One execution saves hundreds of Russians from destruction and thousands of Muslims from treason.[19]

Yermolov set his aims and methods accordingly:

I desire that the terror of my name should guard our frontiers more potently than chains or fortresses, that my word should be for the natives a law more inevitable than death.[20]

The main flaw in relying solely on the use of violence and terror is that, to paraphrae Abraham Lincoln, one can terrorise all the people some of the time, or some of the people all the time, but not all the

---

[16] Umar Yarichev, 'Dadi Yurt' in *Lavina vremeni. Stikhi* (Groznyi, 1990), pp. 41–4.
[17] Quoted in Leslie Blanch, *The Sabres of Paradise* (London: John Murray, 1961), p. 93.
[18] Tsitsiianov (the second Governor of Georgia) to Alexander I as quoted in Baddeley (note 2), p. 65.
[19] Ibid., p. 97.
[20] Ibid., *loc. cit.*

people all the time. Indeed, Yermolov found it beyond his power and ability to subdue the Chechens. The best he could do was to carry out his devastating punitive expeditions. The 'Proconsul' thus instructed the commander of the new Sunja line, Nikolai Vasil'evich Grekov, to continue such expeditions, which he did, devoting 'himself heart and soul to the execution of Yermolov's policy and instructions,' i.e., 'to destroy *auls*, hang hostages, and slaughter women and children'[21]—welcome tasks for a man who was more than Yermolov's equal in vanity, brutality and cruelty:

[Grekov] looked at [the Chechens] from a very mean point of view, and in speech as well as in official papers had no other name for them than rascals, and [called] any of their representatives either robber or cheat.[22]

Between February 1819 and July 1821 Grekov carried out four punitive expeditions, destroying time and again the major villages of Greater Chechnya—Great Chechen, Shali, Germenchuk, Avtury, Geldigen, Mayurtup—and dozens of smaller ones. In addition he carried out four forest-felling expeditions. This was to facilitate a plan devised by Yermolov's able Chief-of-Staff, Vel'iaminov, in response to lessons learnt from the Pieri and Bulgakov disasters. According to this system, wide avenues—twice a rifle range in width—were cut through the primeval forests of Chechnya, either between Russian fortifications or in the direction of the major populated centres of Greater Chechnya, to facilitate the quick and secure movement of Russian forces. A fifth felling expedition was conducted by the commander of the Caucasian Line, General Stahl, in November 1820. Unable to force the Chechens to do the felling for him, Stahl reverted to treachery. He invited fifty elders from the villages on the Kachkalyk range for negotiations. As soon as they arrived he arrested them and held them hostage until their co-villagers finished felling the avenues he had planned. Such acts of treachery on the part of Russian generals were a common occurrence during the conquest of the area. Obviously 'Asiatics' and 'Tartars' were 'savages' to the Russians and as such were not included among those to whom one needed to keep one's word. Such behaviour not only quickly taught the Chechens—and other Caucasians—not to trust the Russians, but also increased their contempt and hatred for their new uninvited neighbours.

[21] Ibid., pp. 147–8.
[22] Ibid., p. 144.

Such deeds and operations were accompanied by the draconian set of rules Yermolov forced on those Chechens who 'preferred' to accept Russian rule in order to stay on their land. According to these rules, 'The Chechens were obliged to supply guard details and keep them everywhere. These details always had to be ready to fight their own so-called "unpacified brethren".'[23] Yermolov, on whom 'nothing has any influence ... except his own vanity',[24] boasted,

There has been no precedent yet of someone being able to force a Chechen to fight his co-tribesmen; but the first step towards this has already been taken and it has been impressed upon them that this will always be demanded of them.[25]

In his vanity Yermolov did not realise 'that although the crater of the volcano had been cleansed, the internal fire was far from extinguished.'[26] The volcano was soon to erupt again.

The main lesson the Chechens learnt from the events of 1817–21 was the need to unite against the invading enemy. On 5 June 1821 an all-Chechen gathering of elders in the mosque of Mayurtup made the first step towards such a union: it declared Mullah Muhammad of Mayurtup, a renowned *'alim* and a disciple of Shaykh Muhammad al-Yaraghi,[27] chief spiritual leader of the country. It also decided to call upon Beybulat Taymiyev to organise the common struggle against the Russians.

Beybulat was born in 1778/9 in Belty, a hamlet of Geldygen, not far from the great and important village of Shali. His first moment of fame came on 9 October 1802 when he was 24 years old. At the head of six men he crossed the Terek where they met a party of Cossacks and took Colonel del Pozzo prisoner.[28] He continued as a leader, his increasing fame reflected in the growing number of warriors who followed him on each raid. However, on 18 September 1807 Beybulat arrived at Vladikavkaz to negotiate a captain's rank and a yearly salary of 250 roubles offered by the Russians, and on the following day he joined the service of the Tsar. Following that

[23] Kolosov (note 10), p. 43.
[24] Quoted in Whittock (note 1), p. 58.
[25] Quoted in Kolosov (note 10), p. 43.
[26] Quoted in M. Gammer, *Muslim Resistance to the Tsar: Shamil and the Conquest of Chechnia and Daghestan* (London: Frank Cass, 1994), p. 34.
[27] See following chapter.
[28] See chapter 2, above.

he was called to Tiflis where he met the governor and commander-in-chief, Gudovich. Nevertheless, Beybulat's time in the Russian service was short and in January 1808 he returned to the mountains of Chechnya. In 1810 he was again raiding the Russian Line, his party now counting 600 men.[29] However, on 11 June 1811 he was in Tiflis once more, meeting with the governor and commander-in-chief, Tormasov, and the next day rejoining the Russian service.

Beybulat's decision might have been influenced by Tormasov's instruction to 'bribe Chechen elders and clergy' by offering them an annual pension of 250 and 150 roubles respectively. This offer seems to have been a catalyst in the outbreak of an internal struggle among Chechen elders in August 1810[30]—one of the Russians' most successful implementations of a 'divide and rule' tactic. This time Beybulat's stay in the Tsar's service was even shorter. In August 1811 he joined forces with 'Ali Khan of Avaristan against the Russians. Since the joint venture would have taken some time to negotiate, Beybulat must have escaped the Russian camp—taking hostage a Russian major—sometime before the end of June. Although the joint Avar-Chechen force was defeated by the Russians, Beybulat's fame and importance continued to grow and he appears to have become the most important leader in Chechnya. At least this is how the Russians regarded him, since in September–October 1816 Yermolov, on his way to assume command at Tiflis, bothered to meet Beybulat twice. Beybulat was again enlisted and designated the rank of ensign, though this did not entail any duties and 'he could live quietly at his home in Geldygen'.[31] However, Yermolov failed to use Beybulat to control Chechnya and, whether out of preference or the lack of an alternative (though the former seems more likely), he decided to use force. Consequently, within two years Beybulat was active once again. In August 1818 he was the leader who called on the Avars to join in the attack on the fortress being built at Groznaia, and the following October in that same fortress he conducted negotiations on behalf of the Chechens with Grekov.

Now, after the June 1821 gathering in Mayurtup, Beybulat started to raid the Russian Line from the Kachkalyk range—his base of

---

[29] In one of those raids in the summer of that year he was wounded. In fact his life was saved by his nephew.

[30] Aydamirov (note 14), p. 32.

[31] Kolosov (note 10), p. 32.

support. However, not all Chechen leaders accepted Beybulat's supremacy. At the beginning of 1822 one of his major rivals, Mullah 'Abd al-Qadir from Germenchuk, called for a general uprising under his leadership. Consequently, he carried out raids against the Russians from his own base of power—the basins of the Argun and Shavdon rivers.

Grekov's reaction was, once more, a punitive expedition in February that destroyed several Chechen villages. However, on 23 February Mullah 'Abd al-Qadir was killed in battle, which lessened the intensity of Chechen pressure on the Caucasian Line. In November Grekov carried out another expedition, destroying a few villages, but he was blocked by Beybulat's followers reinforced by Daghestanis. All that time Beybulat 'used the good offices' (to use modern terminology) of the Shamkhal of Tarku—one of Russia's Daghestani vassals—to arrange a meeting with Yermolov. This finally took place in Erpeli (one of the Shamkhal's villages) in January 1824, 'but instead of a dialogue there was a monologue by Yermolov, in which Russia once again put forward conditions, or more correctly an ultimatum.'[32]

Several days later, in January 1824, another all-Chechen gathering took place in Mayurtup led by Mullah Muhammad of Mayurtup, Avko of Germenchuk and Beybulat. Once again the gathering decided on a united struggle against the Russians, proclaiming Avko Imam (according to some sources temporarily). The military leadership was left to Beybulat.

Revolt soon spread throughout Chechnya and the Ingush, the Kabartay and the Aksay Kumyks, as well as some Ossets and a few hundred Daghestanis, joined in. Grekov, who at first had dismissed reports of the revolt, soon had to act:

[Grekov] resorted to all his usual methods, but in vain. [In June 1825] one of the popular leaders [Janbulat Chetsoyev] was publicly flogged to death [and his body displayed on the wall of Groznaia], others within an inch of their lives. But no punishment he was able to inflict made any serious impression on the enemy; or rather, his cruelty served only to exasperate them.[33]

In January and again in March 1825 Grekov carried out punitive-cum-felling expeditions, in which he 'marched hither and thither, but the Chechens evaded him or suffered only minor defeats'.[34]

---

[32] Vachagayev (note 15), p. 75.
[33] Baddeley (note 2), pp. 148–9.
[34] Ibid., p. 149.

On 5 June 1825 another general gathering convened in Mayur-tup. This time Sheikh Muhammad of Kudatli, a Daghestani disciple of the Naqshbandi Sheikh Muhammad al-Yaraghi, who had recently settled in Mayurtup, was appointed Imam. Less than two weeks later, on 25 June, Beybulat threatened Gerzel Aul, forcing Grekov to march to its rescue. As soon as the Russians arrived, on 27 June, Beybulat took off. On 4 July he met Daghestani reinforcements who had answered his and Sheikh Muhammad's call. Later that month, on the night of 20–21 July, the Chechens and their allies stormed and destroyed the fort of Amir-Hajji-Yurt (nowadays in Daghestan). Of its 181-strong garrison 98 were killed and 13 taken prisoner. In addition to the rich booty, Beybulat captured a cannon. From Amir-Hajji-Yurt the Chechens and their allies proceeded to attack Zlobnyi Okop and Prigradnyi Stan. Threatened with encir-clement, Grekov was forced to march back to Groznaia.

Once Grekov had departed, Beybulat returned to lay siege to Gerzel Aul. Grekov had to march again in that direction, this time accompanied by his superior, the Commander of the Left Flank of the Caucasian Line, General Lisanovich. On 27 July the Russians arrived at Gerzel Aul, but Beybulat had retreated into the nearby hills. On the following day they invited 318 elders from all the Che-chen and Kumyk villages in the area, intending to arrest them once they had all arrived. Opening the reception, Lisanovich strongly re-buked and insulted the elders in their own language.[35] Then, threat-ening to punish them for treachery, he ordered them to give up their *kinjals* (daggers)—an insufferable insult to a mountaineer's man-hood and pride. A certain Uchar Hajji Ya'qub refused to do so. Grekov lost his temper and slapped Uchar Hajji in the face. Within seconds Uchar Hajji hacked Grekov and two other officers to death and dealt mortal wounds to Lisanovich. However, before expiring the general managed to order the Russian soldiers to kill all the natives. According to eye-witnesses, 'the furious soldiers did not spare any-one in an oriental costume who caught their eye. Even three Geor-gians and several Greben Cossacks were killed.'[36]

On receiving this news Yermolov set out for Vladikavkaz. Pull-ing down forts and building others, he spent the rest of the year

[35] Probably Kumyk, the *lingua franca* in the North-Eastern Caucasus.
[36] Quoted in Vachagayev (note 15), p. 77.

there relocating the Line. Meanwhile the rebellion spread and a number of Russian forts and *stanitsas* were attacked and some of them taken. On 10 September 1825 Beybulat even attacked Groznaia in what looks like a demonstration rather than a real attempt to take it. And on 7 December he almost captured the 'Proconsul' in an ambush. Finally in January 1826 Yermolov started his campaign. Moving back and forth through the country he 'punished the rebellious Chechens, burning their villages, destroying their crops, beating them in skirmishes that never developed into battles and, occasionally, even seeking to win them over by an unwonted display of clemency.'[37]

Since 'to outward appearances his success was complete,'[38] Yermolov returned to Tiflis triumphant. However, this was his last triumph, his career soon coming to an abrupt end following his failure when faced with the Qajar invasion of 1826,[39] and on 9 April 1827 he left the Caucasus never to return. Nevertheless, his actions had ensured that Russo-Chechen relations would never be the same, but in a manner of which all Imperial Russian sources and a great number of Soviet ones remained unaware. Not only did his extremely brutal and cruel methods fail to achieve the intended results, they also increased Chechens' internal resistance to the tactics of terror, virtually eradicating their fear of the Russians. Furthermore his activities had propagated such a hatred of Russia in the hearts of the Chechens that any Russian attempt to win them over by peaceful means had become virtually impossible.

A close examination of the events clearly shows that Yermolov was far from successful. However, this does not mean that the Chechens were victorious. 'One of the reasons for the Chechen failures (the loss of a considerable territory) in the struggle with the Russian empire', wrote a Chechen historian, 'lies in the lack of a united, centralised authority, [in the lack] of co-ordination with the other peoples of the Northern Caucasus, and [in] the discord within the leadership of the movement.'[40] Indeed, on 6 August 1825, in another

---

[37] Baddeley (note 2), p. 153.

[38] Ibid., *loc. cit.*

[39] For an evaluation of Yermolov in the Caucasus, see Moshe Gammer, '"Proconsul of the Caucasus": A Re-examination of Yermolov', *Social Evolution and History*, 2, 1 (March 2003), pp. 166–84.

[40] Vachagayev (note 15), pp. 84–5.

general gathering in Mayurtup, a rift occurred between Beybulat and the other two leaders. This was the real reason for the decline of the Chechen struggle that allowed Yermolov to believe he had won. Beybulat continued to be active until his murder on 26 July 1831. He tried to enlist Qajar and Ottoman help, and in 1826/7 even went to Tehran. In 1829 he visited Tiflis in yet another attempt to find a *modus vivendi* with the Russians. But after 1826 his movement—as also that of Avko, Mulla Muhammad and Sheikh Muhammad—was finished. A new force and a new leadership—the Naqshbandiyya from Daghestan—was to take the stage, and in recognition of that fact the old one took its final bow in the spring of 1830.

5

THE GREAT GAZAVAT

Whether a Naqshbandi or not, Mansur did not introduce the order to the Caucasus. The branch of the Naqshbandiyya that has actually taken root there (mainly, but not exclusively, in Daghestan)—the Khalidiyya—is named after Sheikh Ziya al-Din Khalid al-Shahra-zuri (1776–1827), one of the most important and least studied figures in the history of the modern Muslim world.[1] The message of Sheikh Khalid was carried to the Caucasus in the 1810s by one of his deputies,[2] and by the mid 1820s the order had already become strongly established in Daghestan and was making fast progress in Chechnya.[3]

One of the secrets of the Naqshbandiyya's lightning success in the Caucasus was timing. It happened to arrive at the exact moment the Mountaineers felt their physical and spiritual world was falling apart under the Russians' (especially Yermolov's) blows. Furthermore, it arrived offering not only a solution to their problem, but in particular a set of beliefs and rules of behaviour, a plan of action, religious, social and ultimately political activism, and a new leadership

---

[1] For Sheikh Khalid, see Butrus Abu Manneh, 'The Naqshbandiyya-Mujaddidiyya in the Ottoman Lands in the Early 19th Century', *Die Welt des Islams*, XII (1982), pp. 1–12; Albert Hourani, 'Sufism and Modern Islam: Maulana Khalid and the Naqshbandi Order' in Albert Hourani, *The Emergence of the Middle East* (London: Macmillan, 1981), pp. 75–89.

[2] See Butrus Abu Manneh, 'The Role of Shaykh Isma'il al-Shirwani in the Khalidi Sub-Order' in Moshe Gammer and David Wasserstein (eds), *Daghestan in the World of Islam* (Helsinki, forthcoming).

[3] For the spread of the Naqshbandiyya-Khalidiyya, see Moshe Gammer, 'The Beginnings of the Naqshbandiyya in Daghestan and the Russian Conquest of the Caucasus', *Die Welt des Islams*, 34 (1994), pp. 204–17.

to replace the old one discredited through either failure or submission to Russia.

Even more than Sheikh Mansur forty-four years earlier, the Naqshbandi-Khalidi leaders in Daghestan were far from eager either to assume power and lead local society, or to declare war on Russia. Accordingly they did their utmost to avoid the latter. However, the new Tsar (since 1825), Nicholas I, left them no choice. Drunk with the quick and easy success achieved in the wars with the Qajars (1826–8) and the Ottomans (1828–9), he ordered his Commander-in-Chief in the Caucasus to add to that 'glorious deed, another ... in my eyes as glorious and ... by far more important', that is 'to tame forever the mountain peoples, or *exterminate the insubordinate*' [emphasis added]. This had to be done in one mighty blow, 'as decisive as it should be unexpected'.[4]

Faced with an imminent Russian assault the Naqshbandi leadership, after a bitter debate, declared Ghazi Muhammad (known in Russian sources as Kazi Mullah) Imam, and he in his turn declared holy war on Russia. Thus started the 'Great Gazavat', which would last for thirty years (1829–59).

Ghazi Muhammad's authority was acknowledged by all the Chechen resistance leaders in the spring of 1830 (that is within two to three months of his becoming Imam). In May he sent one of his confidants, Sheikh 'Abdalla of Ashilta (in Daghestan), to rally the Chechens to his cause. Helped by Avko, Beybulat and other Chechen leaders, Sheikh 'Abdalla proved very successful. In October 1830 Ghazi Muhammad himself arrived in Greater Chechnya and, visiting the different villages, strengthened his authority.

In 1831, having established his authority, Ghazi Muhammad went on the offensive, taking advantage of the great depletion in the Russian forces in the Caucasus caused by the Polish revolt. Noticing how slow the Russian army was compared to the swiftness of the Mountaineers, and taking advantage of the fact that he was fighting from internal lines, he initiated a series of surprise strikes in various directions. At the beginning of June he laid siege to Burnaia and by the end of that month he joined 'Abdalla at Vnezapnaia.

[4] V. G. Gadzhiev and Kh. Kh. Ramazanov (eds), *Dvizhenie gortsevv severo-vostochnogo Kavkaza v 20–50 gg. XIX v. Sbornik dokumentov* (Makhachkala: Dagestanskoe Kniznoe Izdatel'stvo, 1959), pp. 58–9, document no. 32. Letter from Nicholas I to Paskevich, 25 September [7 October] 1829. Quotations from p. 58.

While Ghazi Muhammad was operating in Daghestan, 'Abdalla was inadvertently aided by the Russians in his efforts to enlist the Chechens: a series of punitive expeditions during the winter of 1830–1 destroyed about thirty-five villages, and the ranks of 'Abdallah's supporters swelled. On 7 June 1831 the Imam's deputy arrived in the vicinity of Vnezapnaia, blocked the approach roads and by 26 June had started a siege of the fortress itself. On 29 June Ghazi Muhammad arrived to take over command. Only on 11 July did he retreat into the mountains within sight of a Russian relief force. However, this may have been a ruse: the Russian force, led by Emmanuel, the commander of the Caucasian Line, followed Ghazi Muhammad, but on 13 July it was attacked and defeated in a thick forest near Aktash Aukh. Among the 400 Russian casualties was the wounded Emmanuel, who had to transfer command of the Line to Vel'iaminov.

Without delay Ghazi Muhammad set off for Daghestan, where he besieged Darbend in late August and early September. Two months later, by threatening Groznaia, he lured Vel'iaminov to the area between the Terek and Sunja rivers, then on 13 November 1831 stormed Kyzliar. In this 'terrible catastrophe' 134 civilians were killed and forty-five wounded, and 168 people, mostly women, were captured. Their ransom, remarked a Russian source, 'supplied Ghazi Muhammad and his followers with a solid sum of money'.[5]

No wonder the Imam's fame spread throughout the Caucasus and people flocked to his banner from its various eastern districts: Kumyks, Kara Nogays, Karabulaks, the Kabartay and the 'semi-pagan Ingush, who had nothing in common with the *shari'a*,[6] now interrupted communications along Russia's lifeline across the Caucasus—the Georgian Military Highway leading from Vladikavkaz to Tbilisi. The new commander-in-chief in the Caucasus, Baron Rosen, on his arrival in Tiflis on 20 October 1831 had to deal urgently with the challenge posed by Ghazi Muhammad. Rosen decided—or rather was ordered by the Tsar—to carry out a concentrated campaign to get rid of the Imam once and for all. But before that Ghazi Muhammad carried out another of his lightning-raids. At the end of March he arrived in the area of Vladikavkaz and

[5] N. A. Volkonskii, F. fon Kliman and P. Bublitskii, 'Voina na vostochnom Kavkaze s 1824 po 1839 g. v sviazi s miuridizmom', *Kavkazkii Sbornik*, XIV, p. 123.

[6] Ibid., pp. 116–17.

even attempted to storm Nazran. Then on 8 April he arrived at Groznaia where, according to a Russian observer,

it caused him no harm to stay ... to cause panic in the nearby *auls* and along the Line, and to see again the Russian forces shutting themselves in the fortress on his account. In addition, such manoeuvres trained the Chechens to obedience, to concentration and marches, increased their ties to the Imam, and gave him plentiful material for future thought without taking any risk at all.[7]

Having conducted several punitive expeditions in Chechnya since the summer of 1831, the Russians started their overall assault in August 1832. During that month two columns of about 10,000 men each, commanded by Rosen and Vel'iaminov, criss-crossed Lesser and Greater Chechnya and systematically looted and destroyed about eighty villages, their gardens and fields. From Chechnya the unified force crossed to Daghestan where on 29 October it stormed Ghazi Muhammad's fortified position near his native village of Gimry. Trapped in a nearby house, the Imam with about fifty followers resisted to the last, although two miraculously survived. The spot where Ghazi Muhammad was killed is now a *mazar* (place of pilgrimage) and small mausoleum has been built there.[8]

It is difficult to overstate the importance of Ghazi Muhammad, who as the first Naqshbandi Imam established many, if not all, of the policies, practices, strategies and tactics followed by his successors. He was, for example, the first to use, explicitly against the Russians, the twin strategies of, on the one hand, uniting all the Mountaineers in total struggle and, on the other, attempting to reach an accommodation with them from a position of 'nuisance value'. He was also the first to build on Mansur's experience, pointing out the Russians' weak points and demonstrating how to exploit them with swift movements and surprise attacks, as well as by defending fortified positions. Most crucially he taught his successors the importance of taking the initiative.

According to a shrewd Russian commentator, Ghazi Muhammad consciously prepared the Mountaineers for a long struggle, trying

---

[7] Ibid., *Kavkazkii Sbornik*, XVI, pp. 456–7.
[8] Alexandre Beningsen and Chantal Lemercier-Quelquejay, *Le sufi et le commissaire. Les confréries musulmanes en URSS* (Paris: Seuil, 1986), p. 186.

'to bind together this scattered raw material … to train [them] to single-minded actions'. In his campaigns he endeavoured to accustom them to long manoeuvres beyond their home areas. He even devised a sophisticated way of misinforming the Russians by spreading false rumours, while keeping his intentions secret. He was also responsible for urging the Chechens to move out of their large villages and scatter among the many hamlets in the midst of their primeval forests. He also advised them to grow maize instead of wheat:

This advice was of extraordinary importance: […] Henceforward the Chechens would live in the midst of inaccessible forests. […] They would lose nothing when their huts were destroyed, and would be able to rebuild them promptly. […] The forests would provide shelter for their families, livestock and the little property they had. […] The change from wheat to maize was calculated to preserve the inaccessibility of the country by limiting the cultivated area. The rich crops of maize … could easily feed the population and replace the loss of bread.

All these measures, the Russian commentator concluded, were intended to make the Chechens 'vigilant, always ready to fight or run, and little sensitive to destruction. […] A well-conceived system of popular war was being organised against us, which could not be better suited to the local conditions and the Chechen tribes' primeval way of life.'[9]

Russian hopes that the death of Ghazi Muhammad would put an end to his movement were soon dashed. A short time after his death, a new Imam was proclaimed—Hamzat Bek. However, during his short reign (November 1832–September 1834) the second Imam was engrossed in the affairs of central Daghestan and was, therefore, hardly involved at all in the affairs of other parts of Daghestan, much less of Chechnya. Nevertheless, Ghazi Muhammad's work did not stop there. It was continued by a new generation of Chechen war leaders who had grown under the first Naqshbandi Imam and his deputy, Sheikh 'Abdalla. The most outstanding among them was Tasho Hajji (known in Russian sources as Tashev Hajji).

Tasho's place of birth and even his nationality are a matter of debate. In local chronicles (written in Arabic) he is known as 'al-Indiri', meaning 'from the village of Enderi'. As such he could be either a Kumyk or a Chechen, since Enderi was a Kumyk village

---

[9] Volkonskii, fon Kliman and Bublitskii (note 5), pp. 457–70.

with a sizeable Chechen minority among its population. However, he is buried in Sayasan in Chechnya (near Nozhay-Yurt), and since Chechens, like all North Caucasians, make great efforts to ensure they are buried in their ancestral villages, Chechen historians regard him as a Chechen and Sayasan as his place of birth.[10] Whatever his background, the first mention of Tasho in available sources places him in Enderi, where he had been the Mullah, in 1831 by which time he had probably already performed a pilgrimage to Mecca since the title Hajji had been added to his name. At about that time he joined Ghazi Muhammad as a Naqshbandi disciple. In fact, it was he who introduced the Naqshbandiyya into Chechnya.[11]

After the death of Ghazi Muhammad Tasho Hajji was slow to recognise his successor. Only in the summer of 1834—shortly before the assassination of the second Imam on 19 September 1834—did Tasho Hajji recognise Hamzat Bek as Imam and accept his authority. It was probably then—and not after the death of the second Imam, as a Soviet historian dated it—that Tasho Hajji called on 'all the Muslims' to follow the *shari'a* and stated that 'now the time has arrived for us to return to the domains of the Imam Hamzat.'[12]

Within a few days of Hamzat's assassination, the third Imam was proclaimed in Ashilta (Daghestan). This was Shamil, a co-villager, distant relative by marriage, and close friend of Ghazi Muhammad and one of his first followers. Shamil was destined to lead the resistance for the next twenty-five years, and bring it to unprecedented peaks of success. He became its most famous leader, whose name would be known and admired far beyond his native land.

But all this was still to come. At the moment Shamil was far from being acknowledged as Imam, even in Daghestan. In Chechnya Tasho Hajji felt strong enough and senior enough to challenge Shamil and proclaim himself Imam. In fact, at first he was far the stronger of the two, at least with regard to the number of warriors under his command. In challenging Shamil—who enjoyed a broader base of legitimation—Tasho Hajji had two advantages, on which he now tried

[10] e.g. A. Aydamirov, *Khronologiia: istorii Checheno-Ingushetii* (Groznyi: Kniga, 1992), p. 43.

[11] Bennigsen and Lemercier-Quelquejay (note 8), p. 186; A. Bennigsen and S. E. Wimbush, *Muslims of the Soviet Empire: A Guide* (London: Hurst, 1985), p. 187.

[12] Quoted in A. B. Zaks, *Tashev-Khadzhi. Spodvizhnik Shamilia* (Groznyi: Kniga, 1992), pp. 12–13. The proclamation, found in 1937, is undated.

his hardest to capitalise: his fame as a war leader (or guerrilla leader in modern terms) and his tenacity in enforcing the *shariʻa*. Tasho Hajji therefore launched frequent small scale raids to harass the Russian Line. According to a Soviet historian, he

....tried to introduce the elements of system and order into the spontaneous, uncoordinated actions of the local Chechen detachments. He started to regulate the mobilisation of troops: each house had to supply one man to the militia. In each of the annexed areas a fortified point was established, using at the same time the gathering place of the local militia. [...] These fortified points were by no means fortresses but only shields to keep the enemy at bay thus giving the population time to find shelter in the forests. As a rule, such fortified places were constructed not inside *auls* but in their vicinity.

In order to regulate government Tasho Hajji nominated a leader over each of the annexed areas. [...] Thus the prototypes of [Shamil's] future *na'ib*-doms were created. However, this measure was not fortified by a definite administrative system, such as Shamil introduced in the future, and therefore it could not overcome the 'centrifugal' forces in Chechen society or properly promote Chechen unity in their struggle for independence.[13]

One of the reasons for this was the fact that the Russians would not allow Tasho Hajji to consolidate his 'proto-state'. His incessant raids on the Line created an unbearable situation for the Russians:

The daily alarms caused by small raiding parties penetrating through the cordon along the Terek constantly kept the troops constituting the cordon mounted and with muskets in hand. The position of the dwellers of the *stanitsy* [i.e. the Cossacks] was even worse, because they, expecting a raid every minute, could not engage in their agricultural work.

To contain the Chechens our troops used to carry out raids within the foe's territory. We used to burn his [the foe's] villages, seize goats, sometimes capture a number of men and women as prisoners, bring into submission the frightened savages, take hostages from them to keep them in submission, and having accomplished nothing, return to the Sunja with a train of killed and wounded officers and lower ranks. The [destroyed] villages would then be re-established and in our wake Tasho Hajji would reappear among the[ir] devastated inhabitants.[14]

If from the Russian point of view these 'raids' or 'punitive expeditions' did not bring the desired results, for the Chechens they

---

[13] Ibid., pp. 13–14.
[14] I. Drozdov, 'Nachalo deiatel'nosti Shamilia (1834–1836 g.)', *Kavkazskii Sbornik*, XX, p. 275.

were disastrous. 'Hundreds of settlements', wrote a Chechen historian, 'were burnt, the result being thousands of people killed, the absolute majority of whom were civilians—women, old people, children.'[15] In January 1836 Colonel Pullo, the commander of the Sunja Line since 1834, carried out such a 'punitive raid':

About 1,200 regular troops were poised against the village of Kishkeroy, which contained several dozen houses. During the entire day of 27 December 1835 [8 January 1836] Pullo failed to conquer the small village. [...] 'Many locked themselves in with their families [reported Pullo] ... and had to be dislodged at the point of the bayonet. In two adjacent houses four Chechens with two women and three little children [held on] during the entire day and night ... and had to be smoked out by throwing burning hay and firewood through the chimneys. When the house was on fire two of them, dagger in hand, jumped headlong through the doors on the surrounding *jägers* and were bayoneted to death. Two, wounded by our fire, were found burnt. The women and children were saved by our soldiers.' In this battle forty people were taken prisoner: two men (both wounded), thirteen little boys, seven women (one of them wounded) and eighteen girls, aged one to fourteen. The rest of the population were slaughtered.[16]

Such events were not infrequent. They happened each time the Russians managed to fall on the Chechens undetected, giving them no time to save their families and movables by escaping into the surrounding forests. In a great number of such cases resistance was followed by a 'terrible massacre'.[17]

[15] M. Vachagayev, 'Chechnia v Kavkazskoi voine, 1816–1859' (Moscow, 1995), p. 109.
[16] Ibid., pp. 109–10.
[17] The scenes of looting and carnage that followed the conquest of native *auls* were described with great disgust by Tolstoy and even in stronger terms by Lermontov:

> *Auls are burning, their defenders mastered,*
> *The homeland's sons have fallen in battle.*
> *Like steady comets, fearful to the eyes,*
> *A glow is playing 'cross the skies,*
> *A beast of prey with bayonet, the victor*
> *Charges into a quiet dwelling.*
> *He kills the children and the old folks,*
> *And with his bloody hands he strokes*
> *The unmarried girls and young mothers.*
> *But woman's heart can match her brother's!*
> *After those kisses, a dagger's drawn,*

The Russian blows, while not decisive enough to eliminate Tasho Hajji's influence in Chechnya and put an end to his activity, were nevertheless strong enough to force him into the arms of Shamil. Consequently, at the beginning of 1836 Tasho Hajji aligned himself with Shamil, recognising him as an equal. Gradually thereafter Tasho Hajji was compelled to recognise Shamil's superiority and accept his authority. The process speeded up when on 4 September 1836 Pullo managed to destroy Tasho Hajji's stronghold near Zandak. By the end of 1837 Tasho Hajji had become one of Shamil's *na'ibs* (deputies). In the following few years, until his death by natural causes in

---

> *A Russian cowers, gasps—he's gone!*
> *'Avenge me, comrade!' And in just a breath*
> *(A fine revenge for a murderer's death)*
> *The little house, delighting their gaze,*
> *Now burns: Circassian freedom set ablaze!*

(Mikhail Iur'evich Lermontov, 'Izmail Bey', pt. III. Translation by S. Layton, *Russian Literature and Empire: Conquest of the Caucasus from Pushkin to Tolstoy* [Cambridge University Press, 1994], p. 142).

The usual justification of Russian commanders reporting such massacres was that 'the exasperated soldiers had lost control', which reminds one of General Custer's usual order before attacking an American–Indian encampment: 'Spare the women and children, *if you can!*' [emphasis added]. The issue goes further than the question of how fit the officers are who lose control over their soldiers, however. There seems to have been a feeling, an implicit assumption within the Russian army, percolating from generation to generation, from the Imperial to the 'Red', or Soviet army, which was perhaps best expressed by Stalin. Criticising Yugoslav complaints of 'many serious assaults on citizens and on members of the Yugoslav army' by 'men and parties of men in the Red Army', Stalin said:

> Can't he [i.e. Djilas] understand it if a soldier, who has crossed thousands of kilometres through blood and fire and death, has fun with a woman or takes a trifle? (Milovan Djilas, *Conversations with Stalin*. Trans. Michael B. Petrovich [London: Hart-Davis, 1962], p. 81). 'According to complaints filed by citizens,' wrote Djilas, '121 cases of rape, of which 111 involved rape with murder, and 1,204 cases of looting with assault' were recorded (ibid., p. 82).

In the 'civilised' 1830s, unlike the 'barbaric' times of Suvorov and Yermolov (this was the self-image of the Russian élite under Nicholas I, starting with the Tsar himself) such deeds—or rather talking about them—were not *bon ton* any more. This meant that all explicit talk about such deeds was to be suppressed. As for the 'barbaric' acts themselves, the soldiers continued to commit them with the officers washing their hands of them. After all, did not Nicholas I himself, who took such pride in the abolition of capital punishment, condemn people to certain death by sentencing them to run the gauntlet several hundred times?

1843, Tasho Hajji would be among Shamil's most important lieutenants and would play a role in consolidating the third Naqshbandi Imam's rule in Chechnya. Nevertheless Shamil would always
remain suspicious of Tasho Hajji and consider him a threat. After
his death Tasho Hajji's importance continued to be recognised as
his tomb in Sayasan became a major place of pilgrimage.[18]

During the 1830s, under all three Imams, Chechnya—whether
accepting their leadership or not—played a secondary role in the
struggle. All three Imams resided in Daghestan and were engrossed
in securing their rule in that country. Consequently, the Russians
also concentrated their attention and efforts on Daghestan. True to
their 'one blow' strategy, which they deemed so successful in the
case of Ghazi Muhammad, the Russians launched major campaigns
against the second and third Imams, at least whenever the Imams'
successes diverted the Russians' attention from the strategically more
important north-western Caucasus.[19] Campaigns in Chechnya, though
on a much larger scale than before, were clearly subordinate to the
main effort. In 1837 and again in 1839 the Russians launched two
major campaigns against Shamil in Daghestan.[20] In the latter campaign General Grabbe after an 80-day-long siege conquered Shamil's
stronghold Akhulgo, and although the Imam with his family and a
few confidants managed to escape and find shelter in Chechnya,
the Russians considered 'the matter finished'. 'The rebel', reported
Grabbe,

…no longer enjoys any trust in the Mountains or a haven …; nowhere can
he find a place more inaccessible than his previous nest, Akhulgo, or followers braver than those who sacrificed their lives for him. His party is
finally destroyed; his *murids*, abandoned by their leader, perished.[21]

---

[18] Bennigsen and Wimbush (note 11), p. 189; Bennigsen and Lemercier-Quelquejay (note 8), p. 186.

[19] See Moshe Gammer, 'Russian Strategies in the Conquest of Chechnia and
Daghestan, 1825–1859' in Marie Bennigsen-Broxup (ed.), *The North Caucasus
Barrier: The Russian Advance towards the Muslim World* (London: Hurst, 1992),
pp. 45–61.

[20] On this see Moshe Gammer, 'A Switzer in the Caucasus: Faesy's Campaigns in
Chechnia and Daghestan', *Middle Eastern Studies*, 30, 3 (July 1994), pp. 668–82;
Moshe Gammer, 'The Siege of Akhulgoh: A Reconstruction and Reinterpreta-
tion', *Asian and African Studies* (Haifa), 25, 2 (July 1991), pp. 103–18.

[21] *AKAK*, vol. IX, p. 333, document no. 298, Grabbe to Golovin, 24 August
[5 September] 1839, no. 456.

Furthermore, the Russians now considered the spirit of the natives finally broken. The execution of the plans for 1840, according to Grabbe's prediction, 'will meet no resistance [...] No serious unrest or a general uprising need be anticipated.'[22] The time seemed ripe for introducing direct rule into Chechnya. 'Supervisors' [*pristavy*], many of them natives in the Tsar's service and considered traitors by their communities, settled in the Chechens' midst and strictly watched the conduct of the villages under their supervision.'[23]

Soon the Chechens became acquainted with the 'benefits' of Russian rule:

Under the pretext of collecting taxes and fines their best [belongings] were taken; it happened that completely innocent people were arrested because of a denunciation by simple and often ill-intentioned translators; detainees and even hostages were treated inhumanely ... and during [military] expeditions forced collections [of food and livestock] were permitted.[24]

These acts of corruption, probably not greatly exceeding the norm elsewhere in the empire of the Tsars, were unbearable to the Chechens. However, the Russians followed this action with a bigger mistake when they started to confiscate firearms. As already mentioned, weapons for the Mountaineers were more than a practical necessity; they were their pride and signified their manhood and freedom. Weapons were handed down from father to son, and regarded as a man's most precious possessions.

Naturally, the Chechens expected this humiliation to be followed by greater ones. Soon the country was swarming with rumours of Russian intentions to press the disarmed population into serfdom, to conscript the men into the army and, most humiliating, to force the women into domestic service. In this context a few 'careless words' attributed to Pullo had a particularly strong effect: 'Now that

---

[22] Grabbe to Golovin, 19 [31] January 1840, as quoted in M. Gammer, *Muslim Resistance to the Tsar: Shamil and the Conquest of Chechnia and Daghestan* (London: Frank Cass, 1994), p. 113.

[23] V. G. Gadzhiev and Kh. Kh. Ramazanov (eds), *Dvizhenie gartsevv severo-vostochnogo Kavkaza v 20–50 gg. XIX v. Sbornik dokumentov.* (Makhachkala: Dagestanskoe Kniznoe Izdatel'stvo, 1959), pp. 280–91, document no. 154, 'Memorandum on the situation on the Left Flank of the Caucasian Line between 1834 and 1840 and the Necessary Measures to Strengthen Russian Rule There', written by Pullo in 1840, p. 285.

[24] A. Iurov, '1840, 1841 i 1842-i gody na Kavkaze', *Kavkazskii Sbornik*, X, p. 271.

we have taken away their arms, we have only to take off their women's trousers.'[25] Not surprisingly, villages in the mountains that were relatively inaccessible to the Russian army refused to submit and accept 'supervisors'. To subdue them, other villages that had submitted were forbidden to have any contact with them. More specifically, they were forbidden to sell them grain and to let them use their pastures, this being considered an especially effective measure because that year the crops had failed all over the Caucasus.

Soon the Chechens were ready for an armed rising against Russian rule. All they needed was a leader they could all accept—and such a person had been living among them for half a year. Arriving in Chechnya with only seven followers, Shamil settled in the hamlet of Gharashkiti in the community of Shatoy (known also as Shubut). He soon started

...to tame the residents. [...] The Imam's modest work was crowned by unexpected results ...: Rumours about his sagacity, his wise and just resolution of various quarrels and lawsuits spread in the entire area. The residents of Shatoy started to flock to Shamil asking [him] to teach them how to live according to [the principles of] religion and truth. The fame of the Imam grew and spread rapidly [and] the Chechens who were under the administration of Russian *pristavs* could not help but compare Shamil's conduct with the activities of our administration, and once such a comparison had been made it, of course, proved to be far from favourable toward the latter. Then the Chechens, led to extremes by our incompetence and abuses, decided to ask the Imam ... to head their armed rebellion.[26]

Applying lessons learnt from earlier encounters, Shamil and his men used classic guerrilla tactics to exploit their position amid the forests and mountains.

[Shamil] threatened the enemy north, east, [west] and south, kept them continually on the move, dispersed his commandos to their homes, gathered them again as if by magic, and aided by the extraordinary mobility of mounted troops who required no baggage, nor any equipment or supplies but what each individual carried with him, swooped down on the Russians continually where least expected.[27]

[25] John F. Baddeley, *The Rugged Flanks of the Caucasus* (Oxford University Press, 1940), vol. II, p. 78.

[26] A. and N. V. Iurov, '1840, 1841 i 1842-i gody na Kavkaze', *Kavkazskii Sbornik*, p. 278.

[27] J. F. Baddeley, *The Russian Conquest of the Caucasus* (London: Longman, Green, 1908), p. 364.

Furthermore, Shamil and his lieutenants,

> ...establishing a new mode of operations to be consistently followed in the future, almost always successfully avoided pitched battle with our forces, thanks to their amazing speed. In [trying to] chase them our columns were [only] brought to extreme exhaustion.[28]

The Russian reaction was to stick rigidly to their attempts to crush the resistance with a single blow. They therefore mounted successive expeditions in which they 'marched throughout Chechnya, sustained heavy losses, and achieved no results at all'.[29] Reprimanding his generals for failing to eliminate a 'band of robbers', Nicholas I sent in more troops, weapons and money, insisting on repeating the campaigns again and again. The result was greater losses each time. The breaking-point was General Grabbe's expedition of June 1842. The description given by a bitter opponent of Grabbe, though caricature-like, is probably closer to what really happened than Grabbe's own reports:

> Grabbe ... marched from Gerzel Aul on 30 May [11 June] up the defile of the Aksay on the left bank of that river, towards the villages of Shuani and Dargo [Shamil's 'capital'], having under his command over 10,000 men and twenty-four guns. [...]
>
> His intention was to reach Dargo quickly, destroy that village, then cross the range dividing Chechnya from northern Daghestan and subdue Gumbet and Andi. It must be noted that he undertook this movement at a time when he knew already that all Shamil's forces had been directed against Kazi-Kumukh [in Daghestan].
>
> At the same time the very magnitude of the force he collected for this movement served to impair efficiency. He had with him, to carry his military stores and provisions, a large number of carts and some 3,000 horses. On the march this baggage train, owing to the difficult nature of the roads, covered a distance several versts and to protect it even by a thin line of soldiers took nearly half the column. With a couple of battalions for the advance guard and as many for the rear, and the rest broken up to form the protecting lines on each side or help the train along, the whole force became extremely weak, having no man free to support the various units; besides which, it had to overcome very great difficulties, presented not only by nature but by the efforts of the Mountaineers, who quite understood that the march through the deep forests of Ichkeri gave them their

[28] Iurov (note 26), p. 286.
[29] A. I. Gagarin, 'Zapiski o Kavkaze', *Voennyi Sbornik*, 1906, 2, p. 34.

only chance of success, and that once the column emerged from the difficult defile they would be unable to do it any harm.

On 30 May [11 June] the column made only 7 *versts*, though no enemy was met. All that night rain fell heavily, making the roads still worse, and delaying progress to such an extent that up to the evening of the 31st [12 June] after 15 hours' march, fighting all the time, the column had only made 12 versts more, and was forced to bivouac for the night on a waterless plain.

Next day the number of the enemy had increased, though according to trustworthy accounts it reached less than 2,000 owing to their main forces being with Shamil in Kazi Kumukh; the road was yet more difficult, barricades more frequent, and for the second day the troops were without water. There were already several hundred wounded, and the general confusion increased hourly.

In this way the column made only 25 versts in three days, and General Grabbe saw that it was already impossible to continue the advance. On the night of 31 May–1 June [12–13 June] abandoning his enterprise, he gave orders to retreat by the same road.

If the advance was unfortunate, the retirement was infinitely more so.

The troops lost ... spirit; the confusion and want of control became extreme; no one made the proper dispositions, and no one troubled about keeping the column together. The retreat, which necessitated the abandonment or, when time allowed, the destruction of everything that could impede movement, if only to save the wounded, the guns, and perhaps some portion of the impedimenta, assumed the appearance of a complete rout; there were battalions that took flight at the mere barking of dogs. In these conditions the losses were bound to be excessive.

This picture, however sad, presented unfortunately the simple truth, without any exaggeration whatever. [...]

At last, on 4 [16] June, the ... column got back to Gerzel Aul, having lost sixty-six officers and more than 1,700 lower ranks killed, wounded and missing besides one field-gun and nearly all the provisions and stores.[30]

The shock of Grabbe's defeat reached St Petersburg. Prince Chernyshev, the Minister of War, observed: 'The system of our activity, being based exclusively on the use of the force of arms, has left political means completely untried.'[31] The Tsar agreed, and a new

---

[30] [Evgenii Aleksandrovich Golovin] 'Ocherk polozheniia voennykh del na kavkaze s nachala 1838 do kontsa 1842 goda', *Kavkazskii Sbornik*, II, pp. 65–7. Translation based on Baddeley (note 27), pp. 356–9.

[31] V. G. Gadzhiev and Kh. Kh. Ramazanov (eds), *Dvizhenie gortsev severo-vosto-*

commander-in-chief in the Caucasus was instructed 'not to spare money' in order to 'draw to us some of Shamil's brothers in arms', to 'sow discord and contention among the others' and to 'reassure and encourage the pacified and semi-pacified tribes'.[32]

To this end Nicholas I banned completely any Russian offensive operations for two years. However, contrary to the Tsar's expectations, the ban served Shamil who prepared for and launched in September and November 1843 two successful offensives in which he conquered most of the Russian-controlled territories in Daghestan.[33] Infuriated, Nicholas ordered a massive reinforcement of his troops in the Caucasus and a full-scale offensive that would 'deal Shamil a few strong blows', turn 1844 into 'a year for requiting the enemy' and 'satisfy the honour of our arms'.[34] Seeing no results in that year the Tsar nominated a new commander-in-chief to the Caucasus, giving him augmented authority and the official title of Viceroy.

Against the advice of generals experienced in the affairs of the Caucasus, the new Viceroy led a force of about 18,000 men to Andi and Dargo in an attempt to get rid of Shamil once and for all. The Russian force was allowed to reach both destinations, only to find itself in a trap. It was saved from annihilation only by good luck and the adroitness of the commanding officer of the Left Flank of the Caucasian Line, who dashed to Vorontsov's rescue.[35] Even so, this was an unprecedented defeat, which once and for all put an end to the 'one blow' approach of the Russians.

---

chnogo Kavkaza v 20–50 gg. XIX v. Sbornik dokumentov, Makhachkala: Daghestanskoe Kniznoe Izdatel'stvo, 1959, pp. 352–3, document no. 195, Chernyshev to Golovin, 19 [31] July 1842.

[32] A. Iurov, '1844-i god na Kavakaze', *Kavkazskii Sbornik*, VII, p. 159.

[33] On this see Moshe Gammer, 'Shamil's Most Successful Offensive—Daghestan 1843', *Journal of the Institute of Muslim Minority Affairs, King Abdul Aziz University*, Jeddah, 12, 1 (January 1991), pp. 41–54.

[34] Iurov (note 26), p. 157.

[35] For this campaign see Moshe Gammer, 'Vorontsov's 1845 Campaign: A Reconstruction and Reinterpretation' in Moshe Gammer (eds), *Political Thought and Political History: Studies in Memory of Elie Kedourie* (London: Frank Cass, 2003), pp. 71–90; Moshe Gammer, 'A Forgotten Hero of the Caucasian War—General Freytag', *Annual of the Society for the Study of Caucasia*, 4–5 (1992–3), pp. 33–43.

6

THE VICTORY OF THE AXE

Writing with the benefit of hindsight, Tolstoy described the new viceroy in the following words:

Michael Semënovich Vorontsóv, being the son of the Russian Ambassador, had been educated in England and possessed a European education quite exceptional among the higher Russian officials of his day. He was ambitious, gentle and kind in his manner with inferiors, and a finished courtier with superiors. He did not understand life without power and submission. He had obtained all the highest ranks and decorations and was looked upon as a clever commander, and even as the conqueror of Napoleon at Krásnoe.[1]

Pushkin, who as Vorontsov's subordinate in 1824 experienced personally the Count's attitude to 'power and submission', left a different description:

> *Half hero and half ignoramus,*
> *What's more, half scoundrel, don't forget.*
> *But on this score the man gives promise*
> *That he will make a whole one yet.*[2]

---

[1] Lev Nikolaevich Tolstoi, 'Khadzhi Murat', p. 413 (Chapter IX), in *Short Novels: Stories of God, Sex and Death*, selected and introduced by E. J. Simmons (New York: The Modern Library, 1962). Krásnoye is 'a town thirty miles south-west of Smolensk, at which, in November 1812, the rear-guard of Napoleon's army was defeated during the retreat from Moscow. It is mentioned in *War and Peace*'—loc. cit., translator's note. The latest biography of Vorontsov is Laurence Hamilton Rhinelander, *Prince Michael Vorontsov, Viceroy to the Tsar* (Montreal: McGill-Queen's University Press, 1990). Its main fault, however, is the complete disregard of the war in the Caucasus, which was, after all, high (if not first) on Vorontsov's agenda. Moshe Gammer, '"The Conqueror of Napoleon" in the Caucasus', *Central Asian Survey*, 12, 3 (1993), pp. 253–65, is an attempt to rectify this void.
[2] Transl. by Babette Deutsch in Avraham Yarmolinsky (ed.), *The Poems, Prose and Plays of Alexander Pushkin*, The Modern Library (New York, 1964), p. 59.

Whatever one's opinion of Vorontsov, his character was strong enough to admit that a change of strategy was needed and his position privileged enough to influence the Tsar to decide upon it. Consequently, in a revival of Yermolov's system of siege and attrition, two new defence lines were established: the 'Upper Sunja Line' (established 1845–6) sealed the west, and, more important, the 'Advanced Chechen Line', constructed in the vicinity of the 'Black Mountains' and consisting of Vozdvizhenskoe (the 'Elevated', established in 1844), Achkhoy (1846) and Urus Martan (1848), strengthened control over the heartland of Chechnya—the plain between the 'Black Mountains' and the Sunja. Construction of these lines mainly involved massive felling operations in the Chechen forests, clearing the way for the movement of Russian troops who could now pass without fear of coming under enemy fire. 'The system of the axe' replaced 'the system of the bayonet'.[3]

This shift back to the 'Yermolov system', which gave such weight to subduing the Chechens, also accentuated the growing Russian awareness of the centrality of Chechnya in Shamil's struggle and state. Chechnya was both the breadbasket of Shamil's state and the source of his best and fiercest soldiers. Furthermore, it protected the 'soft underbelly' of Daghestan. Chechnya's importance to Shamil was reflected in the fact that since 1840 all the Imam's 'capitals' were in Chechnya. While at first merely attempting to conquer Shamil's 'capital' the Russians had gradually come to realise Chechnya's centrality. Thus they had decided that in order to defeat Shamil, they had to conquer Chechnya first. Surprisingly, while concentrating on conquering Chechnya from 'below', the Russians never seriously considered also trying to conquer the country from 'above'—from Georgia.[4]

In concert with the forest clearing operations, Russians struck hard at the foundations of the Chechens' village life, demolishing homes, destroying supplies, burning fields and seizing livestock. The Russians aimed to 'force the Chechens … to migrate into our territory, where no-one would disturb them any more'.[5] Or, in Tolstoy's words, the inhabitants of each destroyed village

….were confronted with the choice of remaining there and restoring with frightful effort what had been produced with such labour and yet so

[3] Arnold Zisserman, 'Otryvki iz moikh vospominanii', *Russkii Vestnik*, 1876, 4, p. 424.
[4] Ibid., *loc. cit.*
[5] 'K.', 'Levyi flang Kavkazskoi linii v 1848 godu', *Kavkazskii Sbornik*, XI, p. 349.

lightly and senselessly destroyed, facing every moment the possibility of a repetition of what had happened; or to submit to the Russians—contrary to their religion and despite the repulsion and contempt they felt for them.

The Chechen decision rarely varied:

The old men prayed, and unanimously decided to send envoys to Shamil asking him for help. Then they immediately set to work restoring what had been destroyed.[6]

Consequently the Russians were astonished to find time and again that villages they had razed to the ground only a few weeks and months earlier had been restored as if nothing of the kind had happened. But achieving this had become increasingly difficult for the Chechens. Unable to counter the now annual and increasingly formidable Russian expeditions, the frequently defeated Chechens were left with an unwelcome choice: either to submit or to migrate into the inhospitable areas in and behind the 'Black Mountains'. Indeed, by March 1848 3,000 Chechen families had submitted to the Russians and were resettled near the new forts while the majority migrated into the 'Black Mountains'. And by October 1850 the plain of Lesser Chechnya was fully under Russian control, and by March 1853 Russia was on the verge of gaining control over the plain of Greater Chechnya as well. This was of major significance in the overall battle: not only did the conquest of the plains cause major food short-ages all over Shamil's domains, the it also brought the Russians close to the back door of the 'Mountainland'.

Just how difficult the situation was for the Chechens and Shamil can be learnt from a letter asking for help which the Imam sent to the Ottoman Sultan. 'We have lost our strength,' he wrote, and 'have no force to furnish against our enemies. We are deprived of means and are now in a disastrous position.'[7] Even if the terms of this letter are exaggerated (as one should expect from a request for help) it still shows the situation and state of mind of its author and his people. A Chechen Sufi described the situation more poetically:

Shaytan divided [the people] into several groups. Some were killed, some

---

[6] Tolstoi, 'Khadzhi Murat' (note 1), p. 461.

[7] M. M. Gabrichidze *et al.* (eds), *Shamil—stavlennik sultanskoi Turtsii iangliiskikh kolonizatorov* (Tbilisi: Gosizdat Gruzinskoi SSR-Sektsiia Politicheskoi Literatury, 1953), p. 367, document no. 302, Shamil's letter to the Sultan, 1853 [not later than 7 April].

were exiled and some sent to far away places. The mosques of the men and the praying places of the women were turned into pigsties.[8]

In view of this, the outbreak of the Crimean War was like manna from heaven for the Chechens. However, the great hope that the Ottomans and their allies would come and deliver the Mountaineers from the Russians ended in great disappointment and psychological collapse. Abandoned by the outside world, the Chechens (and other Mountaineers) lost their will to resist the Russians any longer. Fatigued by decades of constantly fighting, suffering, having to be on the run and live from hand to mouth, the Chechens (and Daghestanis) raised the option of surrender to Russia. Once news of the Paris peace treaty (which officially concluded the Crimean War) had reached the Caucasus, wrote a Russian witness,

...delegations from all over Chechnya and from almost all the mountain tribes gathered to the Imam and in unison demanded: 'If the Sultan with the French and the English ... could not defeat Russia and did not help us at all, then it is time for us to think of our own security. What hope have we left?' They were so strong in this opinion that Shamil had no choice but to agree, asking only for a delay of two months in order to enquire whether any stipulation in the Mountaineers' favour had been included in the general peace. It was possible [now] to achieve in one moment all that we had struggled for with such futility for fifty years.

Then a single act of folly turned the tables:

It was decided that for the [complete] pacification of the Caucasus it was necessary to transfer the submitting population to Vologda Province or any other empty land, and in a council in Stavropol it was decided to send all the Chechens to Manych. [...]
    This madness was [officially] transmitted to the Chechen elders, Shamil was resurrected. [...] The pacified Chechens stated they would never part with their homeland, whatever the cost. The subjugated population in Chechnya and Daghestan has been returned to the mood of 1843 ... and the only favourable moment to be used has been wasted.[9]

Nevertheless, this could only postpone the final conquest, not avert it. Using the 200,000-strong army massed in the Caucasus

---

[8] 'Abd al-Salam, as quoted in Anna Zelkina, 'Some aspects of the Teaching of Kunta Hajji on the Basis of a Manuscript by 'Abd al-Salam Written in 1862 AD', *Journal of the History of Sufism*, 1–2 (2000), p. 486.
[9] 'Pis'ma Rostislava Andreevicha Fadeeva k rodnym', *Ruskii Vestnik*, 1897, 10, pp. 63–4.

during the Crimean war, the Russians now launched a massive effort finally to defeat Shamil and conquer Chechnya and Daghestan. From three sides a succession of co-ordinated offensives were executed. Chechnya soon proved to be the crucial front where the Russians had the fastest and most important successes. By April 1857 they had regained control over the plain of Greater Chechnya, and during the winter campaign of 1857–8 Shamil's domains were split in half with the capture of the upper Argun defile. The result was felt in April 1858 when ninety-six villages with some 15,000 people in Lesser Chechnya submitted to the Russians. In the summer campaign of 1858 Shatoy and fifteen more communities in Greater Chechnya were brought under Russian rule.

Finally, during the winter campaign of 1858–9 the Russians reached Shamil's residence—New Dargo near Vedeno—taking it on 13 April 1859. Having lost Chechnya, Shamil had little chance of resisting the Russians for much longer—his acceptance of which is revealed in a letter to the Ottoman Sultan.[10] Frustrated in his attempt to make a stand in Ichichale, the Imam with 400 followers entrenched himself at Ghunib, where he was forced on 6 September 1859 to submit to Prince Bariatinskii, Viceroy since 1856 of the Caucasus and a childhood friend of Alexander II.

Shamil's unprecedented (and unsurpassed) success in leading the Chechens almost unchallenged for so many years can be explained by the organisational and ideological backbone that he enjoyed in the form of the Naqshbandi-Khalidi *tariqa*. According to a Chechen historian writing in the mid-1990s, the fact that he was not a Chechen also contributed greatly to his success: the Chechens, he argued, have been unable to unite under a leader from among their own people. Only an external (i.e. non-Chechen) leader, free—and, more important, perceived as free—of clan connections and commitments could unite them.[11]

Seventy-five years of intermittent resistance since Imam Mansur, and more particularly thirty years of intensive struggle under the Daghestani Naqshabandi Imams, caused great changes to the people and country. Among these the most obvious were demographic. Chechen writers of the 1990s and early 2000s argue (in a rather

[10] See ibid., p. 285.
[11] M. Vachagayev, 'Chechnia v kavkazskoi voine, 1816–1859' (Moscow, 1995), pp. 84–5.

exaggerated calculation) that Chechen losses, direct and indirect (i.e. the loss of the potential descendants of those killed), resulting from that period of struggle have exceeded 1,000,000.[12] Furthermore, the confiscation of lands, the settling of Cossacks and the resettlement of Chechens, first by Shamil into the mountains and then by the Russians from the mountains into the lowlands and among the Cossacks and the Russian forts, caused major economic, social, cultural and psychological changes that would then become manifest in the following decades.

The changes in population patterns were accompanied by the despoiling of Caucasian forests.

In a prelude to 'pacification', Yermolov began this assault in 1817 when he widened roads and started constructing Russian forts in Chechnya. But after the Dargo campaign completely discredited the goal of seizing the mountains, Russia undertook to clear forests on a massive scale (as exemplified in young Tolstoy's story 'The Wood Felling'). Pursued right to the end of the war, the tsarist army's program of deforestation was a wanton destruction of nature of the sort encompassed in today's ecologically conscious notion of 'raping the land'.[13]

No less important were the changes introduced by the Daghestani Imams, mainly Shamil, which changed irrevocably both Chechen society and its country. One change, already discussed above, was the switch from grain to maize. A second was Shamil's strict enforcement of the *shari'a* and effort to uproot the traditional, customary law—the *'adat*. During his long rule the third Imam put major emphasis on this subject. He was not content with merely enforcing observance of its tenets in public (and as far as possible also in private). His *na'ibs* and *qadis* were continuously urged to teach the people 'Islam'—both daily obligations (like *namaz* or prayer, reciting the Qur'an etc.) and the underlying principles.[14] Even Chechens' stubborn adherence to their traditions and customs and Russian attempts to re-establish the *'adat* and uproot the *shari'a*

---

[12] L. Usmanov, *Nepokorennaia Chechnia* (Moscow: Izdatel'skii dom Parus, 1997), pp. 71–2. Vachagayev calculates Chechen losses between 1830 and 1860 at over 500,000; Vachagayev (note 11), p. 35.

[13] Susan Layton, *Russian Literature and Empire: Conquest of the Caucasus from Pushkin to Tolstoy* (Cambridge University Press, 1994), p. 189.

[14] See M. Gammer, *Muslim Resistance to the Tsar: Shamil and the Conquest of Chechnia and Daghestan* (London: Frank Cass, 1994), pp. 225–35.

could not undo these efforts of almost twenty years. The *shari'a* remained entrenched in various spheres of Chechen (daily) life. More important, in Chechen consciousness it remained the only alternative general, universal, non-tribal legal system to rival the Russian (and later Soviet) code.

Third, Shamil and his predecessors implanted in Chechnya the Sufi *tariqa*. While it is true that soon after Shamil's surrender the Naqshbandiyya was replaced by another *tariqa*, Chechen society has remained permeated by Sufi brotherhoods which still play a major social, economic and political role.

Fourth, the long struggle and especially the Daghestani Imams' rule advanced Chechen self-consciousness differently from their neighbours to both east and west: in the west, the fact that the Ingush did not on the whole take part in the resistance was the first step in their becoming a separate people, and in the east the Chechens had always been aware of their difference from the Tawhlins (literally 'Highlanders', i.e. the Daghestanis). But thirty years of close (to many Chechens too close) contact with Daghestanis, not to mention enduring their leadership, created resentment that broke out in occasional clashes between the two groups. Notwithstanding these facts—allegiance to a rival Sufi brotherhood and heightened ethnic consciousness—Daghestan would still continue to be looked upon by the Chechens for religious and to some extent political leadership for decades to come.

Finally, these decades of resistance and struggle left a wealth of memories, patterns and images to be drawn upon in the Chechens future relations with Russia, should the Russians fail to reconcile them to their rule. And not surprisingly the Russians did fail to do so.

Part III. UNDER THE TSAR

'Who is ignorant of the predatory, disgraceful mores of the Chechens? Who does not know that the most peace-loving measures undertaken by the Russian government to pacify the agitation of those mutineers have never met with success? Deep-rooted in the discipline of robbery, they always remain the same. An imminent, certain danger calms them for a while; then the same treachery, the same acts of murder are visited upon their benefactors.' (Polezhayev)[1]

---

[1] Quoted in G. A. Tkachev, *Ingushi i Chechentsy v sem'e narodnostei terskoi oblasti* (Vladikavkaz, 1911), pp. 9–10.

7

FROM QUIETISM TO UPRISING

Shamil's surrender did not mark the complete 'pacification' of either Chechnya or Daghestan. Indeed general discord continued to simmer in both countries well into the late 1860s, occasionally boiling over into uprisings. The most remarkable uprisings in Daghestan occurred in the community of Unkratl from October 1860 to August 1861 and again from November 1861 from February 1862, in the Zakataly *okrug* in April 1863, in Tabasaran in August 1866 and again in Unkratl in 1871. In addition, an attempted uprising in Koysubu, led by Shamil's nephew Hamza Muhammad, was foiled by the authorities in the summer of 1866.[2] Most of Chechnya accepted Russian rule grudgingly, although some communities—usually those that had not experienced Russian rule before and/or had been in conflict with Shamil or his *na'ibs*, like Shatoy—gladly welcomed the Russian troops.[3] However, even they were soon driven to the verge of uprising, owing to a large extent to the Russian means of administration.

Soon after the conquest, in 1860, the Russian authorities separated Chechnya from Daghestan. The latter—already a separate military command since the late 1840s—was made into a distinct *oblast* (district). Chechnya was included in the Terek (*terskaia*) *oblast* which was based on the wartime Left Wing of the Caucasian Line. This separation would endure during both the Tsarist and the Soviet periods, though the administrative borders between the two would

---

[2] For these attempts, see A. I. Ivanov, 'Natsional'no-osvoboditel'noe dvizhenie v Chechne i Dagestane v 60–70 kh gg. XIX v.', *Istoricheskie Zapiski*, 12 (1941), pp. 165–99.

[3] See M. Gammer, *Muslim Resistance to the Tsar: Shamil and the Conquest of Chechnia and Daghestan* (London: Frank Cass, 1994), p. 283.

change several times. Within the Terek *oblast* Chechnya was divided into four sub-districts—the Chechen, the Argun, the Ichkeri and the Mountain *okrugs*.[4] In a reshuffle in 1883 most of the Chechen territory was included in the Groznyi (*groznenskii*) *okrug*.[5] Command of the sub-districts and lesser administrative subdivisions—*naibstva* (na'ibdoms)—was entrusted to native collaborators, a proven prescription for trouble.[6]

However, the greatest causes of havoc and resentment were the chores and duties now forced on the population, as well as the redistribution of land. In 1860, by order of Yevdokimov, all the lands of collaborators with Russia confiscated by Shamil were returned to their original owners. In addition, the authorities confiscated from the locals large tracts of land, both arable and pasture, allotting them to native collaborators[7] and to new Cossack *stanitsas*[8] and forts in the occupied territories. Consequently many ordinary Chechens were left with insufficient means. Finally, the Chechens were forcibly 'encouraged' to resettle in the lowland, and some were conscripted into the Terek Cossack *voisko* and settled in its *stanitsas*.

The first insurrection started in May 1860 in the Ichkeri *okrug*. It was led by the community of Benoy and headed by Baysungur, a previous *na'ib* of Shamil, and Sultan Murad. Hiding their livestock and property, the people started guerrilla attacks on the Russians, and were soon joined by almost all the other communities of Ichkeri. An expeditionary force concentrated against them failed to achieve any success, so by mid-January 1861 three forces moved on the rebels: 400 Cossacks and 400 local militiamen from Mayrtup, about 7,000 infantry (8–10 battalions) from Khashi-Shardon and

---

[4] The other three were the Kyzliar (Kumyk), the Osset and the Ingush *okrugs*.

[5] This *okrug* would be the territorial base for the Chechen Republic. Some of the Chechen territories were included with the Kumyks in the Khasav Yurt (*khasaviurtovskii*) *okrug*, which would be annexed by the Soviet authorities to Daghestan. The other two *okrugs*—those of Vladikavkaz and Nal'chik—would also be territorial bases for autonomous republics, North Ossetia and Kabardino-Balkaria respectively.

[6] See, for example chapter 4, above.

[7] Thus in 1860 certain princely (*kniazia*) families received the following allocations: the Taymazovs 4,500 *desiatins*, the Turlovs 2,000, the Bekovich-Cherkaskiis 4,900, the El'darovs 1,400 and the Akhlovs 2,800.

[8] In 1860–1 seven new *stanitsas* were established: Il'inskaia, Bariatinskaia, Fel'dmarshalskaia, Datykhskaia, Umakhan-iurtovskaia, Dzhaltinskaia and Nesterovskaia.

300 local militiamen from Vedeno. The forces united on 21 January near Belgatoy under the command of General Musa Kundukhov, whose assessment of the situation was decidedly realistic: 'There is no way of penetrating the hiding places of the people of Benoy,' he reported. 'I can be everywhere, but am unable to surround and catch them. They will always be able to avoid us.'[9] Thus between 25 January and 11 February he conducted, like so many Russian generals before and after him, the usual 'punitive expedition'. 'The troops of the Ichkeri force', Kundukhov reported on 28 January,

...have done everything possible: At this moment I can state with certainty that on the land of Benoy neither a single [person] who has not submitted, nor a single [standing] house have remained. All the food stores have been destroyed; those [Chechens] who had neither submitted nor been taken prisoner left Benoy to a hitherto unknown destination. Baysungur, abandoned by his band, went into hiding with only his family... Sultan Murad, with his gang, also fled Benoy.[10]

To all purposes the revolt had ended. Baysungur and his family were captured on 1 March, and Sultan Murad with his men joined the rebels in the Argun *okrug*. Kundukhov destroyed fifteen *auls* and their hamlets, resettling in the lowlands all the population he could capture. Baysungur was imprisoned in Khasav Yurt, court martialled and executed in the spring of 1861.

Since the 1990s some Chechen nationalist circles have tried to portray Baysungur as a national hero who resisted to the end and never surrendered, unlike Shamil (and by implication some other Chechen resistance leaders). 'Severely crippled', wrote a modern Chechen author, and 'only able to move and take part in battles when tied to his horse', Baysungur represented '*a model symbol of the Chechen people's physical condition and refusal to submit at that period of time* [emphasis added].'[11]

By the end of June 1860, about a month after the insurrection in Ichkeri, another rebellion broke out in the community of Shatoy

---

[9] Quoted in A. I. Ivanov 'Natsional' no-osvoboditel'noe dvizhenie v Chechne i Dagestane v 60–70 kh gg. XIXv.', *Istoricheskie Zapiski*, 12 (1941), p. 177. Many Russian commanders in the 1990s would agree with him.

[10] Quoted in ibid, p. 178.

[11] L. Usmanov, *Nepokorennaia Chechnia* (Moscow: Izdatel'skii dom Parus, 1997), p. 71.

which just a year and a half earlier had welcomed the Russian troops with joy. It was led by Atabay Atayev (son of Ata), who had been the *na'ib* of the community under Shamil, and Uma ('Umar) Duyev (son of Duva), its *qadi*. On 2 July their forces besieged the forts of Shatoevskoe, Bashin-Kala and Evdokimovskoe. The forts were relieved two days later by Major-General Bazhenov leading a force of about 5,000 Russian soldiers (six infantry battalions and two 'hundreds' of Cossacks) with mountain cannon. Unable to establish contact with the Chechen rebels—as usual they had disappeared into the primeval forests—Bazhenov, during the following two weeks, destroyed fourteen *auls* and moved their population to the lowland. However, this did not put an end to the rebellion and in October 1860 the rebels once again besieged Shatoevskoe. This time they were reinforced by the communities of Chanti, Chamalal and Chaberloy. Colonel Tumanov, the commander-in-chief of the Russian troops in the Argun *okrug,* tried to mobilise local militiamen to fight against the rebels, but they all deserted to join Atabay and Uma.[12] On 6 November Tumanov reported: 'Almost all [the locals] have either already risen in rebellion or are ready to rise.'[13] On 20 November Major Shtange, chief administrator of the *okrug,* reported that he had been left with 'no power, no authority and no means' since all the officials—aides-de-camp, *qadis* and 'peoples' judges'—had fled and no one agreed to replace them.[14]

This time three forces were concentrated to suppress the rebellion: Bazhenov from Vladikavkaz with about 4,500 infantry, two 'hundreds' of Cossacks, four 'hundreds' of local militiamen and an artillery battery; Kundukhov from Urus Martan with five 'hundreds' of Cossacks and five 'hundreds' of local militiamen; and Tumanov from Shatoy with about 3,000 infantry, a 'hundred' of Cossacks, and artillery. They were ordered to destroy all the villages, their fields and food stores, find suitable sites in the foothills for relocating the mountain villages, and generally resettle all the captured population in the lowland.[15] And to the best of their ability this is

[12] A. Aydamirov, *Khronologiia* istorii Checheno-Ingustetii (Groznyi: Kniga, 1991), p. 71.
[13] Quoted in Ivanov (note 9), p. 178.
[14] Quoted in ibid., p. 179.
[15] Quoted in ibid., loc. cit.

what the Russian forces did. However, Atabay and Uma with their forces disappeared in the forests where 'for the next several months Russian forces tried in vain to hunt them down.'[16] But by the spring of 1861 the forces of Atabay and Uma had started to grow again and in March Sultan Murad, the co-leader of the revolt in Ichkeri, joined them with his fighters. In August the rebels in the Unkratl community—their leader, Qaraqul Muhammad, having been captured by the Russians (6 August 1861)—also tried to join Atabay and Uma, or at least that was the Russians' fear.[17] Finally, in October rebels from Lesser Chechnya and from the Qarabulaq community also joined Atabay and Uma.

In that very month the Russians decided to stage yet another campaign against the rebels. A force of about 8,000—infantry, a regiment of local irregular cavalry, a squadron of Dragoons, four 'hundreds' of Cossacks, two 'hundreds' of local militiamen and two batteries of artillery—was concentrated under the command of Kundukhov and Tumanov. An additional force of two infantry battalions and six 'hundreds' of cavalry blocked the mountain passes between the Argun *okrug* and the newly-formed Andi *okrug* in Daghestan. Kundukhov and Tumanov started their campaign on 1 November 1861 by clearing forests, destroying villages and moving their inhabitants down to the lowlands. After Sultan Murad had been wounded and taken prisoner, both Atabay (on 26 November) and Uma (on 26 December) surrendered and were sent into exile in Porkhov (in the Pskov *guberniia*) and Smolensk respectively. With their surrender the rebellion ended.

Using classic 'divide and rule' tactics the Russians employed any Chechen element that would submit in their efforts to 'pacify' the country. One way was to enlist Chechens into *ad hoc* militias and permanent irregular units, then use them against rebels. Thus, for example, on 15 October 1860 the *terskii konnyi polk* ('Terek [Irregular]

[16] Ibid., p. 180.
[17] To prevent it the commander-in-chief of the Russian forces in Daghestan, General Lazarev, occupied the mountain passes with a force of about 2,500 local cavalry, an infantry battalion and four pieces of artillery. There seems to have been constant association, if not cooperation and coordination, between the two communities and their leaders. This might have been one (though neither the only nor the main) of the reasons for the Russian decision to separate in June 1861 the communities of Unkratl, Chamalal, Tekhnutsal and Gumbet from the Terek *oblast* and annex them to the Daghestan *oblast* as the Andi *okrug*.

Cavalry Regiment') was formed.[18] None of the Russians' attempts proved to be of benefit in battle: Chechens, then as in the 1990s, seldom fight other Chechens. In some cases the militias even joined the rebels. However, the 'Terek Cavalry Regiment' and the various other militias had both a political and a practical significance: they removed a great part of the most warlike elements from the reservoir of the rebels. For that specific purpose it was even suggested in 1863 that the 'Terek Cavalry Regiment' and some volunteer militias should be used against the Polish rebels.[19] In 1872 the authorities decided to

...form as many militia regiments as possible from among the native population [*korennye zhiteli*], to enrol in them the most restless elements of Chechnya, Ichkeria, and Aukh and to remove them, with their horses and weapons, as far as possible from the confines of the country.[20]

Another tool of the Russian administration was the Qadiri Sufi *tariqa* (known as 'Zikrizm' in Russian and Soviet literature). The Qadiriyya is one of the four oldest and most prestigious Sufi *tariqas* and probably the most widespread of them all.[21] In other parts of the Muslim World the Qadiriyya arrived earlier than, and in some cases been replaced by, the Naqshbandiyya. However, in the Northern Caucasus the reverse was true. 'Orthodox', though centred mainly on personal rather that communal salvation, and far less centralised and disciplined than the Naqshbandiyya, the Qadiriyya arrived in the Northern Caucasus in the late 1850s, some forty years after the Naqshbandiyya-Khalidiyya, and in Chechnya managed within a few decades to replace it.[22]

The man who brought the new message was al-Shaykh al-Hajj Kunta al-Michiki al-Iliskhani,[23] whose biography and personality

---

[18] A similar regiment was formed in Daghestan.

[19] Report by Loris-Melikov, commander-in-chief of the Russian forces in the Terek *oblast*, as quoted in Ivanov (note 9), p. 180.

[20] Ibid., p. 187.

[21] For the Qadiriyya, see J. Van Ess, 'Ḳadiriyya', *Encyclopaedia of Islam*, 2nd edn, IV (1978), pp. 368–72.

[22] For an overview of the Qadiriyya in Chechnya (and the Northern Caucasus in general), see Moshe Gammer, 'The Qadiriyya in the Northern Caucasus', *Journal of the History of Sufism*, 1–2 (April–May 2000, Special issue: 'The Qadiriyya Sufi Order'), pp. 275–94.

[23] The latest study of Kunta Hajji is Vahit Akayev, *Sheikh Kunta Khadzhi: Zhizn' i*

are shrouded in a mist of legends. From what can be reconstructed, he was born around 1830[24] in the hamlet of Mel'cha-Khi (Isti-Su in the Russian sources). His father Kishi (hence his Russian-given surname 'Kishiev') and his mother Hedi belonged, according to Chechen sources, to the *te'ip* of Gumkhoy.[25] When he was seven years old his family moved to Eliskhan-Yurt in the community of Michik (hence his nickname 'al-Michiki al-Iliskhani'). According to tradition, Kunta displayed from early childhood exceptional characteristics: great piety, a sense of justice, an inclination to solitude, and unusual intellect and grasp for his age. He demonstrated a strong interest in religious studies and by the age of twelve knew the entire Qur'an by heart. In an age preoccupied with resistance and survival this was a very rare phenomenon. Hence Imam Shamil encouraged such inclinations. Thus Kunta proceeded to study with the most famous *'ulama* and Sufi Sheikhs and was introduced to the Naqshbandiyya-Khalidiyya by Tasho Hajji al-Indiri.

In 1848–9 Kunta and his father were allowed to perform the *haj*—an exceptional privilege under Shamil's rule. It was probably during this pilgrimage that he was initiated into the Qadiriyya in Baghdad, though no documented details on this have yet become available. The oral tradition of his followers has it that he was taught and initiated by 'Abd al-Qadir al-Gilani himself during a dream in the saint's mausoleum in Baghdad, which probably reflects the Qadiri initiation ceremony in which 'the candidate for admission to the Order sees 'Abd al-Qadir in dreams'.[26]

On his return Kunta started to proselytise the new *tariqa*. However, he soon clashed with the Naqshbandi-Khalidi doctrines and practices, and thus with Shamil. In particular Kunta's teaching was anathema to the Naqshbandi-Khalidi on four counts: first, on the ritual plane Kunta introduced the loud *dhikr* performed by chanting

---

uchenie (Groznyi: Nauchno-Issledovatel'skii Institut Gumanitarnykh Nauk Chechenskoi Respubliki, 1994).

[24] Ibid., p. 29. Other sources give an earlier date of birth—'the Beginning of the 19th century'—e.g. Yavus Ahmadov, 'Dvizhenie Kunta Khadzhi', paper delivered at the First International Conference on Shamil and the Anti-Colonial Struggle in the Caucasus, Oxford, March 1991, p. 3.

[25] e.g. ibid., *loc. cit.*

[26] D. S. Margoliouth, 'Ķadiriyya', *EI²*, IV, 63–4 (Leiden, 1973), p. 381, quoting John Porter Brown, *The Dervishes: or, Oriental Spiritualism* (London: Trübner and Co., 1868).

and 'dancing'. Although the Naqshbandiyya does not exclude the loud *dhikr*—the Naqshbandiyya-Khalidiyya in the Caucasus and Shamil himself used to perform it to mobilise support and strengthen morale—it prefers the silent *dhikr*. Secondly, on a more important level Sheikh Kunta, being a Qadiri, emphasised individual rather than communal salvation. Thus he appealed to his fellow Muslims to withdraw from worldly affairs and concentrate on prayer and on individual effort to improve one's own morality. According to Sheikh Kunta,

[Each Muslim had to] clean his soul and interior from the dirt and every-thing that is forbidden and … from evil intentions and falsehoods. Then remember Me and call Me for help, and he will surely find Me in his soul and heart. Indeed My dwelling is the human heart and if [a servant] cleans his heart and fills it with recollection of Me [*dhikr*] then I will instantly enter his soul and will find him before he finds Me.[27]

While these two doctrines made the new Sheikh a competitor and challenger to the Naqshbandiyya-Khalidiyya and its leadership, the following two made him a deadly threat to the resistance it led and the state it had built. The third issue related to collective affairs—or politics; here Kunta demanded a halt to the resistance to the Russians, which he deemed not only futile but also a sin against God. He even predicted the downfall of Shamil's Imamate. Contrary to what both Shamil and the Russians might have thought, this did not mean acquiescence in Russian rule, but rather dissociation from it: 'As for the teaching of the *'ulama* that the faithful should not communicate with the infidels and should separate themselves by prayer, it is true indeed.'[28] Consequently, Sheikh Kunta had created a third, more realistic option for the desolate Chechens, and this was the fourth point of contention for the Naqshbandiyya-Khalidiyya, who called upon the Chechens to choose resistance rather than submission, the latter being equal to apostasy. Sheikh Kunta told them that thus was not necessarily so: they could submit to Russia's superior might yet still remain 'good Muslims':

God almighty out of His mercy gives those imprisoned or captured or held by the infidels recompense as if they performed the pilgrimage or recited the Qur'an, and [treats them] like children who do not have to per-

[27] 'Abd al-Salam, as quoted in Zelkina, 'Some Aspects', p. 491.
[28] Ibid, p. 492.

form religious rituals, but who still perform them, and [grants them] as if they had undertaken all *nawa'if.*[29]

He thus offered a people approaching the limit of their ability to suffer and on the verge of falling into bottomless despair a way out of the abyss. He supplied them with the religious legitimation to end their armed struggle and gave them hope of salvation. Further- more, Sheikh Kunta took care to ensure that those opting for his course could be proud: according to him they were the best Mus- lims and their faith was superior to that of the Meccans 'because here [in Mecca] you have only one enemy [*Shaytan*] and there we have three—*Shaytan, kafirun* [infidels] and *munafiqun* [hypocrites, that is collaborators with the Russians].'[30] No wonder the number of his followers swelled rapidly. It is also not surprising that Sheikh Kunta Hajji was invited three times to Shamil's 'capital' near Vedeno, where he had long debates with the Imam and other religious authorities. Having failed to be persuaded to toe the Naqshbandi- Khalidi line, the Qadiri Sheikh in 1858 was made 'an offer he could not refuse': to leave for a second pilgrimage to Mecca.

'The Son of Kishi', as he is referred to by his followers, returned to the Caucasus in 1861–2 with the blessing of the Russian author- ities, who tried to use Kunta Hajji's 'pacifist' views and influence to eliminate finally all remnants of resistance in Chechnya. However, within less than a couple of years the Russian administration had made a 'U-turn'. Official reports now termed the new movement 'fanatical' and extremely dangerous to Russian rule in the Caucasus. 'The teaching of Zikrizm', reported Loris-Melikov, 'being in many respects consistent with *gazavat,* is serving now as the best means for popular unity, which once recuperated will only be waiting for a more propitious moment to become transformed into a fanatical re- awakening.'[31] Furthermore, the usual structure of the *tariqa* was now interpreted by the Russian authorities as a 'parallel secret Zikrist administration' aimed at 'promoting the fanaticism and unity of all the Muslim population … in order to overthrow Russian rule.'[32]

---

[29] Ibid., p. 494.

[30] Ibid., *loc. cit.*

[31] Quoted in Ivanov (note 9), p. 180.

[32] Grand duke Prince Michael, the Viceroy in the Caucasus, in an interview with *Russkii invalid* and in a report to St Petersburg, as quoted in Akayev (note 23), pp. 35 and 42 respectively.

One important reason for the change of heart must have been the suspicion, so deep-rooted in Russian governments, of anything and anyone not fully controlled by the authorities. 'Fanatic' was a label assigned to any such group, whether consisting of Russian 'Old Believers' sticking to their faith, though otherwise fully loyal to the state, Hassidic Jews refusing to send their children to state schools, or of Muslims attempting to observe the commandments of their religion. Sheikh Kunta Hajji's rapidly expanding fame and influence and the swift spread of his movement must have triggered that reflex. Another reason must have been the change of Viceroy in the Caucasus on 18 December 1862. The new Viceroy (1862–81) was Alexander II's younger brother, Grand Duke Michael, who tended to mistrust the natives more than both his brother and his predecessor.

Whatever the reason, the change of attitude soon found expression in action. On 15 January 1864 Kunta Hajji, his brother and several followers were surprised and arrested in a village near Shali. They were transferred under heavy guard via Groznyi and Vladikavkaz to the military prison in Novocherkassk, where they were put to hard labour for about six months. The difficulties of the journey were described by a *murid* who accompanied his *ustadh*.

Then during the month of Ramadan we could not fast because we were travelling with the infidels. [...] We made up the fast a month later. We could not pray regularly in peace and quiet, but we performed prayer in our hearts, shortening and compounding it. Sometimes we could not find water, and even if we found it, we were forbidden to purify ourselves. [...] Sometimes we were forbidden to pray and we prayed without *rak'as*. Because of many turnings in our journey we often could not decide where the *qibla* was and we turned our faces in the direction in which our hearts were inclined.[33]

By decree of Alexander II 'the deported ... resident of the Chechen sub-district, Sheikh-Kunta' was 'resettled for life under police supervision' in the town of Ustiuzhkino in the Novgorod *guberniia*.[34] In that remote town the originator of the Qadiriyya in the Caucasus

---

[33] 'Abd al-Salam, as quoted in Zelkina (note 27), p. 486.

[34] Akayev (note 23), p. 61. The other prisoners were scattered under similar conditions all over the Russian Empire. Sheikh Kunta Hajji's brother managed to escape to the Ottoman Empire and finally settled in Syria.

practically starved to death for almost three years,[35] dying according to official Russian documents on 31 May 1867.[36] However, his followers still refuse to believe that he died; according to a disciple, 'he travels all over the world incognito. He might sit next to you in the aeroplane without you suspecting it.'[37]

As soon as the followers of Sheikh Kunta Hajji heard of his arrest they started to flock to Shali, believing 'the son of Kishi' was detained there in the Russian fort. Three delegations approached the commander of the fort, but their request to release him was flatly refused. By 26 January 1864 about 3,000 men and women had gathered in Shali. After the third delegation was rejected they started a continuous *dhikr.* On 30 January the crowd, having completed their morning ablution and prayer, threw away their firearms and moved towards the fort. The Russian troops forming a *carrée* in front of the citadel fired volleys at the approaching men and women. Under fire, the Chechens stormed the troops with their daggers, but were met by grapeshot. Russian sources give different figures for the Chechens killed that day, ranging from 100 to 'more than 400' of whom four to six were women.[38] The Russian losses were reported as eight killed and thirty-three wounded.[39]

Although the Russian accounts call it an uprising, it is clear from those same accounts that '*sha'ltan tom*'—'the Battle of Daggers', as the event has since been remembered by the Chechens—was a peaceful demonstration.[40] Furthermore, the Sheikh's arrest was a

---

[35] In a letter dated 15 February 1865 Kunta Hajji wrote to his wife: 'Please be kind enough to send me ten silver roubles, because I have no means to live. I receive as pocket money only six *kopeks* per day, while bread is very expensive and so are other groceries.' Quoted in Akayev (note 23), p. 62.

[36] Y. Ahmadov, 'Dvizhenie Kunta Khadzhi', Paper delivered at the First International Conference on Shamil and the Anti-Colonial Struggle in the Caucasus' (Oxford, March 1991), p. 10.

[37] Conversation with a *murid* in Eliskhan-Yurt after a *dhikr* in May 1992.

[38] Akayev (note 23), p. 73.

[39] Ibid., p. 72; Ivanov (note 9), p. 181.

[40] 'O podavlenii vosstaniia v Terskoi oblasti v 1864 g.' quoted in ibid., *loc. cit.* Russian and Soviet historiography—including that of Chechen historians—followed this cue and described the event as a straightforward attack by the Sheikh's followers on the Russian troops. The fact that they had thrown their firearms away is explained by attributing to them the belief that the supernatural powers of their *ustadh* would protect them from Russian fire (e.g. quotations in Ahmadov, note 36, p. 8). The possibility that by throwing away their weapons the

transparent provocation, the authorities being fully aware (and perhaps even hoping) that 'the removal of Kunta Hajji might bring forward among the Chechens a leader of a rebellion rather than the head of a sect.'[41] Russian documents clearly stated that the arrest was aimed at prompting the Chechens into an action that would give the Russian command the needed excuse to 'eradicate the Zikr from within the Chechen tribe'.[42] Thus throughout 1864 'the rebellion in Shali' was followed by massive arrests, in which eighteen Qadiri leaders and dozens of *murids* were banished and the performance of *dhikr* prohibited on pain of deportation.[43]

However, this was only part of a larger plan. Grand Duke Michael pursued a more 'active' policy than his predecessor *vis-à-vis* the natives, which found expression in what would nowadays be termed 'ethnic cleansing'. During the final conquest of the north-western Caucasus, in 1864–5, between 0.5 and 1.5 million Circassians were 'encouraged'—sometimes at gunpoint—to leave for the Ottoman Empire.[44] The new Viceroy and his aides intended to pacify Chechnya by similar means. Indeed, he strongly urged his subordinates

---

Chechens were signalling to the Russians that their intentions were peaceful has not even been considered. In fact, there is a possibility (though by far not a certainty) that all they might have intended was to hold a massive *dhikr*, or another form of non-violent demonstration, near the fort. What makes this explanation plausible is the fact that the Sheikh wrote in captivity a letter calling on his followers and all Chechens to keep calm and abstain from violence (Akayev, note 23, p. 39). Even if it was written under Russian coercion, as Akayev believes (*loc. cit.*), it still might have expressed the *ustadh*'s genuine will and belief. Thus the Zikrists' actions might only have been in obedience to their master's letter.

[41] Report by Loris-Melikov as quoted in Ivanov (note 9), p. 180.

[42] Quoted in Akayev (note 23), p. 59.

[43] Ahmadov (note 36), p. 9.

[44] For the expulsion of the Circassians to the Ottoman Empire, see Halil Inalcic "Čerkes", *EI²*, II (Leiden: E. J. Brill, 1983), pp. 21–5; Paul B. Henze, 'Circassian Resistance to Russia' in Marie Bennigsen-Broxup (ed.), *The North Caucasus Barrier: The Russian Advance towards the Muslim World* (London: Hurst, 1992), pp. 99–105; Willis Brooks, 'Russia's Conquest and Pacification of the Caucasus: Relocation Becomes a Pogrom in the post-Crimean War Period', *Nationalities Papers*, 23, 4 (1995), pp. 675–86; Austin Lee Jersild, 'From Savagery to Citizenship: Caucasian Mountaineers and Muslims in the Russian Empire' in Daniel R. Brower and Edward J. Lazzerini (eds), *Russia's Orient: Imperial Boundaries and Peoples, 1700–1917* (Bloomington: Indiana University Press, 1976), p. 112; Kemal Karpat, 'The Hijra from Russia and the Caucasus' in D. F. Eickelman and J. Piscatori

'at the first opportunity to take the same measures against these people as are now being taken to pacify the tribes of the Western Caucasus.'[45] However, the Russians did not intend to induce such a massive
exodus. Rather they wanted to 'remove from among the Chechen
... the most untamed [men] and [all those] inciting the people to
insolence',[46] and a plan to that effect was indeed prepared.[47]

Such an opportunity now being at hand, the authorities did their
best to push the Chechens and Ingush, especially the followers of
the Qadiriyya, to emigrate to the Ottoman Empire. Indeed,

...according to an agreement with the Turkish government signed in
1865, the Ottoman Porte agreed to accept the migrants into Turkish territory and promised to settle them in Asia Minor, near Diarbakir and Sivas,
far from our border. In view of this, during the summer of 1865 the mass
of the most vigorous and fanatical among the Chechen population, some
5,000 families containing up to 20,000 souls of both sexes, left to live in
Turkey.[48]

A great many of the forced migrants were relatives, disciples and
followers of Sheikh Kunta Hajji. 'The most hostile tribe, the Chechens, having lost some 20 per cent of its numbers, has become
markedly more pacified' reported the Grand Duke with satisfaction
on 4 September 1865.[49] According to a Chechen historian writing
in the early 1990s, 'the most energetic, the most freedom-loving
part of the population' emigrated. It was, he lamented, 'an ethnic
catastrophe that deprived the people of its finest sons'.[50]

(eds), *Muslim Travellers: Pilgrimage, Migration, and the Religious Imagination* (London: Routledge, 1990), pp. 132–5; A. Uner Turgey, 'Circassian immigration into
the Ottoman Empire, 1856–1878' in W. B. Hallaq and D. P. Little (eds), *Islamic
Studies Presented to Charles J. Adams* (Leiden: E. J. Brill, 1991), pp. 193–217.

[45] Quoted in Akayev (note 23), pp. 77–8.
[46] Ibid., *loc. cit.*
[47] Ivanov (note 9), p. 181.
[48] Quoted in E. Eshba, *Aslanbek Sheripov* (Groznyi: Serlo, 1929), p. 62. And cf.
Ivanov (note 9), 90; Ahmadov (note 36), p. 11; I. Bennigsen estimates the number of emigrants at 30,000 at least (Alexandre Bennigsen, 'The Qadiriyyah
[Kunta Hajji] *Tariqah* in North-East Caucasus: 1850–1987', *Islamic Culture*, LXII,
2–3 [April–July 1988], p. 66).
[49] Quoted in Ivanov (note 9), p. 181.
[50] Ahmadov (note 36), p. 11.

In the long run the events of 1864–5 greatly affected the future relationship between the Chechens and Russia. If the Russian authorities had ever hoped to mould the Chechens into loyal subjects, their policies prevented it. Furthermore, they failed to uproot the Qadiriyya. What had happened with the Naqshbandiyya some thirty-five years earlier was now repeated only in an aggravated form: the Naqshbandiyya, which in no way could be described as a quietist movement, had not put the struggle against Russia at the top of its agenda until forced to do so by the Russian advance. The Qadiriyya, which had started as a movement resigned to Russian domination, had now turned into a sworn enemy of Russia, or at least of the Tsarist regime. This opposition to Russian rule must have facilitated the Qadiriyya's spread among the Chechens and Ingush—as it had done two generations earlier with the Naqsh-bandiyya-Khalidiyya—adding its share to their ongoing insubordination towards the Russian authorities. Indeed, after a period of confusion following its Sheikh's arrest the Qadiriyya re-emerged, albeit underground. By the 1890s it had all but replaced the Naqsh-bandiyya among the lowland and foothill Chechens and recruited the hitherto pagan Ingush. Henceforth the Qadiriyya would take part in all the uprisings against Russian rule—Tsarist and Communist alike—and lead some of them.

However, this was in the distant and unforeseeable future. At the moment the Russians seemed to be successful, for in the absence of its founder the Qadiriyya had ceased to be a united movement and split into several branches. In May 1865 a disciple of Kunta Hajji, Toza Akmirzayev from the *aul* of Kharachoy (near Benoy), proclaimed himself 'Imam of the Believers'[51] and sent proclamations throughout Ichkeri calling the people to gather in Kharachoy by 5 June. Forewarned by their agents, the Russian authorities arrested Toza and seventeen of his followers. A court-martial sentenced Toza to death, but this was reduced to twelve years' hard labour. No one could have guessed that this would be not only the first Qadiri-lead rebellion but by no means the last one.

Satisfied with their success, the authorities proceeded with the consolidation and standardisation of Russian rule in Chechnya.

---

[51] Most probably '*Amir al-Mu'minin*'. For his rebellion, see 'O zhitele Ichkerin-skogo okruga Terskoi oblasti aula Kharachoi, Taze Ekmirzaeve', *Sbornik Svedenii o Kavkazskikh Gortsakh*, IV, 4 (1870), pp. 55–62.

Step by step the authorities turned the Terek *oblast* into a regular administrative unit, while Russian officials gradually replaced native ones. In 1864 a district court of law was opened in Vladikavkaz. In 1867 the codex regulating the administration and the courts was introduced. In October 1869 the administration was adjusted to conform to that of the Empire in general, and in 1871 the (all-Russian) 1864 court and the 1868 notarial regulations were adopted. In 1876 the directorate of education was established and made responsible for all schools with the exception of the religious ones.

While these steps might have had a positive influence on those Chechens who collaborated with Russia, the mass of the population were adversely affected in their daily subsistence, first and foremost because of the shortage of land which for rural society was the prime means of survival. In addition to the land confiscated in 1860 that of the deportees and the emigrants to the Ottoman Empire was also expropriated. Some was distributed to Chechen collaborators who had proved their loyalty,[52] and some to Russian officials.[53] However, most was reserved for the use of the Cossacks. In 1870 a law was passed securing each ordinary Cossack 30 *desiatins* of land per household member. The garrisons of the forts in many cases simply 'annexed' land officially belonging to neighbouring Chechen communities. In 1866 an official report stated:

The local residents have pretensions to the Kurin regiment, which being quartered in the forts of Vedeno and Ersenoy in the Ichkeri *okrug* lead their horses and cattle to pasture on Chechen lands, and even crop hay, which squeezes the inhabitants considerably.[54]

Already that year an official report had stated that

...the economic mode of life of the Chechens is far from flourishing. Agriculture is very limited. Maize is the main staple food of the people. Haymaking is almost unknown. There is no land at all either for cattle or for cultivation. [...] Pasturelands are extremely limited, and therefore ani-

---

[52] In 1866 the following were allocated: Qasim Kuramov, Artsu Chermoyev and Alkhanov—556 *desiatins* each; Bata Shamurzayev—576 *desiatins*. In 1876 some 1240 *desiatins* near Vozdvizhenskoe were distributed among thirty-four persons.

[53] In 1866 1,017 *desiatins* were given to Colonel Belik. In 1875 1,000 *desiatins* were granted to Ippolitov, the Chief Administrator of the Argun *okrug*, who married a Chechen woman.

[54] Quoted in Ivanov (note 9), p. 166.

mal husbandry is in decline. Trade, crafts, fruit gardens are almost completely non-existent.[55]

Several commissions were established to solve this problem but achieved nothing. Clearly this problem was not high on the agenda. As if to confirm the authorities' apparent indifference to the plight of the population, the collection of tax in cash per household, as practised everywhere in the Empire, was introduced in 1866 in the Terek *oblast*. Economic, religious, political and other tensions had gradually been building up, making Chechnya (and Daghestan) a powderkeg waiting to explode. The Russo-Ottoman war of 1877–8 was the match that ignited it.

[55] Quoted in ibid., p. 167.

8

THE LESSER GAZAVAT

The crisis that had been unfolding in the Ottoman Balkans since 1875 and the growing tension between St Petersburg and Istanbul, which led to the Russo-Ottoman war of 1877–8,[1] could not but affect the Caucasus. As the clouds of war gathered, the populations of Chechnya and Daghestan became increasingly restless and the authorities became correspondingly apprehensive. Rumours of Ottoman envoys trying to stir up the population abounded, some of them probably being true.[2] In May 1876 the Russian authorities in Daghestan discovered and foiled a joint Chechen-Daghestani plot 'to liberate all the natives of Chechnya and Daghestan from Russian rule'. It was headed by Ghaziyaw from Archu in the community of Karata (in Daghestan) and Musalaw Shu'ayb, the *qadi* of Mayrtup later proclaimed Imam. Its motives were given as the continued deportation of Mountaineers to Central Russia, the growing burden of taxation and the threat of being conscripted into the Russian army.[3] In December 1876 an uprising broke out at Gubden, in Daghestan, but it was immediately quelled.[4]

Towards the end of April 1877 'the Administration of Chechnya became troubled by unusual excitement' among the Mountaineers. 'Not only the wide masses, even the leaders' displayed an 'evident reluctance to show their former obedience to the authorities'.[5] Dada

---

[1] See Matthew Smith Anderson, *The Eastern Question, 1774–1923: A Study in International Politics* (London: Macmillan, 1966), pp. 178–219.

[2] See, for example, A. I. Ivanov, 'Natsional'no-osvobotitel'noe dvizhenie v Chechne i Dagestane v 60–70 kh gg. XIVv', *Istoricheskie Zapiski*, 12 (1941), pp. 185–6.

[3] Ibid., pp. 186–7.

[4] Ibid., p. 186.

[5] N. Semenov, 'Khronika Chechenskogo vosstaniia 1877 goda', Appendix to *Terskii Sbornik*, Vypusk I (Vladikavkaz, 1891), p. 13.

Zalmayev, the headman of Chobakhkenroy in the community of Chaberloy, was arrested for 'plotting "something" against the government and gathering a party'. However, since the authorities lacked proof of their suspicions he was released on bail 'in order not to cause inappropriate apprehension among the population'.[6] Naturally, such incidents only served to spread awareness of Russian insecurity and weakness. (Once the revolt started, at the beginning of May, Dada Zalmayev joined the rebels.)

The Russian sources connected the rebellion of 1877 exclusively to the Russo-Ottoman war, officially declared on 24 April 1877. According to them, 'the Muslims of the mountain *okrugs*' got word of the declaration of war 'well in advance of the local administration'.[7] On that very night

…about 60 people, residents of different villages of the Vedeno *okrug*, gathered in the forests near the *aul* of Sayasan and took a mutual oath to proclaim their independence. Then, from among this small group, Sultan Murad from Benoy and 'Alibek Hajji, native of Zandak, were brought forward as leaders, and on the spot the latter was proclaimed Imam.[8]

However, this conclusion, based as it is on circumstantial evidence, seems to overstate the Chechens' connections with the Ottomans, not to mention their means of communication. This is not to say that there were no connections, or that the Ottomans did not try to stir the Chechens and Daghestanis up to rise against Russian rule. In fact, the Ottomans gave Ghazi Muhammad, the second son of Shamil who had lived in the Ottoman Empire since 1872, the rank of General and command over a division of Caucasian volunteers that fought on the Caucasian front. Ghazi Muhammad, who in March 1848 had been officially declared Shamil's heir, obviously had his own reasons for fighting Russia and reaching Daghestan. According to both Russian and Chechen sources he sent at least one messenger to the Terek *oblast*—a certain Jambar, a native of the village of Ansalta (in Daghestan), who under the name 'Abbas Pasha had served as an officer in the Ottoman army.[9]

[6] Ibid., pp. 13, 14.

[7] Ibid., *loc. cit.*

[8] Semenov (note 5), pp. 13, 14.

[9] Smekalov's report for 18 [30] August–1 [13] September 1877 quoted in Semenev (note 5), p. 55; Goytakin Rasu from Benoy, 'Istoriia o tom kak Albik-Khadzhi stal Imamom', *Respublika* (Groznyi), 8 August 1991, p. 6.

Despite this, the same Russian source, while overstating the Chechens' connection with the Ottomans, understates, or rather disregards other, local and therefore more important reasons for the revolt, here revealed by a Chechen source:

On the night of Monday, 1 Rabi' al–Awwal 1294 [16 March 1877] Albik ['Alibek] Hajji gathered people secretly at Savrag'an Mohk [near the village of Sayasan] and raised the question of the obstacles raised by Tsar Alexander II to [the practice of] Islam and the *shari'a* as well as other prohibitions. At that time the Russian authorities publicly forbade the performance of loud *dhikrs* in the mosques; they prohibited *hajjis* from wearing the special *khalats* [robes] and *chalmas* [turbans] signifying pilgrims; and they outlawed gatherings of people in large numbers to call for rain and other purposes. The people present at that gathering, and especially Albik Hajji, strongly condemned these prohibitions. They decided to elect Albik Hajji as *Imam*. In order to strengthen his authority they decided to nominate his *na'ibs* to all the provinces. They also resolved that exactly two weeks later, on Monday [that is 19 Rabi' al–Awwal/3 April], Albik Hajji would publicly announce the plan and bless it by prayer.[10]

Russian sources detail almost no information about Albik ('Alibek) Hajji 'Aldanov', apart from his age—twenty-two—which must be a mistake. It is clear from the title Hajji that he had performed the pilgrimage to Mecca; hence he must have been considerably older and probably had a religious standing. Indeed, according to his chief *qadi*, Albik Hajji was an *'alim*.[11] The events of the uprising seem to indicate that he was also a Sufi, probably a Qadiri leader. Soltamurad (Sultan Murad), the son of Solumgiri from Benoy, was about seventy years old in 1877. He had participated in the resistance to Russia under Shamil and Baysungur and served as the *ma'zum* (a *na'ib*'s deputy) of Benoy under the Imam.

Once news of the gathering became public knowledge, Albik Hajji's forces started to grow rapidly. Russian reports estimated them at 200 on 30 April and at 500 a day later. 'The Mutineers', wrote a Russian source, 'advanced from *aul* to *aul*', mobilising their inhabitants 'partly by the use of threats, but mainly drawing on the sympathy of the population'.[12] By 2 May the revolt had

[10] Ibid., *loc. cit.*
[11] Ibid., *loc. cit.*
[12] Semenov (note 5), p. 15. According to a Chechen source, in one case force was

...engulfed 47 *auls* [and their hamlets] in eastern Ichkeri, with a population of roughly 18,000 people, and threatened to spill over into Salataw,
Aukh and Chaberloy. The population of Greater Chechnya was very unreliable and its representatives openly confessed that they would side with
the stronger party.[13]

The uprising caused great apprehension within the administration
since among other things it caught the Russians with depleted
forces. Some units had been moved from Chechnya and Daghestan
to the Ottoman front and their replacements were not due until 7
May. Having proclaimed the Terek *oblast* a war zone on 1 May, the
Russians moved two detachments to block Albik Hajji's advance to
Shali fearing that the joining of that *aul* to the movement 'would
have served as a signal for a general uprising of all Chechnya'.[14] On
3 May these forces clashed with the Imam near Mayrtup. 'After several successful salvos by our artillery', reported the Russian commander, Colonel Nurid, 'the mutineers fled into the mountains.'
Later, however, 'huge masses of mounted and foot mutineers'
attacked Nurid's transport, but failed to prevent the force from
'crossing the river bank. [...] Hit by the fire of our infantry, and
especially of the artillery, they suffered a complete defeat and were
forced to seek refuge in the forests and ravines.'[15] The Russians were
obviously checked and forced to retreat.

Two days of heavy rain prevented Albik Hajji from moving back
to Mayrtup,[16] but once the rain ceased on 5 May he did exactly that
and once again threatened to enter Shali. The Russian commander
'used every effort to keep Shali in submission, threatening that
otherwise he would not leave a single stone there unturned.'[17]
Adjutant-General Svistunov, the head of administration and commander-in-chief of the Terek *oblast*, wrote that these threats and,

---

used. On 15 Rabi' al-Awwal, when entering Zandak he ordered three people
killed who had opposed him. Goytakin Rasu (note 9), p. 6.

[13] Semenov (note 5), p. 15.

[14] Svistunov's order of the day no. 254, quoted in Ivanov (note 2), p. 284.

[15] Semenov (note 5), p. 16. According to the Chechen account, the artillery fire
caused no damage at all. Then, 'under the pressure of incessant attacks from the
troops of Albik Hajji, the enemy retreated ... and returned to its camp.' Goytakin
Rasu (note 9), p. 6.

[16] Ibid., *loc. cit.*

[17] Semenov (note 5), p. 18.

more important, the arrival of reinforcements 'persuaded the *aul* of Shali to meet on 28 April [8 May] the party of mutineers with fire.'[18] Albik Hajji, 'realising he could not win',[19] retreated but was then surprised by a Russian force. The Imam decamped into the inaccessible forests of Samsir at the juncture of the borders of Ichkeri, Salataw and Awkh. Svistunov boasted:

All of Chechnya has now been given proof that our forces are able to appear everywhere—and in strength fully sufficient to destroy rebel hordes, whatever their numbers—and that our armament gives us the ability to cause them incalculable casualties while suffering relatively insignificant ones ourselves. The terrible panic that had befallen the *auls* in view of these casualties forced the vacillating ones (Avturi, Geldygen, Kurchaloy and others) to join our side, and those guilty of taking part in the mutiny to submit and beseech forgiveness.[20]

Having put down the uprising in Chaberloy, led by Dada Zalmayev, 'in two to three days', Svistunov now reported that 'peace in the *oblast* may be considered fully restored.'[21] Nevertheless, in order 'not to let the mutineers collect themselves and venture some new attack', Svistunov decided to surround the Samsir forest and capture the rebels. Of the troops at his disposal (24,409 infantry, 2,261 Cossacks and 1,100 local militiamen, with 104 cannon[22]) he employed 17,500 infantry, 1,200 Cossacks and 32 cannon. These were divided into two columns advancing from Groznyi and Khasav Yurt. A third column of about 3,000 infantry, three 'hundreds' of militia and four cannon advanced from Daghestan in the south under the command of Nakashidze and was put at Svistunov's disposal by the head of administration and commander-in-chief of the Daghestan *oblast*, Adjutant-General Prince Melikov. However, Svistunov's plan was not limited to the use of the troops. It involved 'divide and rule' tactics combined with 'punishment': the commanders of the various forces were ordered to tell the Chechens that 'in order to atone for their crimes' they had to send people 'to capture Alibek and Soltamurad along with their band. Only after this proof of their obedience and repentance will they hear how much mercy they can

---

[18] Svistunov's order of the day no. 254, quoted in Ivanov (note 2), p. 284.
[19] Goytakin Rasu (note 9), p. 6.
[20] Semenov (note 5), p. 19.
[21] Ibid., p. 20.
[22] By mid-May all the units had been reinforced and brought to war-time strength.

expect from the authorities.'[23] The communities of Benoy and Dargo had no choice but to obey, but the men sent to capture the Imam 'proved completely incapable' of fulfilling their task: 'At the first shots in their direction from an insignificant party of mutineers they turned their backs and looked for cover behind the [Russian] troops.'[24]

Svistunov started his campaign on 22 May 1877. Four days later he had to suspend it when news reached him of an uprising in Salataw. Forced to leave, Svistunov 'told the inhabitants that even though he had not yet granted them a final pardon, they might earn it by … not allowing malefactors in and by meticulously complying with the commands of the authorities.'[25] The operation in Salataw lasted a fortnight. 'Bearing in mind that the people of Almak, Burtunay and Dylym'—the centres of the uprising—were 'chronic rebels', Svistunov ordered 'not only those *auls*, but also all the eighty hamlets along both banks of the Aktash' to move to the lowlands.[26] A delegation of 350 elders, who begged for mercy 'on their knees, heads uncovered and without weapons', did not 'shake his determination. […] Telling the petitioners that they would remain in the fort as hostages … he ordered that the villages be destroyed.'[27]

Leaving his subordinate Nakashidze to complete the transfer of the population of Salataw, Svistunov returned to Groznyi in order to punish Ichkeri, 'which he deemed impossible to put off' because of 'rumours that the people of Ichkeri boasted of having been unpunished'.[28] The *aul* of Zandak was singled out especially because its people were suspected of secretly supplying Albik Hajji with provisions. Svistunov sent Colonel Batianov there to 'demand once again that they either unconditionally surrender all the leading culprits of the disruption or catch and deliver Alibek with his gang.'[29] However, 'assuming that neither demand would be carried out' the General 'intended to inform the people of Zandak that their disobedience was the reason for the *aul*'s immediate relocation to the lowland.'[30]

[23] Semenov (note 5), *loc. cit.*
[24] Ibid., p. 21.
[25] Ibid., p. 22.
[26] Ibid., *loc. cit.*
[27] Ibid., *loc. cit.*
[28] Ibid., pp. 22–3.
[29] Ibid., p. 23.
[30] Ibid., *loc. cit.*

These extreme punitive measures caused the revolt to spread further. On 27 May 1877 Gumbet—the closest area of Daghestan to Chechnya—rose up and some of the insurgents proceeded to assist the people of Salataw. Nakashidze was forced to turn back. By 9 June he had put down the rebellion with sword and fire. 'The main rebellious villages were punished [in other words destroyed]' Melikov telegraphed to Svistunov, and 'the residents will be evicted.'[31] About a week later another revolt broke out in the community of Dido in south-western Daghestan, keeping Nakashidze occupied until the end of June. At more or less the same time, 13 June, the *auls* of the upper Bass 'completely unexpectedly drove down their horses from the mountain [pastures] and gathering in crowds in the mosques started to sing the *dhikr.*'[32]

Under these circumstances Svistunov tried to form a militia of Chechen volunteers to 'seize these desperate fanatics'. To facilitate mobilisation the volunteers were offered 10 roubles per month and forage at discount prices and promised rewards of 'several thousand roubles for delivering Alibek dead or alive to the authorities, and of several hundred for Soltamurad and Dada Zalmayev. For each of the other *abreks* the reward was 25 roubles.' Nevertheless, only a few joined the militia and those proved to be 'very unreliable where active pursuit of the mutineers was concerned'.[33] Thus on 30 June Albik Hajji broke through 'almost unhindered'.[34] Svistunov now finally concluded that he could not count on Chechens to extradite Albik Hajji.

One has to acknowledge that, even if not all the Chechens unconditionally sympathise with Alibek and wish him success, the entire population without exception sees in him a victim suffering for the holy cause of religion and whom, therefore, every believer must help, at least stealthily.[35]

Batianov, with a force of some 5–6,000 infantry and several cannon, was sent in pursuit. On 6 July he encountered Albik Hajji's force in a 'fortified and inaccessible position' on Mount Kozheltenduk.

[31] Ivanov (note 2), p. 190.
[32] Semenov (note 5), p. 25.
[33] Ibid., p. 23.
[34] Ibid., p. 24.
[35] Ibid., *loc. cit.*

'One could not count on taking or destroying the gang,' ran the Russian report, but the Chechens

…shouted at the troops that the Russians sent only Muslims [i.e. Chechens] into the forests because they themselves were afraid to confront the Imam. Since such impertinence could not be left unpunished, Colonel Batianov deemed it necessary to send the troops to storm the mountain.[36]

'Killing and wounding several dozen attackers', the Chechens 'disappeared in the forests.'[37]

Soon enough, on 25 July 1877, Albik Hajji carried out another feat. Having 'punished' the *auls* along the upper Bass in their usual way, the Russians captured 'in the burnt *aul* of Makhketa the 135 principal instigators and sent them to Vedeno'.[38] They were guarded by a force of about 1,250 infantrymen and two cannon. Learning of that, Albik Hajji ambushed the convoy and, causing it heavy casualties, released the prisoners, though not before some of them were shot by the Russians.[39] News of this and of Russian setbacks on the Ottoman front[40] reverberated throughout the Caucasus. Spontaneously the people of Shali started to 'sing the *dhikr*'. The communities of Shatoy and Chaberloy joined Albik Hajji and the Russians feared that Lesser Chechnya would 'cross over to the mutineers, which in turn, would be the beacon for an insurrection not only of Greater Chechnya, Awkh and Ichkeri, but also of the Kumyks, the Ingush and the Kabartay.'[41] Under these circumstances, decided Svistunov,

…merciless punishment of the guilty was the only way to re-establish peace in the *oblast*. The destruction of *auls*, fields, cattle and everything at hand should strike the mutineers as just retribution and by denying them

---

[36] Ibid., *loc. cit.*

[37] A. I. Ivanov, 'Vosstanie v Chechne v 1877 g.', *Istoricheskie Zapiski*, 10 (1941), p. 287. The Chechens had two killed. Goytakin Rasu note 9, p. 6.

[38] Semenov (note 5), p. 24.

[39] As might be expected, the Chechen source claims the Russians started shooting the prisoners as soon as they realised they were under attack, while the Russian source claims the prisoners were trying to escape and were only then shot at (ibid., p. 25 and Goytakin Rasu (note 9), p. 6).

[40] See W. E. D. Allen and P. Muratoff, *Caucasian Battlefields: A History of the Wars on the Turco-Caucasian Border, 1828–1921* (Cambridge University Press, 1953), pp. 105–51. For the rest of the war, see pp. 152–217.

[41] Semenov (note 5), p. 25.

means for survival should force them to come out of the forests and submit.[42]

In addition, the General ordered his subordinates to take *amanats* (hostages) from suspect villages, which he 'deemed the most useful measure'.[43]

With a column from Daghestan once more available, the Russians moved on 26 July from four directions to 'pacify' the areas in revolt. However, their actions only served to spread the revolt further. On 29 July Uma Hajji joined Albik Hajji. Uma Hajji, then about eighty years old, had reached the rank of *na'ib* under Shamil and led an uprising in 1860–1.[44] The direct reason for his action, wrote Uma Hajji to two friends in Daghestan, was 'the wrong-doings of the infidels against the believers' or, more specifically, their 'deeds against the community of Nozhali, the villages of which were burnt and destroyed'.[45] Although Uma Hajji was wounded a few days later and consequently disabled for a while, his men constituted a considerable threat. A fortnight later on the night of 13–14 August Suleyman of Tsentoroy proclaimed himself Albik Hajji's *na'ib* and raided the Cossack *stanitsa* of Vodianaia Balka.

By the second half of August the movement reached its peak. It now engulfed forty-seven *auls* with a population of 18,000. Albik Hajji himself arrived on 22 August in Tsentoroy, from where he moved to Benoy and down the Khulkhulaw, where he occupied Nozhay Yurt on the 24th. The Russians concentrated all their available forces and used any measure, threat or promise at their disposal. Thus the *auls* along the Bass were told that their complete submission and full obedience might yet win them the right not to be resettled. A new measure was now introduced into Greater Chechnya, where all the *auls* were divided into several groups, the villages in each one being responsible for the others' behaviour. A Russian source reported:

All these measures successfully localised the uprising almost exclusively to Ichkeri. Naturally this brought home the need to send there considerable

---

[42] Ibid., p. 26.
[43] Ibid., p. 29. The Russian source adds in a footnote: 'Prince Melikov [...] did not attach to this measure equal importance and even deemed it harmful.'
[44] See previous chapter.
[45] Letters to Ismail of Botlikh and to Girey of Andi, translated in full in Semenov (note 5), pp. 28, 29 respectively.

military forces and at the same time to nominate over all the detachments deployed there, including the Daghestani task force, a commander-in-chief who due to his service record *would enjoy sufficient authority to be able to control fully the activities of all the other commanders and, eliminating harmful bickering among them, to coerce them to comply with the plans and obey his orders* [emphasis added].[46]

Since the nominee also had to be 'fully acquainted with local conditions', Svistunov appointed on 24 August 1877 his deputy, Major-General Aleksei Mikhailovich Smekalov to the position, instructing him:

Take into account that our aim should be to pluck out all the untrustworthy people from the *auls* and to exile them and their families to Russia forever. The taking of hostages should be merely a temporary measure. In general [we should] pluck out as many as possible and in the most oppressive manner. The entire population of Benoy and Zandak should be exiled to Siberia and if these rascals refuse, they should all be exterminated in the winter like cockroaches and starved to death. Send the hostages from Zandak to me as I want to exile them to far away *guberniias* as soon as possible. [.... Send them] with their hands not merely tied but twisted in such a way that the left palm touches and is tied tightly to the right shoulder and vice versa. Under no pretext should they be untied on their way and in case of the smallest resistance by anyone, beat them all up. I must add: my strong wish is for the latter possibility to happen.[47]

On the very day of his nomination Smekalov arrived in Vedeno to find 'all the population of Ichkeri in full revolt ... with the exception of Tsa-Vedeno, which thanks to its proximity ... did not openly join the mutineers [but] kept a suspicious attitude.'[48] Taking charge of the forces there—6,100 infantry, a 'hundred' of Cossacks, five 'hundreds' of infantry and four-and-a-half 'hundreds' of mounted (native) irregulars and artillery—he moved immediately. On 26 August he marched with his main force on Dyshni Vedeno, sending a diversion towards the range of G'amara Kort (Gemerduk in Russian). In both places the Russians encountered bitter resistance:

In the *aul* they used every possible cover, and held with extraordinary stubbornness the cemetery, the artillery fire notwithstanding. On the Gemer-

[46] Ibid., p. 34.

[47] Svistunov to Smekalov, 18 [30] August 1877 as quoted in Ivanov (note 37), p. 290.

[48] Smekalov's report for 12–16 [24–8] August 1877—Semenov (note 5), pp. 35, 36.

duk range they even tried to counter-charge [... They] charged in frenzy, sword in hand [and] at a certain moment they hung on to the bayonets and perished on them.[49]

According to a Chechen source,

Albik Hajji's *na'ibs* and army displayed furious resistance, killing many enemy soldiers. Realising he was not going to win, the Russian commander retreated to his camp. [...Nevertheless,] the followers of Albik Hajji gradually fell out, until he remained with only a handful of adherents.[50]

On 28 August, having destroyed the village completely, Smekalov moved on to Tsentoroy. He found it deserted, and the forces of Albik Hajji, Soltamurad, Sulayman and the Daghestani Rajab 'Ali on the surrounding heights. This, he reported, 'was the factual base for the rumours in Daghestan that our forces were surrounded and almost completely annihilated.'[51] The General intended to fight the rebels in order 'to destroy the [population's] fear of the names of Albik and the other leaders'. However, 'since the mutineers [...] avoided pitched battle ... it was decided to send small columns against each of them separately.'[52] The Russians managed to force the Mountaineers from their positions mainly by the massive use of artillery. Retreating, Albik Hajji and Sultamurad took up a position on the ridge of Gendyrgen, commanding Smekalov's route to Benoy. However, since the people of Benoy decided to surrender they retreated to the Samsir forest. The General told the elders of Benoy that the authorities demanded the resettlement of the entire community of Benoy to the plains, after which their lands would be confiscated.[53] In the meantime the villages that had not hastened to surrender were destroyed and those that had done so were obliged to supply sheep to feed the force. On 2 September the people of Benoy started to move to the plains. 'Since the planned, combined operation with the force of Colonel Batianov could not be carried out', Smekalov decided to return to Vedeno. The submitting villages

---

[49] Ibid., pp. 42, 41 respectively.
[50] Goytakin Rasu (note 9), p. 6.
[51] Smekalov's report for 18 [30] August–1 [13] September 1877—Semenov (note 5), p. 45.
[52] Ibid., p. 46.
[53] Ibid., p. 50.

were warned that 'if they should let through a party or any of the leaders of the mutiny, their hostages would be hanged and the villages mercilessly destroyed.'[54]

Back in Vedeno on 5 September, he immediately sent the force of Nakashidze to Makhketa against Uma Hajji. In one of the ravines en route the Russians encountered 'amazingly, excellently and masterfully built fortifications' which were 'devised for defence from two sides and to cover each other'.[55] In a three-hour-long battle the Chechens 'made every possible effort to put down the artillery, literally saturating the men and their covers with bullets.' At a certain point they were successful: the commander of the battery was severely wounded and 'the soldiers, stricken by the absence of their beloved commander, stopped firing for a few moments'.[56] Only 'a determined charge with fixed bayonets dislodged the Chechens from their positions. In view of this dramatic description the reported casualties were amazingly small—four killed and fifteen wounded. Having spent the rest of that day, 6 September, destroying the fortifications, Smekalov proceeded on the following couple of days to destroy the *auls* of Elistanji, Khatun, Makhketa and Tauzen. At this point 'prolonging the stay of the Daghestani force in the Terek *oblast* had for many reasons become impossible.'[57] So on 9 September Smekalov returned to Vedeno, having to fight his way through the same ravine, losing five killed, six wounded and sixteen horses in the process. Nakashidze moved back to Daghestan and reached Botlikh on 12 September, a day after the outbreak of the rebellion there.

'The necessity of sending off the Daghestani force prevented the conclusion of the affair with the *auls* along the Bass and the breaking of their stubbornness.'[58] However, Smekalov resolved to return, especially since Uma Hajji continued to threaten the Russian hold

---

[54] Ibid., pp. 52, 50 respectively.

[55] Ibid., p. 55. 'Clearly', continued Smekalov in his report, 'the fortifications were erected by an experienced man. This proved to be the same Jambar of Ansalta [in Daghestan] who had been an Ottoman officer and came to the Terek *oblast* under the name 'Abbas Pasha with messages from Ghazi Muhammad and the Ottoman government.'

[56] Ibid., p. 54.

[57] Ibid., p. 55.

[58] Smekalov's report for 2 [14]–25 September [7 October] 1877—ibid., p. 59.

on both the Argun *okrug* and the plains. According to an elder from Shali, 'the people's soul was with Uma, only their body at their place of residence.'⁵⁹ On 14 September Smekalov moved to Elistanji and on the 15th he started to transfer the population to the plain. This was followed by the resettlement of the villages of Makhketa (from 20 September), Tauzen (from 21 September) and others.

Smekalov was successful in this operation because he seems to have gone back—intentionally or not—to the tactics used by Yevdokimov in 1856–9. In addition to the transfer of the population, he engaged in wide-scale forest felling and—more important—in outmanoeuvring his rival rather than actively looking for pitched battle. Outflanked time and again by superior forces and firepower, Uma Hajji had no choice but to retreat. Finally on 1 October he left the Bass ravine. Followed by Russian forces from several directions, he managed on the night of 5–6 October to slip away to the Samsir forest.

Enjoying huge superiority both in firepower and in numbers—now being amassed in the Terek *oblast* were '27,991 bayonets, 3,361 sabres, 104 pieces of artillery and 5,000 volunteers mobilised in Daghestan, Chechnya and Ingushetia'⁶⁰—Smekalov dared to 'divide the force into several columns [and] move along the ranges and the ravines [... thus] forcing the enemy to break up his forces.'⁶¹ 'This system of military operations', he wrote to his superior, 'of sending small columns into groups of hovels gave excellent results and proved to be the only military means of forcing the population of such an environment as Ichkeri to submit. This system', he added, 'has to be applied on a larger scale when clearing the forests of Benoy and Samsir.'⁶²

Indeed, on 7 October Smekalov moved again with a force of some 1,500 infantry, 500 Cossacks, five artillery pieces and local irregulars. His aim was to attack the hamlet erected by Albik Hajji in the Samsir forests, in which the Imam had gathered provisions in large enough quantities to last the winter. The immediate reason, however, was a clash on 4 October between the Imam's followers

---

⁵⁹ Ibid., *loc. cit.*
⁶⁰ A. Aydamirov, *Khronologiia istoni Checheno-Ingushetii* (Groznyi: Kniga, 1991), p. 87.
⁶¹ Smekalov's report for 2 [14]–25 September [7 October] 1877—Semenov (note 5), p. 70.
⁶² Ibid., p. 72.

and the people of Datakh, immediately following which Albik Hajji attacked and burned their village. While sending one force to Datykh, the General moved to the vicinity of Benoy. On the night of 7–8 October he attacked and dispersed Sultamurad's band and during the following days sent search–parties into the forests to capture the hiding population and burn all the stores they could find. On 11 October

…on the slope leading to Greater Benoy the band of Sultamurad robbed two [native messengers] and a militiaman [carrying a letter from Svistunov]. The event took place in plain view of the residents, who not only failed to come to the rescue [of the victims], but did not bother to inform me about it. [….] I ordered the arrest of all the people of Benoy present in the camp and sent to the *aul* … a force to gather all the residents and bring them to the camp. The force returned with seventy-five men and women, who were told that they would not be released until they found the letter taken from the messenger.[63]

Two days later Smekalov announced to the people of Benoy, who had been allowed to come and harvest their fields, that 'they are forbidden to stay longer in the lands they own and have to leave immediately'.[64] In the following three days he despatched numerous search–parties which destroyed all the hamlets, fields and stores.

All this time Smekalov's intelligence was keeping him informed of Albik Hajji's moves. On 8 October, after long hesitation, the Imam accepted the invitation of some people from Andi (in Daghestan) and moved to Gogatl. However, two days later, having met resistance, he returned to the Samsir forests. Now Smekalov decided to deal the rebels a final blow. On 16 October the Russian forces advanced on Albik Hajji's position from four directions, with local militia blocking possible escape routes. The troops arrived at sunset and caught the Chechens, who were performing the evening prayer, by surprise. They surrounded the place 'so tightly that Albik Hajji was left to either take off into the air or crawl under the earth', wrote one of his followers. One of the attacking forces

…came across the house of Albik Hajji. […] Finishing the *namaz*, Albik Hajji jumped out of the house, sword in hand. The surrounding soldiers lost their heads and froze in amazement and Albik Hajji was spared. Hear

---

[63] Smekalov's report for 25 September [7]–10 [22] October 1877—ibid., p. 79.
[64] Ibid., p. 80.

ing of this, the enemy troops started to comb the forest, arresting anyone they came across and killing anyone offering resistance. [... In] the terrible battle [that ensued] countless Russian soldiers were killed, while the troops of Albik Hajji suffered insignificant losses.[65]

Naturally the Russian report gave a diametrically opposite account:

The results of the battle of Samsir were more than fifty Mountaineers killed, according to the native guides, the complete rout of the band, the destruction of the huge stores amassed by Albik Hajji and the capture of more than 1,000 cattle and horses and a huge mass of other objects.[66]

In one respect the Russian victory was incomplete: 'Albik Hajji, his parents, brothers and wife were all safe.'[67] Only his nephew was captured by the Russians.[68] However, to all intents and purposes the uprising in Chechnya came to its end. On 28 October Svistunov reported to St Petersburg that the Terek *oblast* had been 'purged of mutineers' and that all military operations had come to an end.[69] The theatre of action now moved to Daghestan.

On 10 September 1877 Sheikh 'Abd al-Rahman Hajji al-Tsughuri, the most prominent Naqshbandi-Khalidi master and scholar in Daghestan, convened a gathering of *'ulama*, Sufi Sheikhs and other notables in Sogratl (Tsughur).[70] The meeting declared *jihad* against infidel rule and proclaimed 'Abd al-Rahman's son, Muhammad Hajji, Imam of Daghestan. Within less than a month the revolt had spread throughout almost the whole of Daghestan; according to a Russian report, 11,642 out of 13,140 households (*doma*) took part in the revolt.[71] Even if this number is exaggerated—it was used for collecting fines—it is clear that the 1877 revolt also engulfed areas not affected by the resistance in the 1830s–1850s.

It was thus to Sogratl that many of the leaders of the Chechen revolt—Albik Hajji, Sultamurad, Suleyman, Uma Hajji, Dada Zalma-

---

[65] Goytakin Rasu (note 9), p. 7.

[66] Semenov (note 5), p. 88.

[67] Goytakin Rasu (note 9), p. 7.

[68] Semenov (note 5), p. 85.

[69] Ivanov (note 37), p. 292.

[70] For further details of Sheikh 'Abd al-Rahman Hajji al-Tsughuri, see M. A. Abdul-laev, *Deiatel'nost' i vozzreniia sheikha Abdurakhmana-Khadzhi i ego rodosloviia* (Makhachkala: Iupiter, 1998).

[71] Quoted in Amirhan Mahomeddadayev, 'Dagestanskaia diaspora v Turtsii i Sirii. Genezis i problemy assimiliatsii' (Makhachkala, 1996), p. 188.

yev and others—as well as 'Abbas Pasha now fled to continue their struggle. However, the Russian authorities acted with determination. In possession of large forces in Daghestan, reinforced by units from the Terek *oblast*, from the Baku *guberniia* and from Krasnovodsk across the Caspian, they immediately started reconquering the country. By the beginning of November 1877 the Russian forces had 'pacified' central Daghestan, and on 13 November they surrounded Sogratl.[72] On the following day they stormed the *aul* and after a bitter battle that lasted the whole day succeeded in destroying one of its defence towers.

Then the people of Sogratl negotiated a secret agreement [with the Russians] to capture and extradite Albik Hajji, Uma Hajji and the Chechens accompanying them. In accordance with their plot, the participants in this settlement caught Uma Hajji, his sons and his comrades and handed them over to the Russian troops.[73] Not giving himself up to them, Albik Hajji and his brothers were able to slip away and went back to the Samsir forests. There Albik Hajji with his family, brothers and parents lived as before. [...][74]

[While they were there,] friends of Albik Hajji and people he trusted arrived and informed him that if he came to the authorities in peace he would be allowed to retain his freedom. Believing the promises and following these people, who had deceived him, he came to the commander of the fort of Vedeno [on 9 December 1877]. The commander immediately arrested him and sent him to the city prison [of Groznyi].[75] Soon

---

[72] Vasilii S. Krivenko, 'Vosstanie v Dagestane v 1877 Godu', *Russkii Vestnik*, 1892, 3, pp. 167–84; A. P. Andreev, 'Vosstanie v Dagestane v 1877 godu', *Istoricheskii Vestnik*, 1903, 11, pp. 548–53; G. I. Kovalevskii, *Vosstanie v Chechne i Dagestane v 1877–1878 godakh* (St Petersburg, 1912.); A. A. Takho-Godi, 'Vosstanie Chechni i Dagestana v 1877 g.', *Krasnyi Dagestan*, 1925, nos 215, 252, 254, 257, 259–62, 269; R. M. Mahomedov, *Vosstanie gortsev Dagestana v 1877 g.* (Makhachkala: Dagestanskoe Knizhnoe Izdatel'stvo, 1940); Kh. Kh. Omarov, 'Vospominaniia Abdurazaka Sogratlinskogo o vosstanii 1877 g.' in D. Kh. Hajieva (ed.), *Izuchenie istorii i kul'tury Dagestana: Arkheograficheskii aspekt. Sbornik stat'ei* (Makhachkala: Dagestanskii Filiial AN SSSR, Institut Istorii, Iazyka i Literatury, 1988), pp. 88–100.

[73] In fact the people of Sogratl agreed to hand over to the Russians all the leaders of the rebellion, Daghestanis as well as Chechens. During 15 to 17 November 274 people were delivered to the Russian forces, including such eminent co-villagers as the 100-year-old Sheikh Abd al-Rahman Hajji and his son, the Imam of Daghestan Muhammad Hajji.

[74] Goytakin Rasu (note 9), p. 7.

[75] The Russian authorities had from the very beginning no intention of keeping their promise to grant pardons. As early as 20 August 1877 Svistunov wrote to

afterwards twelve *na'ibs* of Albik Hajji were arrested, as were all those [270] people deemed guilty by the Russian authorities.[76]

Between 16 and 18 March 1878 the seventeen main leaders of the Chechen rebellion were court-martialled in Groznyi. Six of them were sentenced to twenty years' hard labour. The others—including Albik Hajji, Uma Hajji, his son Dada (Umayev) and Dada Zalmayev—received death sentences and were executed three days later. Hearing his sentence Albik Hajji said: 'From now on it is crystal-clear to all the people how perfidious the Muscovite Tsar is.'[77] Of the major leaders only two avoided Russian vengeance: Sulayman managed to escape to the Ottoman Empire, while Soltamurad

...did not make peace with the Russians and did not go to them. Letting no one but his relatives know his location, he was constantly on the run. He fell ill and died without making peace with the Russians and was buried with great honour in the graveyard of Benoy.[78]

But Russian punishment was not limited to the leaders. Obeying the government's order 'not to leave a single rebellious nest unpunished',[79] the authorities took harsh measures. To start with, each of the households accused of taking part in the rebellion had to pay compensation of 3 roubles in silver. From this the authorities raised 31,113 roubles in Daghestan alone.[80] Then any suspect was exiled to inner Russia or Siberia. Sometimes they were banished on their own, sometimes with their families. Moreover, entire villages were moved to inner Russia, and their lands and the lands of villages moved into the plains were confiscated and granted to the Cossacks and to natives who took part in quelling the rebellion. 'It seems impossible', wrote a Soviet historian, 'to determine the exact number of Chechens exiled to Russia, because the official documents are inconsistent. They sometimes list villages, sometimes families and sometimes individuals. In any case they were in the thousands.'[81]

Avalov: 'Let it be said between the two of us: at the moment compliance is necessary, but the overall reckoning will come.' Ivanov (note 37), p. 293.

[76] Goytakin Rasu (note 9), p. 7.

[77] Ibid., *loc. cit.*, also for the full list of those sentenced to death and their last words. Also, Ivanov (note 37), p. 293.

[78] Goytukin Rasu (note 9), p. 7.

[79] Ivanov (note 2), p. 196.

[80] Mahomeddadayev (note 71), p. 188.

[81] Ivanov (note 37), p. 293. Nevertheless, in another place he came up with a partial

Thus far no studies have been made of the Chechen exiles in inner Russia and only one piece of evidence has to date been published—that of Goytakin Rasu from Benoy, a *qadi* under Albik Hajji. 'If I described in detail', he wrote, 'all the affronts by officers and soldiers all through our journey from town to town, even my enemies would have mercy on me.'[82] However, one can get an impression of their fate in exile from an article examining the destiny of about 5,000 Daghestanis, the population of entire villages who were moved to the Saratov and Astrakhan *guberniias* on the Middle and Lower Volga respectively, allotted land and told to establish new settlements.[83] Yet the Daghestanis stubbornly refused to work the fields they had been assigned and fell into complete demoralisation and disorientation. A *qasida* (poem) written in Arabic by one of the exiles describes their state:

> *I was upset when I saw*
> *the prisoners who hoped to return [to their homeland]*
> *and refused the money and cattle the Treasury*
> *had assigned to them. [...]*
> *The judges in Saratov*
> *were angry with us and*
> *shut the door of compassion,*
> *making us taste punishment*
> *by letting us starve and not letting us leave [...]*
> *Some prisoners were happy to take the land [they were allotted],*
> *but they only began to indulge to drinking.*
> *How hard Fate hit the prisoners,*
> *it struck them with strange things.*
> *These are the woeful afflictions that take away our youth.*
> *How many of us are hungry and weep*
> *and wail in our weakness.*
> *How many of us are naked and barefoot*
> *without any of the clothing we need?*
> *How many scholars began to wander*

---

figure of about 7,630 exiled of whom about 450–500 were from the Terek *oblast* and 6,900 from Daghestan. Ivanov (note 2), p. 197.

[82] Quoted in Mahomeddadayev (note 71), p. 192. For a more detailed description, see Goytukin Rasu (note 9), p. 7.

[83] Austin Jersild, 'Imperial Russification: Daghestani Mountaineers in Russian Exile, 1877–83', *Central Asian Survey* 19, 1 (2000), pp. 5–16.

with their bags on their shoulders,
despised in the streets, ridiculed
by strangers, desperate, suffering [...]
But a group of fools among us
began behaving like a pack of wolves,
prowling the streets at any time
and stealing whatever they could find.[84]

This demoralisation and disorientation, coupled with diseases and the extreme change of climate and altitude, made exile, to use the words of the Imperial Interior Minister, 'almost equivalent to capital punishment'.[85] 'Most of the Mountaineers', reported an officer assigned to inspect their situation in the spring of 1878, 'are exhausted by diseases and smitten by their misfortune and homesickness to such a degree that to leave them in the severe climate and unfamiliar conditions of life means to doom them to a more or less prolonged agony.'[86] Because the number of the exiles continued to decrease at a terrible rate—in the *guberniia* of Novgorod, for example, 429 out of 1,625 (26.4 per cent) died within a few months of their arrival[87]—the government was compelled to abandon the project of mass resettlement. Then after the accession of Alexander III in 1881 the Caucasian exiles were pardoned and a month later allowed to return to their homeland.[88]

While at least some of those exiled to inner Russia returned to the Caucasus, the thousands who emigrated to the Ottoman Empire (where they formed the second wave of immigration) never returned. A few of them were escaping Russian punishment. Many more chose to emigrate out of despair and because all the prohibitions against the free practice of religion were reintroduced. Yet many others were simply 'encouraged' by the authorities to do so.

---

[84] Poem written probably in 1881 and sent to Hasan 'Ali al-Alqadari, who included it in his *Diwan al-Mamnun* (Temir-Khan-Shura, 1913), pp. 167–8. Translation based on one by Michael Kemper, 'Daghestani Shaykhs and Scholars in Russian Exile: Networks of Sufism, *Fatwas* and Poetry' in Moshe Gammer and David Wasserstein (eds), *Daghestan in the World of Islam* (Helsinki, forthcoming).

[85] Minister of the Interior, 28 October [9 November] 1878, as quoted in Ivanov (note 37), p. 294.

[86] Colonel Germesen as quoted in Ivanov (note 2), pp. 197–8.

[87] Ibid., *loc. cit.*

[88] Goytakin Rasu (note 9), p. 6.

Like those exiled to Russia, many of the émigrés were followers of both Sufi *ta'ifas*—the Naqshbandiyya and the Qadiriyya—which the Russian authorities tried once again to eradicate. The attempt was doomed to failure.

9

THE EMPEROR'S INSUBORDINATE SUBJECTS

From the Russian point of view the brutal suppression of the 1877 uprising and the massive retributions that followed achieved the desired effect and the authorities could claim that, as in the Bible, 'the land had peace for forty years'. Indeed between 1878 and 1918 no large-scale revolt broke out in the Northern Caucasus. Even the revolution of 1905–7, which engulfed all the surrounding areas, was of rather minor interest in Chechnya and Daghestan.[1] This encouraged the Russian authorities to move parts of the country gradually from 'special' military to a more 'normal' civilian administration. Nonetheless, throughout the entire period the 'natives' remained under special military control. Despite several internal administrative boundary changes, Chechnya remained until 1917 part of the Terek *oblast* centred on Vladikavkaz. Thus the Chechens remained separated from Daghestan and joined the Ingush, Ossets, Kabartay and Kumyks as well as the Cossacks and the growing non-indigenous population.[2] This latter group increased at an accelerated rate following the discovery of oil.

J. J. Etienne Lenoir's invention in 1859 of the internal combustion engine and its further rapid development and employment turned an already rising demand for oil and its refined products—mainly petrol—into a galloping one. Many places where oil was discovered immediately became 'modern age Eldorados' attracting large numbers of men seeking their fortune, or at least hoping to

---

[1] Luigi Villari, *Fire and Sword in the Caucasus* (London: T. Fisher Unwin, 1906), pp. 24–5.
[2] See Chapter 7.

make a living. The Russian Empire, or more precisely the Caucasus, was one—perhaps the major one—of these 'Eldorados'.

The existence of easily accessible oil along the Caspian shores of Azerbaijan had led to its extraction and use since time immemorial. However, from 1859 oil extraction became an industry using modern technologies and refineries.[3] Consequently Baku, 'at mid-century still a sleepy port on the Apsheron Peninsula', became in the 1870s 'a typical boom city with the highest rate of population increase in the Russian Empire'.[4] With such a concentration of wealth and a population of multi-ethnic, -religious and -cultural composition Baku became what one might call a 'Levantine city' on a par with Tangier, Alexandria, Beirut, Izmir/Smyrna, Aden, Odessa and Shanghai.[5] A buzzing cultural, political and ideological centre, Baku radiated its influence far beyond the Caucasus—as far as Tehran and Istanbul—and became the cradle of Armenian, Azerbaijani and Iranian nationalisms as well as several other political and ideological movements.[6]

Oil was first found in Chechnya in the mid-1880s and has affected its fate ever since. By 1890 shallow pits in the ground were already producing over 263,000 barrels per year. This naturally drew the attention of Western prospectors and in 1893 the first two gushers were struck.[7] According to a report published in London in 1911,

---

[3] For the history of the oil industry, see Essad Bey, *L'épopée du pétrole* (Paris: Payot, 1934); Jean-Jacques Berreby, *Histoire mondiale du pétrole* (Paris: Editions du Pont Royal, 1957).

[4] Tadeusz Swietochowski, *Russian Azerbaijan, 1905–1920: The Shaping of National Identity in a Muslim Community* (Cambridge University Press, 1985), p. 21.

[5] 'Levantine cities' according to this concept were major ports, which following their economic centrality also became major cultural, political and ideological centres where Western and local cultures mixed. For a short description of Beirut in this perspective, see Kemal S. Salibi, *A House of Many Mansions: The History of Lebanon Reconsidered* (London: I. B. Tauris, 1988). Still, similarly detailed indepth studies of Beirut and other similar cities are yet to appear.

[6] Baku as a Levantine city and as the cradle of various cultural, political and ideological movements is yet to be studied. A summary of the demographic and social changes following the oil boom can be found in Alex Kamaisky, 'Hatmurot bHitpathut haHevra ha'Azerit tahat haHashpa'a haRusit veHishtaqfutan baHistoriografiya ha'Azerit haModernit [The Changes in the Development of Azeri Society under Russian Influence and their Reflection in Modern Azeri Historiography]' (Tel Aviv, 1997), pp. 32–3.

[7] Charles van der Leeuw, *Oil and Gas in the Caucasus and Caspian: A History* (London: Curzon Press, 2000), pp. 74–82.

[The oilfield] is situated about eight miles [*c.* 13 km.] from the city of Grozny, and has been worked for a long time, but it was not until 1893 that rational methods of working were adopted, with most favourable results. [...] The number of wells in exploitation at Grozny is now [1910] over 200, and produce an average of 50,000,000 poods [5.9 million barrels] yearly.[8]

What made Groznyi oil especially attractive was the fact that it was—and still is—'of the paraffinous description';[9] in other words, it is rich in petrol and needs little refining. Indeed, the production of petrol leaped from 17,900 barrels per annum in 1901 to 47,500 in 1913.[10] It was now the turn of Groznyi, a 'normal', civilian town since 1870, to become a 'boom town'. Earnings from the sale of petrol alone multiplied by 70 in twelve years, from 93,000 roubles in 1901 to 6.5 million roubles in 1913.[11] Unlike Baku, however, Groznyi never grew into a large cosmopolitan city or became a cultural centre. It remained a small provincial town, not unlike many Texan towns experiencing the oil boom at the same time. Not only

[8] John Mitzakis, *The Russian Oil Fields and Petroleum Industry* (London: Pall Mall Press, 1911), p. 35. The annual production of oil in Groznyi between 1900 and 1917 was as follows:

	barrels (m.)		barrels (m.)
1900	3.6	1907	4.7
1901	4.1	1908	6.2
1902	4.0	1909	6.7
1903	3.9	1910	8.3
1904	4.8	1912	8.0
1905	5.1	1915	10.5
1906	4.7	1917	12.5

Sources: Mitzakis, p. 35 (for the years 1900–10); Van der Leeuw (note 7), p. 76 (for the years 1912–7).

[9] Mitzakis (note 8), p. 88.

[10] Groznyi Petrol Market (average prices in kopeks, volumes in million puds)

	1901	1905	1907	1909	1911	1913
Output	0.15	1.0	1.9	3.6	4.7	6.5
Price	62.0	50.0	90.0	110.0	65.0	100.0

Source: Mitzakis (note 8), p. 88.

[11] Ibid., *loc. cit.*

did it not enjoy a large hinterland, a long history or attraction to the native population, but the quantity of oil produced, but the economic activity it generated were insufficient for Groznyi even to replace Vladikavkaz as the administrative and cultural capital of the *oblast*.[12]

By the time of the Russian conquest Baku was a long-established major political, economic and cultural centre. Therefore, it was natural that following the oil boom it attracted large numbers of Muslim workers from throughout the Caucasus and beyond. Groznyi on the other hand had been established by the Russians as, and remained, largely a Russian town. It attracted mainly Russians and other Slavs and was not merely unattractive to the neighbouring Caucasian highlanders, but made them feel unwelcome. Consequently very few Chechens, Ingush or Daghestanis found work in Groznyi or its oilfields, much less settled in the city. Thus on the whole the Chechens did not enjoy the fruits of the economic boom, even to the limited extent that Azerbaijani rural society did.[13] But the exclusion of the Chechens (and other Caucasian communities) also had an internal reason—self-isolation—and each process reinforced the other. The overwhelming majority of Chechens refused to open up to the ways of the modern world—connected in their mind with the Russian infidel—and preferred to stay in their villages and continue their traditional way of life. Thus, for example, even though they had the opportunity to send their children to

---

[12] Even in the 1990s Vladikavkaz still had the atmosphere of its old Imperial past: 'The centre of Vladikavkaz ... with its trams, enclosed balconies and mock towers has real charm [... and] a relatively cosmopolitan feel to it.' Sebastian Smith, *Allah's Mountains: Politics and War in the Russian Caucasus* (London and New York: I. B. Tauris, 1998), pp. 106–7.

[13] This does not mean that individuals did not enjoy the fruits of the economic boom. Several Chechen entrepreneurs did accumulate capital, either directly from oil extraction or from other economic activities. These included officials and officers in Russian service, like Chermoyev, and Sufi Sheikhs and other religious leaders. Among the latter were the Naqshbandi Sheikh Abdul Aziz Shaptukayev (known as Dokku Sheikh), who established the oil company Staroiurtovskaia Neft', the Naqshbandis Yusup Hajji Baybatyrov from Koshkeldi and Deni Arsanov from KenYurt, and the Qadiri 'Ali Mitayev, who were engaged in widescale economic activites. Julietta Meskhidze, 'Die Role des Islams beim kampf um die staatliche eigenständigkeit Tschetscheniens und Inguschetiens, 1917–1925' in Anke von Kügelgen, Michael Kemper and Allen J. Frank (eds), *Muslim Culture in Russia and Central Asia from the 18th to the Early 20th Centuries*, vol. II: *Inter-Regional and Inter-Ethnic Relations* (Berlin: Klaus Schwarz, 1998), pp. 458–9.

receive a modern education free of charge in Russian schools, only a tiny minority did so.[14] Rather, almost all boys were sent to the traditional *maktabs*, where they learned at least the basics of Arabic and Islam.[15] Even most of those in the Russian service—officials, interpreters and soldiers[16]—preferred to do the same. The result was that by 1914, while nearly all Chechens were literate in Arabic, and some had a working knowledge of Russian, only a trivial number among them had a modern 'Western' education and could be counted among the ranks of the 'intelligentsia'.[17]

However, isolation does not necessarily mean stagnation or lack of change. Indeed, a major change did take place in Chechen society in those years, but in a different direction to that desired by the Russian authorities. It was the spread of the Qādiriyya. In spite of active persecution by the authorities—or perhaps because of it—this *ta'ifa*, after an initial period of confusion following the arrest of Kunta Hajji, enjoyed a somewhat clandestine re-emergence. As stated earlier, by the 1890s it had all but replaced the Naqshbandiyya among the lowland and foothill Chechens and recruited the hitherto semi-pagan Ingush to Islam and the *tariqa*. According to Soviet sources, by the mid 1920s about 70–80 per cent of the

---

[14] In 1863 a two-class school for well-to-do Chechens already operated in Groznyi. By 1871 two primary tuition-free schools were functioning in Vladikavkaz, and from 1876 a directorate of public schools supervised a network of such institutions in the Terek *oblast*. By 1914 ten primary schools were operated by the directorate, mainly in Groznyi. M. A. Karataeva, 'Reaktsionnaia ideologiia musul'manskogo dukhovenstva Checheno-Ingushetii i bor'ba s nei v 1920–1931 gg.', *Sotsiologiia, Ateizm, Religiia* (Groznyi), I, 1 (1972), p. 87.

[15] According to Russian sources, there were 140 'religious [Muslim] schools' in Chechnya in 1917 (ibid., p. 86, quoting archival reports).

[16] As mentioned above, Caucasian Mountaineers were not conscripted into the Russian army, although volunteers were welcome. In addition to the above-mentioned two Daghestani and one Chechen irregular mounted regiments, the Emperor's guard included a Mountaineers unit, and a regular army division was formed known as 'the Wild Division' (*dikaia diviziia*), known among other things for the invention of 'Russian roulette'.

[17] A major and early Chechen modern intellectual was Umalat Laudayev, who had published since 1872 ethnographic studies of his people. The appearance of jedidists among the Chechens has yet to be studied. For a highly critical and distorted piece about them, see A. A. Mankiev, 'Iz istorii musul'mansko-klerikal'noi mysli v Checheno-Ingushetii', *Sotsiologiia, Ateizm, Religiia* (Groznyi), I, 1 (1972), pp. 36–62.

Chechen population were followers of the various Sufi Sheikhs,[18] and the number of '*murids*' (of both *tariqas*) was well above 60,000.[19] In the absence of its founder, however, the Qadiriyya split into several branches. The large majority of followers deny the fact that Shaykh Kunta Hajji died and believe he has gone into a state of hidden existence from which in due time he will re-emerge to redeem his people. They accept him as their *murshid* and deny any other interim leader as a temporary substitute. However, three groups followed their leaders—all *vekils* (deputies) of Kunta Hajji, though none of them, it seems from the available sources, had been authorised by him to disseminate the *tariqa*—and accepted them as temporary *ustadhs* until the *murshid*'s return. These disciples of Kunta Hajji established each a *vird* (sub-order) of his own, the leadership of which has been transmitted to his descendants.

The group established by Bamatgiri (Bammat Giray), son of Mita (thus 'Mitayev') from Avturi, is the largest of the three and is spread throughout Chechnya and among the Ingush. The main area of diffusion of the second largest *vird*, established by Battal Hajji from the Ingush *te'ip* Belhoroy (thus 'Belkhoroyev'), is Ingushetia, though it also has followers in Chechnya and Daghestan. The smallest group is that established by Chim Mirza ('Taumirzayev') from the *aul* of Mayrtup, and is spread mainly in Ichkeria. In the early 1920s the Soviets estimated the number of their *murids* as being about 10,000,800 (probably a misprint for 8,000) and 2,000 respectively.[20]

The various branches of the Qadiriyya as well as the Naqshbandiyya, all being strictly orthodox, reinforced the people's self-isolation. Becoming intertwined with the fabric of society and enjoying moral and spiritual leadership, the *ta'ifas* guided the Chechens to be better Muslims, to live according to the *shari'a* and to shun the infidels in order to avoid their ways. Naturally, both *ta'ifas*' tradition of hostility to Russian rule was another important reason for their preference for isolation. (On the other hand, this hostility facilitated

[18] Meskhidze (note 13), p. 480, note 56.

[19] In 1917 their estimated number was 60,000; in 1925 it was 61,200; Karataeva (note 14), pp. 86, 92. However, one must take into account the highly confused way such terms were used by Russian and Soviet sources. Thus what was meant could well be the number of followers rather than of disciples.

[20] Ibid., p. 97. For further details see Gammer, 'The Qadiriyya in the Northern Caucasus', *Journal of the History of Sufism*, 1–2 (April–May 2000), pp. 275–94.

the Qadiriyya's spread among the Chechens and Ingush.) In their turn, both *ta'ifas* with their hostile attitude to the infidel authorities added to Chechen (and Ingush) defiance.

The fact that between 1878 and 1917 no large-scale revolt broke out in the Northern Caucasus did not necessarily mean that the country was pacified. On the contrary, by the turn of the twentieth century the Northern Caucasus was the wildest province in the Russian Empire. Indeed, if Groznyi may be compared to a Texan oil town then Chechnya and a great part of the north-eastern Caucasus was Russia's 'Wild West', where, according to an Englishman intimately familiar with the country, the 'chord or triad' of 'brigands, rifles and revolvers proved to be the *leitmotif*, so to speak, of existence'. Especially 'bad' in this respect was Chechnya, the Chechens (and Ingush) being 'addicted' to 'brigandage', which 'was with them the very breath of their being'.[21] But even here banditry was mainly experienced in the lowlands, 'especially near Grozny'.[22] In that town 'the talk going and coming was, inevitably, as to 20 per cent, or thereabouts, of brigands and, as to the remaining 80 per cent, of oil.'[23] In the mountains of Chechnya brigandage was very rare:

The very men who would rob and kill without compunction within sight of Vladikavkaz or Grozny would, if, as well might be the case, they came from the higher and remoter districts, refrain in their home-land from any such crimes. [...] The net result was that to drive or ride—no one, of course, walked—in the lowlands of Tchetchnia was always to run a very

[21] J. F. Baddeley, *The Rugged Flanks of the Caucasus* (Oxford University Press, 1940), vol. I, pp. 8, 19. Another Western traveller wrote of Vladikavkaz: 'I have rarely seen a place more full of ruffians than the bazaar, and murders and robbery were everyday occurrences. Only two days ago a band of Ingushes had come into the town, murdered several people, plundered a couple of houses and ridden off undisturbed.' Villari (note 1), p. 321. That banditry was common in other parts of the Caucasus as well is testified to by Russian accounts, for example D. S. Baranovskii to Viacheslav Konstantinovich fon Pleve 'Prichiny razboev, grabezhei i drugikh besporiadkov v Zakavkaz'e i sposoby k ikh iskoreneniiu', 23 November [6 December] 1903, published by Galina Georgievna Lisitsyna, 'Dva dokumenta o polozhenii na Kavkaze' in Galina Georgievna Lisitsyna and Ia. A. Gordin (eds), *Rossiia i Kavkaz skvoz' dva veka* (St Petersburg: Zhurnal 'Zvezda', 2001), pp. 329–39.

[22] Baddeley (note 21), vol. I, p. 8. 'The night before I arrived a band of seventy Chechens had held up a train near Groznyi, murdered fifteen passengers and two guards, and made off with a large amount of booty.' (Villari, note 1, p. 321).

[23] Baddeley (note 21), vol. I, pp. 8–9.

serious risk of being robbed and murdered, and the nearer the town the greater the danger; whereas, once you had entered the mountain regions, if only you knew the ways of the people, you were as safe—even safer than—in the most civilized countries of Europe.[24]

A Russian author described this restlessness of the Chechens and attributed it to their collective nature:

The Chechens are a lively and passionate people. A quiet and regular life is not to their liking, and therefore they always ramble, always surround themselves with an exceptional atmosphere of lively phenomena. As soon as they have finished cultivating their fields—mainly maize—in the summer, behold the season of fights between *jigits*—sometimes because of the most nonsens reasons—has already started in the autumn. And what fights! *Kinjals* and pistols are used, with the usual outcome being either death or mutilation for life.

This season is followed without respite by another—that of the valiant exploits of the *jigits* in the struggle against the principle of private ownership, or simply the season of theft. They steal not out of need but partly out of love for an easy gain and mainly out of passion for exceptional and intense sensations. A moonless night spent in a ravine, in dense grass, in the reeds; the careful, silent climb over a fence, or overcoming one obstacle or another to the tempting object, so silent that one can hear one's own heartbeat; taking possession of this object and retreating with it along thieves' ravines overgrown with dense bushes; the fear of pursuit intertwined with a maliciously fearless readiness to face it at any moment and fight even the devil himself—this is to the true Chechen the glory of nocturnal hunts on someone else's property generating the desired moments of passionate sensation.

This is the main pastime during the entire autumn. In the winter the hunt of someone else's bulls and horses must unwillingly stop or at least reach the minimum. In the winter attempts to steal someone else's property are first completely unprofitable and second extremely risky. At this time of the year cattle—the usual object of theft in Chechnya—are in their owners' yards, in the stable, guarded by vicious dogs; the owner himself is also home and awake, and even when he is asleep, it is such a light sleep that at the first rustle or the slightest noise in the yard he arises as if out of the ground in front of the uninvited guest, armed with a *kinjal* and a pistol loaded with a huge portion of grape-shot. Other obstacles to the accomplishment of thieves' achievements are also to be met: the nights are usually bright while the perfidious snow, which in itself neither hinders

---

[24] Ibid., vol. I, p. 9.

nor slows the thief, silently betrays him in the morning exactly to those into whose hands he would not at all like to fall.

In sum, in the winter theft is a no-win game. Yet, how should our mountaineer quench his irresistible thirst for intense sensations at this time of year? And so he starts at leisure various pursuits, asks often very bizarre, questions, and first and foremost plunges into politics, into that peculiar Chechen politics which has caused us so many alarms and trouble to this very day. It is not in the spring, as is usually thought, but in the dead winter, in the season of snow and cold, that the socio-political surprises presented to us with the advent of warm weather, are created in Chechnya. In the winter the Chechens look over the past, analyse the present and fantasise over the future. In the winter all kinds of ideas are aired among them. And if, for example, in the early spring there is talk in Chechnya of resettling to Turkey, or under the cover of the newly green-clad forests the religious dance known as '*zikr*' or '*zikro*' is being danced, someone acquainted with the people would have no doubt at all that both of these phenomena are nothing but the realisation of fantasies developed during the winter.[25]

This description is obviously partial and partisan. It exaggerates the internal contests among *jigits*—the use of arms among Chechens has always been rare—and it flatly denies what most Russian sources ignore: the economic background to this banditry. As already mentioned, the Chechens (and Ingush) remained a traditional rural agricultural community suffering a spiralling shortage of land and resources in the face of a population explosion. Even to those Chechens living in the rich, fertile lowlands, and usually regarded as better off then their brethren in the mountains, hunger was not an unfamiliar guest. Already before 1877, as a Russian source reported, 'the density of the population' caused

...a great shortage of land and means of livelihood. The need, conditioned by custom and religion, to feed the multitude of beggars who come down from the mountains from September until April and even later puts the residents of the lowland in an even more difficult situation. Only the unusual moderation in food enables them to help their hungry co-tribesmen.[26]

---

[25] N. Semenov quoted in G. A. Tkachev, *Ingushi i Chechentsy v sem'e narodnostei terskoi oblasti* (Vladikavkaz: 1911), pp. 11–13.

[26] N. Semenov, 'Khronika Chechenskogo vosstaniia 1877 goda', Appendix to *Terskii Sbornik*, Vypusk I (Vladikavkaz, 1891), p. 9. For a detailed survey of Upper Chechen communities, see N. S. Ivanenkov, *Gornye Chechentsy. Kul'turno-ekonomicheskoe issledovanie Chechenskogo raiona nagornoi polosy Terskoi oblasti* (Vladikavkaz: Terskoe Oblastnoe Pravlenie, 1910), Appendix, pp. 183–223.

The new prosperity generated by oil, so near and yet so far out of reach by other means, was a temptation many could not resist. Still, economic distress has not caused widespread banditry in many other societies throughout history. So to this must be added the Chechens' sense of betrayal by the Russian authorities. During the final conquest of Chechnya, in the late 1850s, the then Viceroy, Prince Bariatinskii, promised the Chechens that they would retain the lands they owned. This promise was completely ignored by successive emperors and viceroys.[27]

Yet another reason for the existence of such banditry is caught well in the above description—the *jigit* spirit behind raiding and brigandage. In this martial society raids had always been more than just a means to supplement one's livelihood. They were and still are both an outlet for the energies of the young and a means for them to prove their value as warriors. 'Ancient traditions, customs and worldview', wrote a Bolshevik observer, had always regarded 'a perfidious and courageous raid and robbery [as] the expression of manly heroism. The Caucasus was always a nest for romantic robber gangs.'[28]

But there was yet another dimension to this banditry: it was an expression of resistance to, or rejection of Russian rule. 'I cannot help smiling', wrote J. F. Baddeley,

…when I read in the books of certain European visitors to the Caucasus that when not too well received by the natives it would in all likelihood have been worse but for the presence of the 'brave Cossack' provided for them by the local Russian authorities. The very reverse was the case![29]

To the Chechens, though they harboured no tender feelings towards these neighbours of theirs, the Cossacks were under these circumstances plainly representatives of the authorities. The hatred was not necessarily directed against individual Russians:

At the station, before catching the 6 p.m. train to Vladikavkaz, I obtained from the restaurant-keeper, a Russian, a very different account of the

[27] As late as 1916 a request by a Chechen loyal to the Russian authorities and serving in the army to approve his ownership over his land was rejected; see documents published by Daliara Ibrahimovna Ismail-Zade, 'Zemli… budut otdany vam v vechnoe vladenie…' in Lisitsyna and Gordin (eds) (note 21), pp. 357–68.

[28] Klara Tsetkin (Clara Zetkin), *Kavkaz v ogne* (Moscow: Moskovskii Rabochi, 1925), p. 24.

[29] Baddeley (note 21), vol. II, p. 82, n. 1.

much-abused natives. To hear him talk one would think the Tchetchens, at least, the mildest-mannered and most charming people on earth. He had been there for years and had never had any trouble with them, though he frequently went shooting amongst them alone. All that was necessary was to speak their language, know how to treat them and take a little trouble to make good friends—a '*kounak*' or two—then all would be well.[30]

Perhaps the clearest expression of this political, anti-Russian character of Chechen banditry is the phenomenon of *abreks* (bandits of honour). Before contact with Russia *abreks* were fugitives usually escaping a vendetta hiding high in the densely forested mountains. During the 'great *gazavat*' the term acquired a negative meaning in Russian usage and of course a positive one among the Chechens, of a highlander, in many cases a fugitive from Russian law, fighting the Russians. By the second half of the nineteenth century the *abreks* became, in the popular image, Robin Hood-like folk heroes, only to transform during the Soviet period into full-fledged national heroes of resistance to the Russian (though later also the Soviet) authorities. That most *abreks* had been forced into their status not out of political or ideological reasons had little bearing on how they have been perceived.[31]

Admired and protected by the population, the *abreks* attacked state installations, raided private property and robbed travellers on the roads and trains. According to a young Chechen who joined the Bolsheviks,

...the authorities terrorised the peaceful population, and the *abreks* terrorised the authorities. Obviously the people regarded them as fighters against the persecutions and atrocities of the authorities.... The most audacious and successful *abreks* so strongly influenced Chechen psychology that they were regarded as continuers of Shamil and his *na'ibs*. At a certain time

[30] Ibid., vol. I, p. 19.

[31] 'As to brigandage, there was none in Daghestan, and any there might be in the mountains, generally, resulted more often than not from the application of the Russian penal code to blood-feud cases. A man who had killed his enemy, quite rightly, even ineluctably, from his own and his countrymen's point of view, would when threatened with the Siberian mines for a period of years, take to brigandage instead and become an *abrek*.' Baddeley (note 21), vol. I, p. 5. For the latest study of the *abrek* phenomenon, see Vladimir Bobrovnikov, 'Abreki i gosudarstvo: kul'tura nasiliia na Kavkaze', *Vestnik Evrazii*, 2000, 1 (8), pp. 19–46.

rumour had it that Zelimkhan[32] would declare himself Imam and expel the Tsarist authorities.[33]

As true heroes and symbols of resistance they were supposed to fight to the end and die in battle. Furthermore, being national heroes, *abreks* could be captured only through the treachery of Chechen quislings and killed only by a vastly overwhelming Russian force. This is how an early-1990s Chechen chronicle describes the death of an *abrek*:

1865—following the treachery of the *pristav* of Chaberloy, Gudanat Mudarov, the famous Chechen *abrek* Vara Gekhinskii was killed in Atagi after a three-hour-long single-handed battle with a huge Tsarist force.[34]

A song was composed about Vara, and along the roads piles of stones were erected; each passer-by was expected to throw a stone on it and curse Gudanat for his treachery.[35]

The most famous *abrek* was Zelimkhan Gushmazukayev of Kharachoy (born January 1872), 'who led the struggle against Tsarist autocracy between 1901 and 1913'.[36] Officially admitted into the pantheon of 'progressive' heroes by early Soviet historiography—later retractions could not undo this step—Zelimkhan has become the hero of both populist histories and oral folk tales. According to Dakha Gaisultan, 'a local amateur historian who clearly liked his subject', Zelimkhan's career started when a 'quarrel with the Russian-installed village head over a girl escalated into a blood feud':

Zelimkhan and his father were arrested and taken to Grozny by the Russians. [...] Zelimkhan managed to escape, digging out of the prison and from then on lived in the mountains—he was an *abrek*. It was 1901. Everyone knew him and he could stay anywhere with friends, who would hide him and look after him. He started to fight against Russian soldiers, who were seen as invaders and Christian infidels, and whenever he needed men, he could find them.

One day he sent a note to the colonel at the Russian fort in Kizlyar and said 'Don't hide like a woman, come and meet me in Kizlyar'. The Rus-

[32] See below.

[33] Sheripov, quoted in E. Eshba, *Aslanbek Sheripov* (Groznyi: Serlo, 1929), p. 69.

[34] A. Aydamirov, *Khronologiia istorii Checheno-Ingushetii* (Groznyi: Kniga, 1991), p. 76. For a more detailed description of Vara and his capture, see Eshba (note 33), pp. 66–8.

[35] Ibid., p. 68.

[36] Aydamirov (note 34), p. 80.

sians laughed and said 'How could he ever get into Kizlyar, a fort?' So Zelimkhan took sixty men and they dressed up like Cossacks and rode right into Kizlyar and robbed the bank. Before leaving, Zelimkhan left a note to the colonel saying, 'I waited for you. Where were you?' That was in 1907. He got back to the mountains and handed the money to his people and some to the orphans.[37]

Zelimkhan's activity brought to the fore the phenomenon alluded to in the last paragraph—Chechen mass insubordination or, perhaps more precisely, rejection of Russian rule in the form of the population's massive support for the *abreks*. Thus his activity prompted the authorities into action:

In 1911 a murderous attack was made on a road-party of government engineers and others, some of whom were killed, others wounded, by the notorious bandit Zelimkhan. The scene of the outrage was the Malo-Kerketski *pereval* [pass], [...] Zelim himself being a native of Khorotchoi, and that wild country his constant refuge and defence. His crimes were many, but on this occasion he surpassed himself and succeeded in rousing, at last, the anger of the central authorities in Tiflis. The Viceroy, who had sent General Shatiloff to report on the whole affair, came to the conclusion that the brigand's immunity was due in the first place to the almost universal protection and assistance afforded him by the Tchetchen population at large. Hardly less serious was the fact that the particular sect known as Zikrists supplied his band not only with arms and munitions but with recruits from the ranks of its fanatical followers.[38] A third factor was the very large number of *khoutors* (isolated shepherd's huts and small farms) that had sprung up in the mountain districts of Grozny and Veden, without authority and beyond the scope of police supervision. In view of all this and to punish the inhabitants for their 'uninterrupted twelve years' harbouring of Zelim' the Viceroy ordained that troops, put at the disposal of the local authorities for that purpose, should be quartered on all those places in the said districts where Zelim had found refuge; that seven of the most guilty *sheikhs* with their families as well as his own relations be exiled for five years, though not until their guilt had been established;[39] that the

---

[37] Sebastian Smith, *Allah's Mountains. Politics and War in the Russian Caucasus* (London: and New York: I. B. Tauris, 1998), p. 14. For the raid on Kyzliar, see N. V. Markelov, 'Where Martial Plunder Prowls the Mountains (Prisoners of the Caucasus)', *Russian Social Science Review*, 44, 2 (March/April 2003), p. 9–26.

[38] Indeed, it seems that he was a follower and protégé of Bamatgiri Hajji (V. Akayev, *Sheikh Kunta Khadzhi: Zhizn'i uchenie* (Groznyi: Nauchno-Issledovatel'skii Institut Gumanitarnykh Nauk Chechenskoi Respubliki, 1994), p. 92).

[39] In fact, some thirty men, among them the three founders of the *virds*, and the

owners of the *khoutors* which had harboured him be deported; that government 'elders' be appointed in all the village communities noted for his activity; finally, that a fine of 100,000 rubles be exacted from the whole Tchetchen population of the Grozny and Veden districts in favour of the families of Zelim's victims.

A month later the newly-appointed commandant of Veden, Prince Karaloff, succeeded in locating Zelim and two or three companions in a cave in one of the rocky cliffs. The entry was closed by an iron door so strong that, after a day's desultory firing and the loss of two of his men and four wounded, Karaloff sent to Veden for pyroxylin with which to blow it in; but this being accomplished it was found that the brigands had escaped, just as the insurgent leaders had done in 1877 in the same locality and possibly from the same cavern.[40]

Zelimkhan was 'treacherously killed' two years later, on 26 October 1913,[41] 'when he was still young, in his forties. He became ill and had to see his relatives in Shali. It was there that one of his own relatives—on his mother's side—sold him out and he was killed fighting.'[42] A statue of him, riding his horse stands outside the village of Serzhen Yurt. As for the thirty religious leaders, among them the three founders of the Qadiri *virds*, who had been arrested and sent with their families into exile in inner Russia, most were released and returned home in 1916. No wonder, therefore, that none of them shed tears when the *ancien régime* was toppled less than a year later, in March 1917.

Naqshbandis Deni Arsanov, Dokku Sheikh, Kana Mulla Khantayev from Lakha Nevri, Mahomet Nazirov from Novyi Yurt, Suhayp Mulla, Uzun Hajji from Salty and Yusup Hajji (that is, all the religious leaders) were rounded up and sent to either Kaluga, Astrakhan or Siberia. Aydamirov (note 34), p. 80; Meskhidze, (note 13), p. 459.

[40] Baddeley (note 21), vol. II, pp. 90–1, summarising *Novoe Vremia*.

[41] Aydamirov (note 34), *Khronologiia*, p. 80.

[42] Smith, *Allah's Mountains*, p. 14.

Part IV. BETWEEN THE HAMMER AND THE SICKLE

'There was one nation which did not surrender to the psychology of submission—not distinct individuals or a few mutineers but the entire nation. These were the Chechens.' (Alexander Solzhenitsyn)[1]

> *You deprived us of sunrises, Stalin,*
> *you deprived us of sunsets, Stalin,*
> *you deprived us of our motherland, Stalin,*
> *may God speed you into your coffin*
> *so that you are deprived of sunrises, Stalin,*
> *so that you are deprived of sunsets, Stalin,*
> *so that you are deprived of all that is most precious to you*
> *just as you deprived us of our native land.*
> *Should we forget that morning?*
> *Should we forget that evening?*
> *We shan't forget our native land*
> *and that black day which befell it.*
> *The bleating of sheep, the whine of dogs,*
> *the weeping of children and old men,*
> *we shall not forget them*
> *as long as we live on this earth.*
> *(Chechen folk song[2])*

---

[1] Aleksandr Solzhenitsyn, *Arkhipelag GULag, 1918–1956. Opyt khudozhestvennogo issledovaniia*, Paris: YMCA Press, 1973, pt. 6, chapter 4.

[2] Quoted in *Zhivaia pamiat'. O zhertvakh stalinskikh repressii* (Groznyi: Ministerstvo Kul'tury ChIASSR, 1991), p. 21.

10

THE LAST GAZAVAT

On 24 February (8 March) 1917 a mutiny started in Petrograd (as St Petersburg had been renamed in an outburst of patriotism in 1914). Four days later, on the 28th (12 March), Tsar Nicholas II was forced to abdicate. The 'February Revolution' began a period of internal struggle within Russia, which led to the 'October Revolution' (7 November 1917), in which the Bolsheviks seized power, to the civil war of 1918–21, and to foreign intervention. The Bolsheviks described this war in a simplified, simplistic way as being between 'revolutionaries' and 'counter-revolutionaries' or, in a more widely accepted terminology, 'Reds' against 'Whites'. This description became dogma in Soviet historiography and was fairly widespread even in the West. But things were not so simple or straightforward. In fact, these three or four years were among the most—if not the most—chaotic in Russian history. A huge number of participants in ever-changing coalitions were involved in what amounted to a war of all against all. Ideological, political and social struggles on every conceivable level, from the entire country to a single village, were intertwined with religious, national and ethnic conflicts becoming more complex with the intervention of foreign powers. And to complicate the matter further, almost every single participant in the civil war at some time experienced an internal, often armed struggle within its own ranks.[3]

Chechnya, like the entire Caucasus, was not spared this experience. In March 1917, immediately after the Tsar's resignation, the viceroyalty of the Caucasus was disbanded and replaced by civilian

---

[3] Even the Bolsheviks were divided into rival factions struggling with one other. And see Stephen Blank, 'The Formation of the Soviet North Caucasus 1918–1924', *Central Asian Survey*, 12, 1 (1993), pp. 13–32.

administrative bodies. In the Terek *oblast* a Civilian Executive Committee (EC; *oblastnoi grazhdanskii ispolkom*) was established. However, as in the centre, the EC's authority was challenged by other bodies. Among them were the Cossack Host Provisional Government (*kazach'e vremennoe voiskovoe pravitel'stvo*), the Civilian EC of Groznyi (*groznenskii grazhdanskii ispolkom*) and the Council (*sovet*) of Workers, Peasants and Soldiers, in and through which the Bolsheviks strove to grab power.

'With no single strong authoritative government,' wrote a Daghestani Bolshevik,

...the peoples of the Terek ... bristled up like beasts ready to tear each other to pieces. [...] The main protagonists were the Ingush and Chechens versus the Cossacks. The basis of it was, of course, the land problem between the Mountaineers and the Cossacks. Each looked for allies among the other peoples [of the *oblast*]. The Ingush and Chechens experienced difficulties in finding friends, since both townspeople and villagers ... were extremely angry with them for their robberies. Only the Muslim Ossets supported them.[4]

Thus the Vaynakhs hastened to organise as well. The Chechens held a Congress in Groznyi on 27 March at which they elected a Chechen Council (*chechnskii sovet*) and chose Tapa ('Abd al-Majid') Chermoyev, the only Chechen oil magnate, a former officer of the imperial guard and son of a general in the Tsar's service, as chairman. However, as Chermoyev moved into other spheres (see below), another Chechen National Council (*Chechenskii Natsional'nyi sovet*) was elected on 12 May in Goyty with Ahmethan Mutushev as chairman. In March the Ingush also formed an Ingush National Council (*ingushskii natsional'nyi sovet*), headed by Vasan Girey Jabaghi.

More broadly there was an attempt to unite all the Mountaineers (*gortsy*). Between 14 and 23 May 1917 the First All-Mountain Congress (*pervyi vseobshchii gorskii s'ezd*) was convened in Vladikavkaz, which then decided to establish the Alliance of the United Mountaineers of the Northern Caucasus (*soiuz ob'edinenykh gortsev Severnogo Kavkaza*; AUMNC) as a self-governing body. The congress elected a Central Committee (CC) to run the newly-created Alliance and approved the constitution and the programme of the AUMNC, as well as reform projects.

[4] A. Takho-Godi, *Revoliutsiia i kontrrevoliutsiia v Dagestane* (Makhachkala: Nauchno issledovatel'skii Institut, 1927), pp. 84–5.

The AUMNC and various national organisations were established and headed by Russian-educated Mountaineers—*intelligentsiia*, entrepreneurs and former officers in the imperial army. These included *inter alia* Basiyat Shakhanov (a Balkar lawyer and chairman of the congress), Pshemakho Kosok (Kotsev; a Kabartay horse-breeder), Kh. Chizhokov, Nauruzov and Atazhukin (Kabartay), Mistulov, Kibirov and Bayev (Ossets), General Safarbi Mal'sagov and Vasan Girey Jabaghi (Ingush), Ahmethan Mutushev, Musa Kurumov, Ibrahim Chulikov and Tapa Chermoyev (Chechens), and Prince Nukhbek Tarkovskii and General Khalilov (from Daghestan). Most of them envisioned a Western-type secular democracy.

However, all these people were generals without armies and rulers without a country. The major cities in the Northern Caucasus—most of them Russian—were firmly controlled by Russian political and military forces. The 'troops' could be supplied only by the Islamic religious leaders, first and foremost the Sufi sheikhs. While some of these, like the sons of Battal Hajji Belhoroyev, refused to have anything to do with the 'secularists', most of them co-operated with the Western-oriented group. Among these were the Qadiri 'Ali Mitayev and the Naqshbandis Deni Arsanov, Dokku Sheikh, Suhayp Mulla, Yusup Hajji, 'Abd al-Vahhap Hajji, Uzun Hajji al-Salti and Najm al-Din al-Hutsi (Gotsinskii). They demonstrated their power by 'supplying' 10,000 participants for the Congress of the Chechen people in Groznyi and some 20,000 for the second All-Mountain Congress in Andi (Daghestan) in August 1917, as compared to 400 participants in the first congress.[5]

The Islamic leaders were interested in securing the monopoly of the *shari'a* over life in the mountains. In the Chechen congress in Groznyi they had already raised the questions of enforcing the *shari'a* and establishing a Terek Muftiate. Neither issue was resolved. Thus they were raised again at the First All-Mountain Congress where Najm al-Din was proclaimed Mufti of the Northern Caucasus. In June 1917 Uzun Hajji visited Chechnya calling for Najm al-Din to be proclaimed Imam. Indeed, in the Second All-Mountain Congress in Andi Najm al-Din tried unsuccessfully to force the issue.[6]

---

[5] Thus they 'dumped' the Congress and made it unmanageable. The Bolsheviks were quick to adopt this technique in future congresses. On the legitimacy of the Andi Congress see below.

[6] Najm al-Din had himself proclaimed Imam of the Northern Caucasus, but this

On 7 November (new style) 1917 the Bolsheviks seized power in what would be dubbed the 'October Revolution' (which has since been called a 'coup' in the countries of the former Soviet Union). Eight days later, on 15 November, the new regime issued a 'Declaration of the Rights of the Peoples of Russia' in which it recognised their right to self-determination and to secession. On 3 March 1918 the Bolshevik-led government signed the peace treaty of Brest-Litovsk with the Central Powers, in which it made far-reaching territorial concessions. These events led to the disappearance of the last trappings of government in the country and to the chaos of the Civil War.

In the Terek *oblast*, having already formed a 'Socialist group' with other left-wing parties, the Bolsheviks moved to consolidate their power. On 7 February and from 16 February to 15 March they convened two Congresses of the Peoples of the Terek *oblast*, in Mozdok and in Piatigorsk respectively. The second congress established the Terek Republic (*terskaia respublika*) with 'people's power' (*narodnaia vlast*). 'People's Power', wrote a Bolshevik leader later, was 'a temporary concession'. In fact, it was 'Soviet power led by the Communist party'.[7] On 4 May 1918 the republic was renamed the Terek People's Republic (*terskaia narodnaia respublika*) and declared part of the Russian Soviet Federated Socialist Republic (RSFSR).

From the very beginning the AUMNC adopted a strong anti-Bolshevik stand. If until the 'October Revolution' it had envisaged itself as part of a Caucasian federation within a federated democratic Russia, it now started to move towards independence, though still striving to be part of a Caucasian federation.[8] However, one of the first steps of the Provisional Government of the AUMNC was very controversial: it joined the Terek Cossack Host (*terskoe kazach'e*

---

was overturned in the second Congress in Vladikavkaz (see below). Also the Bolsheviks in Daghestan counteracted al-Hutsi's move and overturned this decision in the All-Daghestan Congress (*vsedagestanskii s'ezd*) convened in Temir-Khan Shura soon after the congress of Andi. They did so by using al-Hutsi's rival, the Naqshbandi Sheikh 'Ali Hajji al-'Aqushi (Akushinskii), whom they put forward as candidate for Mufti. And cf. below.

[7] Takho-Godi (note 4), p. 85.

[8] Julietta Meskhidze, 'Ob idee Kavkazskoy Konfederazii (1918–1921)', *Istoricheskaia psikhologiia i mental'nost'. Epokhi. Soziumi. Etnosi. Liudi* (St Petersburg: Institut Sotsial noi Pedagogiki i Psikhologii, 1999), pp. 217–24.

voisko) and the Alliance of the Towns of the Daghestan and Terek Oblasts (*soiuz gorodov Terskoi i Dagestanskoi oblastei*) to form the Provisional Terek-Daghestan Government (*vremennoe Tersko-Dagestanskoe pravitel'stvo*), which aimed at establishing the South-Eastern Alliance of the Cossack Hosts, the Mountaineers of the Caucasus and the Free Peoples of the Steppes (*iugo-vostochnyi soiuz kazach'ikh voisk, gortsev Kavkaza i vol'nykh narodov stepei*).[9]

This decision soon proved pointless since it had little chance of success, coming *inter alia* at a time when the struggle between the Chechens (and Ingush) and the Cossacks was quickly deteriorating into warfare. The conflict, manifested in a series of raids and counter-raids, reached its peak with the murder in Groznyi on 8 January 1918 of Deni Arsanov, probably the most influential Naqshbandi Sheikh in Chechnya at the time, with thirty-five (according to other sources twenty-eight) disciples. But the effect of the decision was far more serious: since many activists strongly resented the move, it caused a split among the Chechens and Ingush, 'secularists' and 'Islamists' alike. In fact it was a significant factor (though far from being the only one) in the decision of some young Chechen and Ingush activists to join the Bolsheviks. One of them said of the AUMNC's decision: 'Chermoyev enjoyed the greatest authority during the first months of the revolution' until 'they concluded an alliance with the Cossacks—and made no efforts to get land for the people.'[10]

This split expressed itself organisationally as well. Since Deni Arsanov was the real power behind the Chechen National Council, new elections had to be called. On 28 January 1918 a Congress convened in Urus Martan. It elected a *majlis* (council) and chose Ahmethan Mutushev as its head. Starye Atagi was chosen as its headquarters. In the spring of 1918 Mutushev resigned and Ibrahim Chulikov replaced him. This reflected the fact that 'Ali Mitayev had by now become the real power behind the *majlis*. In August this was further demonstrated when the *majlis* moved from Atagi to Shali. In response the Goyty National Soviet (*goitynskii natsional'nyi sovet*)

[9] For its aims see Meskhidze, 'Die Role des Islams' in A. von Kügelgen, M. Kemper and A. J. Frank (eds), *Muslim Culture in Russia and Central Asia from the 18th to the Early 20th Centuries*, vol. II (Berlin: Klaus Schwarz, 1998), pp. 466–7, note 2.

[10] A. Sheripov, 'Revoliutsiia v Chechne', *Narodnaia Vlast*, 3 August 1918, as quoted in E. Eshba, *Aslanbek Sheripov* (Groznyi: Serlo, 1929), pp. 98, 100.

was established in Goyti, and Tashtemir Eldarkhanov was chosen as its head. However, the real power was wielded behind the scenes by Suhayp Mulla, probably the leading Naqshbandi Sheikh in Chechnya following Sheikh Deni Arsanov's death. Chechnya was thus split between two councils—one pro-South-Eastern Alliance (Shali) and the other increasingly pro-Soviet (Goyty).

The Bolsheviks were relatively late in discovering the potential of the Mountaineer-Cossack conflict. In fact, they at first tried to consolidate their power by uniting all the Russian population against the Chechen and Ingush raids. However, they were soon sucked into the rift between the Cossacks and the *inogorodtsy,* the latter being landless Slavic peasants who had settled in the area during the great colonisation wave of the 1890s–1910s and had to rent land from the Cossack landlords. In late July the Terek government published a decree on redistributing the land. In response, on 2 August the Cossacks attacked and sacked Vladikavkaz, and on that occasion it was the intervention of the Chechens and mainly the Ingush that saved Soviet power. Interpreting the decree as being a return of the ancestral lands that had been distributed by the Tsarist authorities to the Cossacks, the Ingush flocked to help the 'Red Army' and gladly carried on attacking and sacking Cossack *stanitsas.* 'The Chechens and the Ingush', ran a report, 'are nearly all armed and deliver shattering blows on Cossack bands'.[11] Only then did the Bolsheviks realise this potential. The conclusion was obvious:

The Terek *oblast* is a unique phenomenon. Here the national and the class struggle are almost completely identical. The Ingush fights the Cossack not because he is a Cossack, but because the Ingush is landless and poor and the Cossack owns the land. And the correct policy of the Soviet power is to align itself with the Ingush and Chechens.[12]

Accordingly the Cossacks were now punished and the Ingush and Chechens rewarded. The Soviet authorities exiled *en masse* entire *stanitsas,* distributing their land among the Mountaineers or rather accepting the inevitability of its being seized and reoccupied by them. In this way the 'Sunja line', established in the 1820s and com-

---

[11] *Kavkazskii Stol,* Informatsionnyi otdel pri narodnom Komissariate po delam natsional'nostei, 23 December 1918. I am indebted to Arthur Martirosyan for this reference.

[12] Eshba (note 10), pp. 108–9.

pleted in the 1840s, was abolished and the vacant land taken over by the Ingush. This policy would pay the Bolsheviks enormous dividends in the following year.

But in the mean time things had been changing fast in the Caucasus. In March 1918, following the Brest-Litovsk peace treaty and the collapse of the Russian front, Ottoman forces moved into the region. At first, in view of the costs of keeping regular forces in the Caucasus, they deployed only in the south against the British troops in Persia.[13] In other parts of the area an irregular 'Army of Islam' was established, commanded by Nuri Pasha, the half-brother of Enver Pasha who was the Minister of War and leader among the triumvirate ruling the Ottoman state. The core of the 'Army of Islam' was the Ottoman 5th infantry division.[14] By August 1918 further regular Ottoman forces entered the Caucasus to fight alongside the 'Army of Islam'. Under the direct command of Khalil Pasha, Enver's uncle and commander on the Eastern front, the Ottoman forces occupied Baku on 16 September and then moved further north.[15]

Almost all the Muslim Mountaineers, a few Bolsheviks or 'white' officers aside, welcomed the news of the Ottoman advance–although the reception of Ottoman troops wherever they happened to reach was often very different. To them the Ottomans appeared as saviours and as a force that would help them achieve their political aims. The AUMNC was no exception. Already in contact with the Ottoman authorities, the AUMNC sent its representatives to take part in the negotiations between the Ottomans and the Trans-Caucasian delegates at Trabzon and then Batum. Following the declaration on 22 April 1918 of an independent Trans-Caucasian Federation

---

[13] For the complicated situation and the four-way struggle among the Bolsheviks, the British, the Ottomans and the Germans (the latter two officially being allies) see Michael Raynolds, 'The Ottoman-Russian Struggle for Eastern Anatolia and the Caucasus, 1908–1918: Identity, Ideology and the Geopolitical World Order' (Princeton University, 2003).

[14] The usual figures quoted for the strength of the 'Army of Islam'—16–18,000 as in T. Swietochowski, *Russian Azerbaijan, 1905–1920: The Shaping of National Identity in a Muslim Community* (Cambridge University Press, 1985), p. 130—are not very reliable. In fact, relatively few Azeri and Daghestani volunteers joined, and those who did were not highly motivated and many deserted. And cf. Raynolds (note 13).

[15] For the Ottoman advance into the Caucasus, see W. Allen and P. Muratoff, *Caucasian Battlefields: A History of the Wars on the Turco-Caucasian Border, 1828–1921* (Cambridge University Press, 1953), pp. 457–96.

(which under German pressure fell within a month into three independent states—Georgia on 26 May, Azerbaijan and Armenia both
on 28 May), the AUMNC declared the formation of the Independent Democratic Republic of the Mountaineers of the Northern
Caucasus (*nezavisimaia demokraticheskaia respublika gortsev Severnogo
Kavkaza*), in short the Mountain Republic (*gorskaia respublika*).[16]
The declared aims of the new state were 'to isolate' itself from the
civil war and to 'turn life in a democratic direction'.[17]

The CC of the AUMNC became the new state's government,
with Tapa Chermoyev as President, Vasan Girey Jabaghi as chairman of the Parliament and Haydar Bammate (Bammatov, a graduate
of the Law faculty in St Petersburg and probably the best educated
and most gifted among the leaders of the AUMNC) as Foreign
Minister. The new state's territory was defined roughly as the three
oblasts of Daghestan, Terek and Kuban and the two *guberniias* of
Black Sea and Stavropol, which was then divided into seven units—
Abkhazia, Adygeia, Karachai–Balkaria, Kabarda, Ossetia, Chechnya–
Ingushetia and Daghestan. However, the new government controlled only small parts of this territory. 'At this moment', wrote
Chermoyev, 'almost all our territory is under the boot of a small
group of foreign adventurers calling themselves the representatives
of Soviet power.'[18] The military force at its command consisted of the
two (irregular) Daghestan Mounted Regiments (*Dagestanskii konnyi
polk*), established by Russia during its war to conquer the country,
and some elements of the 'Wild Division'. None of these was a
match for the 'Red' units even if they were under the full control of
the Mountain Government (which they were not). Ottoman assistance was therefore essential, and Chermoyev was the first to admit:

Obviously, if we were able to get organised internally and obtain the technical means to fight the Soviet power, the Mountain Government would

---

[16] The official name of the republic in the friendship treaty with the Ottoman Empire was 'The Government of the Union of Caucasian Mountaineers' (*Kafkasya
Cibaliyun-u İttihadi Hükümeti*) in its Ottoman Turkish version or 'The Republic
of the Union of Caucasian Mountaineers' (*La Republique de L'Union des Montag-
nards du Caucase*) in the French one (Raynolds (note 13), p. 495 and n. 134. For
the declaration of independence, see ibid., p. 652).

[17] Meskhidze (note 9), p. 469. Obviously, the first goal of the AUMNC government
was to drive the Bolsheviks out of the North Caucasus and re-establish itself.

[18] Letter from Chermoyev to Prince Nukh Bek Tarkovskii, 25 October 1918 as
quoted in Takho-Godi (note 4), p. 81.

have no reason to look to the Turks for help. [...However,] without this help we cannot get organised, because in order to do so we first of all need to purge our territory of this foreign [*prishlii*] element.[19]

Thus, on 8 June 1918 a Treaty of Peace and Friendship was signed in Batum between the Ottoman Empire and the Mountain Republic. On that very day an Ottoman force of 652 soldiers and officers, commanded by Major Ismail Hakki (Berkok) Bey, reached Daghestan. However, it was too small to make a difference. Following the Ottoman conquest of Baku the Ottoman 15th infantry division moved north to Daghestan. On 12 October it occupied Derbent, where the next day a ceremony of re-installing the Mountain Government took place, and on 8 November it conquered Petrovsk (Makhachkala). An advance Ottoman unit reached as far as Aldi in the vicinity of Groznyi.[20]

However, the Ottoman presence in the Northern Caucasus was too short to overturn the balance of power in favour of the Mountain Republic. On 30 October 1918 the Empire surrendered in the Armistice of Mudros and twelve days later the First World War came to an end with Germany's submission as well. One of the British demands was full Ottoman withdrawal from the Caucasus; thus in November 1918 the Ottoman units withdrew to Anatolia and British forces under General Dunsterville moved into Baku and further north. In December a small British unit occupied Petrovsk and a mission headed by Colonel Rawlinson visited Temir-Khan-Shura (Buinaksk) where the Mountain Government had moved its seat following the Ottoman withdrawal from Derbent. The British presence did not change the *status quo* either, since it too was short—lasting only until June 1919. The change—a drastic one—came only at the beginning of 1919, when General Anton Denikin's *Dobrarmiia* (*Dobrovol'cheskaia Armiia*, 'Volunteer Army') reached the Northern Caucasus.

Founded in Novocherkassk by General Mikhail Alekseyev immediately after the Bolshevik takeover, the *Dobrarmiia* was an organisation of volunteer 'White' officers who wanted to save Russia from

[19] Ibid.
[20] Interview with an 80-year-old Chechen, Groznyi, April 1992. For the Ottoman advance north, see Allen and Muratoff (note 15), pp. 497–509; Raynolds (note 16), pp. 478–96.

the 'Reds'. In one of history's ironies, this army, which remained loyal to Russia's wartime allies, was shielded from the Bolsheviks by the German army of occupation and thus had ample time to grow. Now, with the end of the war and the withdrawal of the Germans, the *Dobrarmiia* went on the offensive. In November and December 1918 Denikin's forces inflicted a series of defeats on the 11th and 12th Red Armies in the Caucasus, and in February they occupied Vladikavkaz and Groznyi and abolished the Terek People's Republic.[21]

Advocating 'one undivided Russia', Denikin refused to recognise any independent states in the Caucasus. Thus the *Dobrarmia* tried to conquer and subjugate the Mountaineers as well. A military regime headed by General Khalilov was established in the mountains. Chechnya was entrusted to the command of General Aliyev.[22] Unable to resist militarily,[23] the new Government of the Mountain Republic, formed in March 1919 by Pshemakho Kosok,[24] tried to negotiate, and in April its delegation met Denikin in person. The 'White' general flatly rejected their claims to independence and demanded loyalty to Russia. In May the *Dobrarmiia* conquered Daghestan, thus putting an official end to the Mountain Republic.[25]

The Chechens, like other Mountaineers, were now facing a dilemma. Sheikh Najm al-Din[26] was the most prominent among the few who regarded the Bolsheviks as the greater danger and were therefore willing to co-operate with the *Dobrarmiia*. However, the overwhelming majority saw the Bolsheviks as the lesser evil. The

---

[21] On the *Dobrarmiia* see Peter Kenez, *Civil War in South Russia, 1918: The First Year of the Volunteer Army* and *Civil War in South Russia, 1919–1920: The Defeat of the Whites* (Berkeley: University of California Press, 1971 and 1977 respectively).

[22] Denikin seems to have tried to pacify the Mountaineers by appointing Muslim officers of local origin to govern them.

[23] In fact the *Dagestanskii konnyi polk* moved to help the Chechens, but it could hardly have been able to stop the *Dobrarmiia*. As it happened, the regiment did not get along with them and returned to Khasav Yurt.

[24] The new government was formed because Chermoyev, Bammate and Gaidarov left for the peace conference in Paris.

[25] For the 'liberation of the Northern Caucasus' by the *Dobrarmiia*, see Anton Denikin, *The White Army* (Gulf Breeze, FL: Academic International Press, 1973), pp. 204–21.

[26] He was head of *shari'a* matters (*glavnoupravliaiushchii shariatskimi delami*) in Kosok's government.

most prominent among these was Sheikh Uzun Hajji, who in April 1919, following the failed mission to Denikin, joined Kosok and Sheikh 'Ali Hajji al-'Aqushi (Akushinskii) in a call to resist the *Dobrarmiia*.[27] Generally the Chechens and other Mountaineers refused to submit to the 'Whites', and in fact the constant low-intensity warfare (to use a modern term) in the mountains distracted a large part of Denikin's forces from the fronts against the 'Red Armies'.

In the mean time many Bolsheviks and Red Army men found shelter in the mountains, where they were received 'with special deference and love' by the 'Muslim-Mountaineers' (*gortsy-musul'mane*).[28] Clearly the Bolsheviks were now reaping the fruits of the events of the summer of 1918 and their declarations recognising the right of self-determination and freedom of religion. Some *auls* were particularly pro-Soviet. In Daghestan it was Kum Torkale, while in Chechnya it was the village of Goyty, which 'turned into a Red Army camp. T[ashtemir] Eldarkhanov, chairman of the Goyty National Council of Chechnya, demonstrated particular devotion to Soviet power and rendered invaluable service to our comrades.'[29]

The Bolsheviks led by Sergo Ordzhonikidze, the 'Soviet proconsul of the Caucasus',[30] and Sergei Kirov now embarked on a campaign to enlist the support of Chechen and Daghestani Sufi leaders. They managed to forge an alliance with 'Ali Mitayev by agreeing that the Soviet government would recognise the *shari'a* as the basis

---

[27] Takho-Godi described Sheikh 'Ali Hajji al-Aqushi in the following words: 'a very old man, one of half a dozen Dargin Sheikhs, the most respected because of his grey hair, humility and learning, whose face according to the Mountaineers shines with '*nur*'—light (because as an example to the peasants 'Ali Hajji has never in his life been exposed to the blazing rays of the sun to do either his own work or a communal-peasant's, but sat in the mosque or at home over 'holy' Arabic books). He joined the revolutionary events and was put forward on the arena of political struggle by the Socialist group in opposition to Najm al-Din al-Hutsi. Since the masses, then still under the influence of the clergy, were drawn to the *shari'a*, a slogan was fashioned: if *shari'a*, then the peaceful one of 'Ali Hajji and not the landowners' counter-revolutionary *shari'a* of Gotsinskii' (note 4, p. 132).

[28] *Pravda*, 14 November 1919. I am indebted to Arthur Martirosyan for this reference and the following one.

[29] G. K. Ordzhonikidze, *Stat'i i rechi v dvukh tomakh*, vol. II (Moscow: Gosudarstennoe Izdatel'stvo Politicheskoi Literatury, 1956), p. 81.

[30] S. Blank, 'The Formation of the Soviet North Caucasus, 1918–1924', *Central Asian Survey*, 12, 1 (March 1993), p. 15.

of future Chechen autonomy (within the Soviet system).[31] With Uzun Hajji, who rejected any rule by *gâvurs* (infidels), they only agreed on cooperation against the 'Whites'. Skilfully the Bolsheviks now coined a slogan for the joint struggle against Denikin: '*Shari'et ve Hurriyet*' (*shari'a* and freedom).

At the beginning of September 1919 Uzun Hajji proclaimed in Vedeno the establishment of the Emirate of the North Caucasus (*Severo-Kavkazskoe Emirstvo*), with himself bearing the titles of both Imam and Emir, and called for *jihad* on the *Dobrarmiia*. Eighty-nine years old at the time, Sheikh Uzun Hajji was among the most influential Naqshbandi Sheikhs in Chechnya and Daghestan. Never accepting Russian rule, he spent fifteen years in Siberia, from where he returned to the Caucasus after the 'February revolution'. Admired even by his Bolshevik rivals as 'highly intelligent, extremely brave, of iron will and totally honest in politics and brave in war', he was nevertheless depicted by them as 'consumed with fanatical fire' and a 'dedicated Pan-Islamist'. Like all his predecessors in resistance to Russian rule, he was said to hate all Russians and to have promised to 'weave a rope to hang students, engineers, intellectuals and more generally all those who write from left to right'.[32]

The Emirate, it seems, was an alliance between secular-nationalists and religious leaders who mistrusted the Bolsheviks and wanted full independence.[33] This is clearly reflected in the fact that Uzun Hajji appointed Inaluk (Mahomet Kyamil Khan) Arsanukov-Dyshinskii to the post of Grand Vezir (Chief Minister). To the secularist nationalists the Emirate was the successor of the Mountain Republic:

After the fall of the Tsars the Muslims of the Northern Caucasus exercised their right for self determination ... through a republic. This aim and this dream were destroyed by the barbaric attack of Denikin's gang. The so-called 'Mountain Republic' was not recognised in the peace conference in Paris. [...] Based on historical facts, the Muslims of the Northern Caucasus

---

[31] Meskhidze (note 9), p. 471.

[32] Marie Bennigsen-Broxup, 'The Last *Gazawat*: The 1920–1921 Uprising' in Marie Bennigsen-Broxup (ed.), *The North Caucasus Barrier: The Russian Advance towards the Muslim World* (London: Hurst, 1992), pp. 114–15.

[33] Thus on 27 October 1919 Arsanukov-Dyshinskii addressed his cabinet with the following words: 'We demand no autonomy, but an independent *shari'a* monarchy. We must die for our independence.' Meskhidze (note 9), p. 472.

... decided to obtain their complete self-determination on the basis of a *shar'i* monarchy [*shariiatskaia monarkhiia*].[34]

However, to the mass of the population its appeal was clearly religious, first and foremost in the form of Uzun Hajji himself. 'Muslims from Ingushetia, Daghestan, Kabarda and Balkaria' started to 'flow' to his 'capital'.[35] A Bolshevik eyewitness described the scene:

Thousands upon thousands of people—on foot and mounted, young and old—moved in a long line to the beautiful wide field of Vedeno. [...] These were the mountain poor, the supporters of the 'Kunta Hajji' sect.[36] They went to pay homage to the rule of 'Imam Uzum-Hajji [*sic*]'. The large square in front of Uzum-Hajji's residence was overcrowded. Under the green banners rhythmic religious dances started, accompanied by religious songs and numerous drums. [...][37] The ecstasy of the dancers increased and many reached exhaustion. Pale, with foam running from their mouths, they were taken by their arms and moved out of the line. [...] The crowd was in the fog of religious excitement. Suddenly, surrounded by armed guards with sabres in hand, a small, very old man with a white beard, dressed in white and in a white turban, was being helped out. This was Uzum-Hajji. In an instant everyone froze in silence.[38]

Indeed, a great many of Uzun Hajji's moves pointed at, and drew legitimacy from, the memories of the heroic Islamic resistance: the title Imam (which also signified a break with Najm al-Din) and the choice of Vedeno—Shamil's 'capital' between 1845 and 1859—for his own were but the obvious ones. So was the division of the Emirate into seven *na'ib*-doms.[39]

By the end of September the 'White' forces were expelled from the mountains. However, the territory of the Emirate did not expand greatly beyond Chechnya, a part of Ingushetia and the north-westernmost part of Daghestan bordering on Chechnya. Meanwhile, the Soviet regime started its counter-offensive against the 'Whites'. In February 1920 the 11th Red Army approached the Northern Caucasus from the north. Most of Chechnya had already

[34] 'Appeal to the Neighbouring Russians and Other Nationalities' by Arsanukov-Dyshinskii (ibid., pp. 471–2).

[35] Ibid., p. 471.

[36] Uzun Hajju was a Naqshbandi Sheikh.

[37] Obviously they were performing a *dhikr*.

[38] Eshba (note 10), pp. 136–9.

[39] Five of these *na'ib*-doms—Shali, Vedeno, Shatoy, Itum Kale and Groznyi—were in Chechnya; Andi was in Daghestan, and the remaining two were in Ingushetia.

been cleansed of the *Dobrarmiia*—only Groznyi was left to be taken ·
on 17 March—and the Red Army men were welcomed as allies.
However, Sovietisation of the country soon began. The Emirate
was abolished and Uzun Hajji was offered the honorary title of
Mufti of the Northern Caucasus. Luckily for both the Bolsheviks
and himself the Sheikh died in May 1920 at the age of ninety.

Four months after their 'liberation' by the Red Army, large parts
of Chechnya and Daghestan were up in arms again, this time against
the Soviets. The reasons, stated 'unanimously' by all the local 'responsible military and civil workers', were the Bolsheviks' own 'mistakes which the leaders of the uprising had exploited so skilfully'.[40]
To start with, 'the Red Army had behaved with the arrogance and
lawlessness of a foreign occupying power in conquered territory.'[41]
Even during the rebellion, when the Soviets had made the utmost
efforts to curb such behaviour, various military commanders and
politruks complained of 'a lack of disciplined soldiers and [their]
inability to respect the religious customs of the Mountaineers'.[42]
'The Kalmyk regiment is unfit for combat,' complained the commander of the front in Chechnya, since it 'is heavily infested with
banditry' and the behaviour of some of its members towards the
peaceful populace was 'scandalous' (*voztmutitel'noe*). Furthermore,
'because of the national frictions between the Kalmyks and the
Chechens, the use of this regiment against the Mountaineers is extremely counter-productive and politically unwise.'[43] The units deployed in the mountains of the Andi *okrug*, stated another report,
'are stealing food, corn, and beasts of burden [*v'iuchnyi skot*], and are
behaving with all forms of illegal violence [*bezzakonnye nasiliia*],'
which 'provoke a justified dissatisfaction with Soviet power and the
Red Army.'[44] 'The drunken and offensive behaviour of the commanding officers', reported the *Cheka* of the Terek *oblast*, 'is alienat-

---

[40] Rossiiskii Gosudarstevennyi Voennyi Arkhiv (Russian State Military Archive;
    RGVA), fond (f) 39247, opis (o) 1, delo (d) 3, Trifonov to Ordzhonikidze, Janu-
    ary 1921. I am grateful to Michael Raynolds for this and all the following refer-
    ences to the RGVA.
[41] M. Bennigsen-Broxup, 'The Last *Gazawat*' (note 32), p. 122.
[42] RGVA, f39247, o1, d101, Telegram from the Commander of the Terek-Daghes-
    tan Group with copies to Ordzhonikidze and Kirov, Petrovsk, 1 February 1921.
[43] Ibid.
[44] Ibid., f39247, o1, d3, 'Revvoensovet Batulin' to Trifonov and Smilge, with copy
    to Ordzhokinidze, Rostov, 24 March 1921.

ing the population and bringing tensions to such a point that an uprising is possible.'[45]

No less important, the civil and party authorities, who were supposed to prevent such behaviour, were gripped by an 'organisational fever',[46] and spent 'more time getting drunk and on banqueting [*pirshestvo*] than on social work'.[47] The flood of Russian cadres, 'with a wide range [*arshinnye*] of powers from centralised institutions', which followed the 11th Red Army, applied stubbornly 'the already obsolete, but still circulating instructions and orders of War-time Bolshevism, ... and ignoring the protests of local workers, ... went on with their essentially counter-revolutionary deeds.'[48] These included 'stupid attacks on patriarchal traditions and Islam, ... punitive raids, police denunciations, blackmail, settling of private feuds, plunder, confiscation of food supplies and fodder, forced conscription into Red regiments, requisitions and destruction of small trade.'[49] 'This is the power of the chicken not the Soviet power,' said the Mountaineers.[50]

In August 1920, when the situation had reached boiling point, Sheikh Najm al-Din al-Hutsi (from the village of Hotso, thus 'Gotsinskii' in the Russian sources) called a gathering in Hidatl, which declared *jihad*. Colonel Kaitmas Alikhanov was elected War Minister of the '*Shari'a* Army of the Mountain Peoples'. Alikhanov was a career officer in the Tsar's army and fought in the 'White Army' during the Civil War. The gathering also issued a call to Sait (Sa'id) Shamil, grandson of the famous Imam,[51] to join and lead the struggle. Indeed, Sait did join the uprising as its nominal leader and was one of two survivors who managed to escape to Turkey.[52] The other leaders of the uprising belonged to two groups: religious leaders,

---

[45] Ibid., f39247, o1, d2, list' (1) 89, Top Secret, Information Bulletin no. 15, for the period of 16 to 22 April 1921.

[46] N. Samurskii, *Dagestan* (Moscow and Leningrad: Gospolitizdat, 1925), p. 107 as quoted in Bennigsen-Broxup (note 32), p. 122.

[47] RGVA, f39247, o1, d2, list' (1) 89, Top Secret, Information Bulletin no. 15, for the period of 16 to 22 April 1921.

[48] Takho-Godi (note 4), p. 142.

[49] Bennigsen-Broxup (note 32), p. 122.

[50] Takho-Godi (note 4), p. 142.

[51] He was the son of Shamil's youngest son, Kyamil.

[52] The other was a Chechen resident of Amman (now in Jordan). His memories of these events were recorded by his son, but never published.

mainly Naqshbandi Sheikhs, and ex-Tsarist (and ex-'White') career officers. But the real leader was Imam Najm al-Din al-Hutsi.

Najm al-Din was the son of Donogo Muhammad, one of Shamil's *na'ibs*, who later served in the Russian administration. He received a classical education and grew up to be a famous scholar (*'alim*) and a poet of great reputation. He also joined the Naqshbandi-Khalidi *tariqa*, becoming one of the major Sheikhs in Daghestan and Chechnya. After finishing his studies in the *madrasa*, he served in the mounted guard of the governor of the Daghestan *oblast*, and later was a member of the 'people's court' (*narodnyi sud*) of Daghestan and then *na'ib* of the Koysubu *okrug*. In 1903 he spent three months in Istanbul, after which he was suspected by the Russian administration of being an Ottoman agent. He thus spent the following fourteen years, until the 1917 revolution, as a *maktab* teacher and a major livestock breeder.

The First All-Mountain Congress in Vladikavkaz chose Najm al-Din as Mufti of the Northern Caucasus. In the Second Congress in Andi, which he forced on the AUMNC leadership and packed with his followers, Najm al-Din had himself proclaimed Imam of the Northern Caucasus. However, the AUMNC leadership did not recognise the Andi gathering and decided to reconvene the second congress in Vladikavkaz, where Najm al-Din was reconfirmed as Mufti, but not Imam. Although in the future Najm al-Din would claim his Imamship from the Andi congress, until April 1919 he exclusively used his official title of Mufti. In the Pshemakho Kotsev government (March 1919) he was chief administrator (*glavnouprav-liaiushchii*) of *shar'i* matters and took part in the delegation that tried to negotiate with Denikin in April. Until then Najm al-Din had been a close ally of Sheikh Uzun Hajji. In fact, the latter had promoted the election of Najm al-Din to Imam. Now, however, their ways parted. While Uzun Hajji regarded the Bolsheviks as the lesser evil and co-operated with them in resisting Denikin's *Dobrarmiia*, Najm al-Din al-Hutsi was strongly anti-Bolshevik and preferred to come to an understanding with Denikin.[53]

When he proclaimed the *jihad* in August 1920 Najm al-Din was about sixty years old.[54] He 'resembled an old eagle, with a sombre

[53] Hajji Murad Donogo, 'Slovo o Nazhmudine Gotsinskom', *Akhul'go*, 3 (March 1999), pp. 4–6.
[54] His year of birth is given in various official documents as 1859, 1862 and 1865—ibid., p. 4.

expression, seldom smiling, proud and domineering.' His was a 'captivating and charismatic personality', and 'he was said to have hypnotic gifts and to be able to interpret dreams. He liked to engage in religious and philosophical debate with his *murids*.'[55]

The uprising engulfed most of the mountainous parts of Daghestan and Chechnya, that is, the western parts of Daghestan and the south-eastern part of Chechnya. The fighting was particularly savage. No quarter was given and no captives taken. The result was a huge number of deaths. According to Todorskii (the commander of the 11th Red Army operating against them) the rebels numbered 9,690 men.[56] All of them (but two) were killed during the fighting or after it. The Red Army lost 10,000 men[57] of an estimated force of 35–40,000.[58] To these must be added an unknown number of civilian casualties. The main theatre of operations was Daghestan. There the Soviets suffered a number of defeats and catastrophes.[59] In Daghestan the struggle also had the character of a civil war. 'Red partisans', mainly from among the followers of Sheikh 'Ali al-Aqushi, who resisted *jihad* and remained loyal to the Soviets, took part in the fighting on the side of the Red Army. In the end the huge Soviet advantage in manpower and technology overpowered the rebels. On 20 May 1921 Hidatl, the rebels' last position, fell and on the 21st the two last rebellious *auls* submitted to the Red Army.

Imam Najm al-Din managed to escape to Chechnya and continue his struggle for four more years. On 17 Ramadan (22 April) 1924 he sent the Soviet authorities the following demands: to evacuate all the Caucasus up to Rostov and to Astrakhan, including the Caspian and Black Seas 'which belonged to our forefathers'; to pay 'compensation for our losses since the day I was elected Imam'; to 'recompense all those who suffered from your unlawful confiscations [*zakhvatnichestvo*]'; and to keep '[your] hand off the Crimea'. If the Soviets met all those conditions, he stated, 'we shall renounce

---

[55] Takho-Godi (note 4), pp. 26–7. Translation by Bennigsen-Broxup (note 32), p. 142.

[56] Quoted in Bennigsen-Broxup (note 32), pp. 116, 135.

[57] *Tainy natsional'noi politiki TsK RKP. Stenograficheskii otchet sekretnogo IV soveshchania TsK RKP 1923 g.* (Moscow: INSAN, 1992), p. 188. I am grateful to Arthur Martirosyan for this reference.

[58] Bennigsen-Broxup (note 32), p. 117.

[59] For the war, see ibid., pp. 121–43; Allen and Muratoff (note 15), pp. 509–27.

independence and enter the government of the Caucasus.'[60] He
finally surrendered in May 1925 and shortly afterwards was tried
and executed. Here is an eyewitness account of his surrender:

Sajid Abdurakhmanov from Gakvari told that during his studies in the
madrasa in the village of Gima (1922–3 [*sic*]) the Soviet authorities offered
a large reward to anyone who would reveal the hiding place of Imam
Najmudin. At last, after several local traitors had pointed to the farmstead
of Chay as the hiding place of Imam Najmudin, several mediators were
sent to offer him the opportunity to surrender and come to Gima in order
to avoid unnecessary losses. The Imam replied that he was ready to accept
the offer if the 'Soviets' released sixteen Chechens who had been arrested
because of him. The Bolsheviks agreed and released the prisoners.

Sajid awaited the arrival of the Imam. As he [the Imam] was coming out
of the forest and approaching the river, he [Sajid] crossed the river to meet
the Imam and talk to him. Sajid hoped that the Imam would relay to him a
vasiyat [will] or a message to his family, but unfortunately a Red Army man
ran over to him and said: 'Hello [*zdravstvuite*] comrade Najmudin.' The
Imam replied in Avar: 'What should I tell them? I don't know their language.' He requested to be taken through the mountains of Daghestan, but
this was declined. Najmudin was taken from Chechnya directly to Rostov.

Here, on the river bank, he made his ablution, prayed a *namaz* of two
rak'as, read a *du'a* [prayer], and then tied a towel around his belly which had
grown thin [his belt, *kinjal* and bullet belts of the *Cherkeska* had been taken
away by the *Chekists*].

Looking briefly at the traitors the Imam said: 'I shall speak to you on the
terrible day of judgement.'[61]

In Chechnya the fighting never reached the scale it had in
Daghestan, and had much more the character of a guerrilla war.
Despite this, or perhaps because of it, the skirmishing lasted for a
longer period. However, guerrilla warfare did not prevent the Soviets from suffering major disasters in Chechnya: on 19 January 1921,
for example, Daghestanis from the Andi region, together with
Chechens from the *aul* of Benoy, suddenly attacked a battalion of
the 292nd Rifle Regiment stationed in Dargo and Belgatoy. The

---

[60] M. Mahomedov, 'Nota Nazhmudina Gotsinskogo Sovetskomu pravitel'stvu',
Akhul'go, 3 (November 1999), pp. 7–9.
[61] Uzunhaji Mukhtarov, 'Predaniia o Najmudine Gotsinskom v Chechne', ibid.,
p. 18.

Regiment suffered heavy losses and was forced to withdraw to join the units of the 291st Regiment garrisoned in Tezen-Qala. Further pressed, both units were forced to abandon Tezen-Qala from where they were driven into an ambush by their Chechen guides, again sustaining serious casualties. Two days later, on 21 January, the élite Cavalry Regiment of the Moscow Cadet Brigade was surrounded near Alleroy in Upper Chechnya. The commanding officer of the regiment, in leading a party that attempted to break out of the encirclement, was the first to be killed. The regiment lost ten officers and eighty-three cadets.[62]

In most cases, however, there was a continuous effort against hit-and-run attacks by small bands, sometimes even individuals. The 'bands, whether politically motivated, criminal or of mixed character', enjoyed the population's 'sympathy and support' because of the people's 'hostility to the Party'. They armed themselves 'by buying weapons from the locals and ambushing Red units'.[63] At least one report mentioned instances of 'rebels purchasing arms and equipment from Red units deployed in Chechnya'.[64]

The Red Army, on the other hand, was operating within a hostile population and was exposed to attacks anywhere and at any time. 'Even the Chechens in the lowlands are unfriendly,' reported the *voenkommissar* of the 33rd Infantry division, the result being that it 'often lost men in the rear'.[65] The endless fighting, and the need to

---

[62] Bennisen-Broxup (note 32), p. 135.

[63] RGVA f39247, o1, d2, ll. 117–18, 'Review of the Banditism in the Terek *oblast* and the Rebellion Movement in Daghestan and Chechnya, for the period up to 25 April 1921.'

[64] Ibid., f39247, o1, d101, Telegram from the Commander of the Terek-Daghestan Group with copies to Ordzhonikidze and Kirov, Petrovsk, 1 February 1921. Surprising as it may seem to anyone not familiar with the 1994–6 war in Chechnya, such behaviour had at least one previous precedent. In March 1846 Prince Vorontsov stated 'military supplies … even cannon shells … have been sold [to the Mountaineers] by army ranks in many places, especially in the units stationed between Vladikavkaz, Evgenievskoe and Temir-Khan-Shura' and warned that 'anyone caught doing so will be treated with all the severity of the law' and 'the punishment awaiting criminals is death.' Vorontsov's Order of the Day, 5 [17] March 1846 (Eshba (note 10), pp. 37–8).

[65] RGVA, f39247, o1, d2, Urgent-Secret, Military Commissar of the 33 Infantry Division to the Chief of Staff and Commander-in-Chief of the Terek-Daghestan Group, Groznyi, 6 March 1921, no. 196. The 33rd Division was known as the

be constantly on guard, took its toll on the Red Army. 'The conditions of battle are nightmarish [*koshmarnye*],' wrote the above commissar. 'All the units have been in battle from the beginning of the
attack and have no hope of rest. [...] There have been cases of suicide even among the commanding officers and of the regimental
commander, unable to tolerate the sight of exhausted Red Army
men, refusing to attack.'[66] Especially costly were attempts to conquer *auls*. 'The fear of repression and confiscation of property',
wrote the commander of the Terek-Daghestan force, 'forces the
rebels to defend their villages fiercely and defiantly, fighting over
every bit of soil in every *aul*. In some villages even women and
children are fighting against the Red Army. Such fighting takes
time and inflicts on us colossal losses.'[67]

One of the major results of warfare, which in turn contributed to
the persistence of the fighting, was the disruption of agriculture.
Thus by the spring of 1921 'a terrible famine' struck the country
with 'heart breaking scenes of poverty'.[68] It was obvious that a 'carrot' had to be offered to the population in addition to the 'stick' of
the Red Army. Indeed the Soviet authorities came forward with
help. They distributed food and seeds to peasants in need and
offered other kinds of aid. This had its effect:

The decisive factor in the feelings of the peasants towards Soviet power
was the fact that it not merely supplied them with the seeds needed for the
autumn sowing, but that it did so quickly and on time. [...] The peasants
welcomed with special satisfaction the orders of the government to
exempt them from taxes proportional to the dimension of the bad harvest,
as well as the reduction of the prices of textiles, boots etc.[69]

In addition to the use of both stick and carrot, the Bolsheviks took
political steps. One of these was to keep Chechnya separate from
Daghestan. On 17 November 1920 Moscow decided to establish a

'Don Cossack Division'. If it was indeed composed of Don Cossacks, the Chechen attitude towards it is self-explanatory.
[66] Ibid.
[67] Ibid., f39247, o1, d101, Telegram from the commander of the Terek-Daghestan
Group with copies to Ordzhonikidze and Kirov, Petrovsk, 1 February 1921.
[68] Tsetkin, *Kavkaz v ogne* (Moscow: Moskovskii Rabochii, 1925), pp. 20–1.
[69] Ibid., pp. 21–2.

Mountain (*gorskaia*) ASSR within the RSFSR, which was officially declared in April 1921. On 20 January the separate ASSR of Daghestan was also established within the RSFSR. Chechnya was part of the Mountain Republic, but not for long: on 30 November 1922 a separate Chechen Autonomous *Oblast* was created. The Soviets' trump card, however, was their success in mobilising the support of Sufi Sheikhs. The most important among these was 'Ali Mitayev, who was asked to be a member of the *Revkom* (*revoliutsionnyi Komitet*, Revolutionary Committee). 'In spite of everything, and not without doubts,' Anastas Mikoyan wrote in his memoirs,

...he gave his agreement to become a *revkom* member. [...] As such 'Ali Mitayev used to come once a week to the *revkom* meeting in Groznyi.[70] Thirty horsemen accompanied him to the *revkom* headquarters and waited there until the end of the meeting. 'Ali Mitayev would come out, mount his horse and return with his companions to his village.[71]

All these tactics and the fatigue of the population had their effect and by 1923 warfare had abated—even if it did not stop completely. A senior Bolshevik, visiting the Caucasus in 1924, testified:

As late as two years ago the incursion of bands of several hundred men who powerfully intertwined ordinary robbery, romantic adventurism and counter-revolutionary aims was quite a common phenomenon. Attacks on Soviet institutions, co-operative shops and trains, and the kidnapping and killing of Soviet servicemen and Communists were not rare. To travel in the Northern Caucasus and the neighbouring *guberniias* was a risky matter. Even last year [1923] quite a few large and small bandit raids occurred. Long excursions, especially into the mountain ravines, could only be carried out with weapons in hand and an armed escort. Now things are different. If such trips are being made today with similar precautions, it is done merely as a decoration, out of habit, or in order to shoot wild birds. Banditry as a political phenomenon has been liquidated. It no longer has [the population's] sympathy. The bandits find neither refuge nor protection among the local peasantry. [...] Soviet policy has won.[72]

---

[70] The headquarters of the state and party administration of the Chechen Autonomous *Oblast* were located in Groznyi, even though the city and the surrounding oilfields had not been included in the Chechen autonomy but remained under the direct control of Moscow.

[71] Meskhidze (note 9), p. 476.

[72] Tsetkin (note 68), p. 24.

'I can state with confidence,' reported Eldarkhanov, head of the Chechen *revkom*, that 'revolutionary power is now solidly established in Chechnya.'[73] The Bolsheviks felt that the time had come to consolidate it.

[73] *Tainy natsional'noi politiki TsK RKP* (note 57), pp. 197–9.

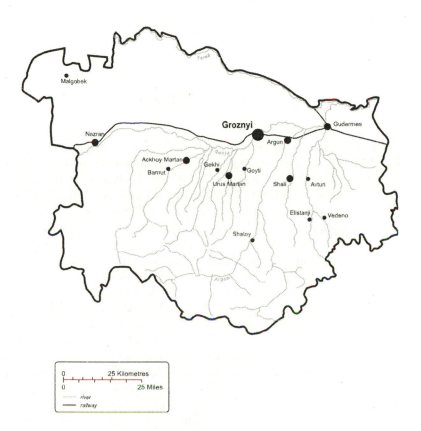

The Chechen–Ingush ASSR before 1944.

11

SOVIETISATION

The first priority of the Soviets was to deal with the Muslim 'clergy'. The Marxist concept of religion as an 'opium of the masses' here joined hands with an intense 'Islamophobia' inherent in Russian society (indeed in all Christian societies): the fear of what in hindsight was clearly no more than the bogey of pan-Islam—plus the actual strength of Islam and its religious leaders in Chechen society. To understand this power one must take into account the fact that before the Revolution Russian reports counted in Chechnya and Ingushetia 850 mullahs who operated 2,675 mosques[1] and 140 religious schools,[2] 38 sheikhs and 60,000 *murids*[3] 'belonging to various sects'.[4] In the mid-1920s these religious leaders received 400,000 roubles yearly in wages and considerable sums in donations, and the average annual income of a sheikh was 1,000 roubles.[5] The Chechens and Ingush obviously preferred their religious leaders to the Soviet authorities, as is demonstrated by the fact that the *zakat* they paid in 1925/6—543,000 roubles—totalled 25 times more than the agricultural tax and 50 per cent more than the sum of all taxes paid to the authorities.[6] Obviously the Muslim clergy, not the Soviets, controlled the people and the economy.

---

[1] The number seems to be exaggerated and probably includes various places of worship, not only mosques.

[2] It is not clear whether the reference here was to *maktabs, madsrasas* or both.

[3] *Murids* here seems to mean followers in general, not disciples.

[4] M. A. Karataeva, 'Reaktsionnaia ideologiia musul'manskogo dukhovenstva Checheno-Ingushetii i bor'ba s net v 1920–1931 gg.'v, Sotsiologiia, Ateizm, Religiia (Groznyi), I, 1 (1972)', p. 86.

[5] Ibid., pp. 92–3.

[6] Ibid.

Clearly, the Muslim clergy had to be dealt with very carefully. Being accomplished masters of political manoeuvring, diplomacy and deception, the Bolsheviks played a sophisticated game of 'divide and rule' with the Sufi sheikhs and other religious leaders. 'Before 1920', a Soviet Chechen historian wrote, 'the lower clergy joined the peasantry in an alliance with the Bolsheviks' to fight 'Tsarism and [foreign] intervention.' Therefore, it was necessary 'to put up' with 'the so-called "*shari'a* regiments"'. During the first years of Soviet power, she continued, '*shari'a* courts, *shari'a* taxes etc.' had to be 'temporarily left intact' because 'the lower clergy joined the peasantry in waging war on the landlords and the bourgeoisie.' Hence, it was 'impossible to launch an immediate attack on the clergy'.[7] In their own words, the Bolsheviks adopted 'the peaceful', not 'the counter-revolutionary *shar'ia* of the landowners'.[8]

At the establishment of the Mountain ASSR, the Soviets tried to drop the *shari'a* from its constitution altogether, but

…the constitutional assembly of the new republic made their recognition of the Soviet government conditional on the *shariat* and the '*adat* being officially acknowledged as the basic constitutional laws of the Mountain Republic, and that the central government should not be intervening in their internal affairs; also on the lands of the Mountaineers, of which they were deprived by the Tsars, being returned to them. Stalin accepted both conditions, after which the delegates officially recognised the Soviet government.[9]

Stalin managed, however, to include the following paragraph: -

taking into account that the mental attitude and socio-economic position of some *shari'a* experts … places them far from the ideals of the toiling masses [… and that] their activity assumes a reactionary character, … the Congress considers a religious struggle [*religioznaia bor'ba*] against such persons and groups who enforce the *shari'a* and the customary law, the '*adat*, … to the evident detriment of the toiling masses, to be inevitable.[10]

[7] Ibid., p. 97.

[8] A. A. Takho-Godi, *Revoliutsiia i Kontr-revoliutsiia v Dagestane* (Makchachkala: Nauchnoissledovatel'skii Institut, 1927), p. 132.

[9] A. Avtorkhanov, 'The Chechens and the Ingush during the Soviet Period and its Antecedents' in M. Bennigsen-Broxup (ed.), *The North Caucasus Barrier: The Russian Advance towards the Muslim World* (London: Hurst, 1992), p. 154.

[10] J. Meskhidze, 'Die Rolle des Islams' in A. von Kügelgen, M. Kemper and A. J. Frank (eds), *Muslim Culture in Russia and Central Asia from the 18th to the Early 20th Centuries*, vol. II (Berlin: Klaus Schwarz, 1998), pp. 474–5.

However, any 'religious struggle' had to be postponed for the time being. Thus, for example, in March 1921 the Second Congress of Councils (*vtoroi s'ezd sovetov*) in Groznyi decided 'to establish cultural institutions, including schools, free of religious influence'. Yet 'in view of the strong influence of religion, the *'adat* and the *shari'a*, it was impossible to prohibit the work of schools in which the teachers were mullahs.'[11] On 3 August 1922 the TsIK of the Mountain ASSR decided to close down the *shari'a* courts. In Chechnya no measures were taken to implement this decision. Nevertheless, once the country became a separate AO, a struggle developed over the position of the *shari'a*.

The main advocate of the *shari'a* was Ali Mitayev, now probably the most influential sheikh in the country, but he was no longer useful to the Soviets. After all, he was a major leader of 'the Kunta Hajji sect', whose 'quantitative growth' and 'enlivened social activity' posed 'a serious threat' to Soviet power, especially because it 'influenced mainly the poor'.[12] Measuring Mitayev with their own yardstick, they suspected he 'had been building up his armed troops and was looking for a suitable moment to rise up.'[13] Thus it was decided to 'liquidate' him. On 16 January 1923 Anastas Mikoyan, Kliment Voroshilov and Semyon Budennyi

...arrived in Urus Martan to 'fraternise with the Chechen people'. [...] In fact it was a well-camouflaged trap set for ... 'Ali Mitayev. [...] In his meeting with the members of the delegation Mitayev repeated that the *shari'a* must be the basis of the [Chechen] autonomy. They replied that they might agree to this demand, but that they must talk on the direct line to Moscow from Groznyi to get a definitive reply. Then they offered the Sheikh to negotiate [on the telephone] in person. He rode with his mounted bodyguards to the railway station in Groznyi, where he was invited to the saloon carriage of the special government train. Immediately the train set off for Rostov. The Sheikh's bodyguards were 'gallantly and nobly' asked to join Mitayev's travel to Moscow, 'to meet Lenin in person'. In fact, a few hours later Mitayev found himself in a secluded cell at the district GPU in Rostov, where he was accused of plotting 'together with Georgian nationalists' a 'joint Chechen-Georgian uprising'. In the following days a growing number of delegations arrived in Rostov to obtain his release. Without delay the Chechen government followed the piece of

---

[11] Karataeva (note 4), p. 86.
[12] Ibid., pp. 99–100.
[13] Meskhidze (note 10), pp. 476.

advice given by Stalin to Mikoyan: 'If you want the Chechens to leave you in peace, give them Mitayev's body.' And in order not to leave any shot wounds, Mitayev was choked to death. His body was delivered to the Chechens with an expression of sorrow, especially since he had died of a heart attack a short while before being released.[14]

The main blow to the Muslim clergy was delivered two and a half years later during the 'disarmament campaign' (*operatsia po razoruzheniu*) between 23 August and 11 September 1925, during which major religious leaders were either arrested or killed. Among them were Najm al-Din Hutsi, Uma[r] Umayev, Belo Haji, Atabi Shamilev, Amin al-Ansalti, Dervish Mahoma, Kahirov, Naid Bekov (killed), Vahap Estemirov, 'Alibulat (killed), Abdul Vahap Hajji and Kaim Hajji.

The Chechens, like all other Mountaineers, resisted disarmament. As already described, weapons to them were not merely a necessity but signified their manhood and freedom. Often masterpieces of craftsmanship and art, weapons were handed down through generations from father to son and were among a man's most precious possessions. Furthermore, the disarmament campaign was a clear violation of their rights according to the *shari'a* and (rightly) interpreted 'as a preparation for forthcoming repressions'.[15] In consequence, of the 242 disarmed *auls* 101 'were subjected to artillery fire' and 16 'to bombardment from the air'. Six Chechens were killed and 30 wounded and '119 houses of bandits were blown up'. In addition, 12 'band-elements' were killed and 5 wounded in exchanges of fire and 39 'band-element leaders' arrested. Of the people arrested 105 were executed before the end of their investigation and 21 'sent to exile'. All in all the Soviets confiscated '25,299 rifles, 4,319 revolvers, 75,566 bullets, a Lyons machine-gun and Morse and telephone equipment'.[16]

---

[14] Abdurakhman Avtorkhanov, *Memuary* (Frankfurt am Main: Posev, 1983), pp. 98–103 as quoted in Meskhidze, note 10, pp. 476–7.

[15] Avtorkhanov (note 9), 156.

[16] RGVA, f25896, o9, ed. khr. 284, ll. 8, ob. 8, 'The Execution of the Operation to Disarm the Chechen Autonomy'. I am indebted to Arthur Martirosyan for this reference. Not only did the Soviets confiscate existing personal weapons, but they also imposed on every house the obligation to hand one firearm to the authorites: to carry out this assignment the Chechens and Ingush bought weapons from Red Army soldiers and from the *Chekists* themselves (Avtorkhanov, note 9, 156).

The campaign was also an opportunity to get rid of the '*padi-shahs*'. These were 'radical intellectuals', like Elderkhanov, Kurba-nov, Tokayev, Oshayev and Arsanukayev, 'who had supported the Bolsheviks from the first days of the Russian Revolution, having been attracted by their promise to give nations the right to self-determination and secession.'[17] All along Moscow had suspected them (like other non-Russians and especially Muslims who had joined the party after the October Revolution) of having a nation-alist agenda and in many cases was right in its suspicions, at least in that these leaders wanted to preserve their autonomy *vis-à-vis* the centre. For the *padishahs* this meant 'complete domestic autonomy in the North Caucasus in the guise of a Soviet Mountain Republic within the RSFSR'.[18] However, these *padishahs* and their likes in other parts of the Soviet Union were of major importance in reach-ing the non-Russian population and in consolidating Soviet power among them. Now that they had lost their usefulness, the *padishahs* were arrested, charged with 'bourgeois nationalism', 'counter-revo-lutionary activity' and supporting 'Ali Mitayev and other Sufi sheikhs. Some of them were executed and the others deported.[19]

In full control of Chechnya, or so it seemed, Moscow could now 'Sovietise' the country. The first moves were not very energetic: *shar'i* courts were abolished in 1926; a Latin-based alphabet was adopted, because the Arabic one was 'an alphabet of exploitation', not 'of culture and progress';[20] and a massive effort was made to establish state schools to attract the children from the traditional 'Arabic' ones. Characteristically such moves were 'in response to demands from below' as expressed in letters to newspaper editors. One typi-cal letter was published in the Chechen newspaper *Serlo*:

The Galanchozh *okrug* has not even a single literate man, unless one counts as literate the Mullahs with their *Qur'ans*, which are written in such ante-diluvian language that even the Mullahs do not understand it. The citizens of the Galanchozh *okrug* request to send them a good village reader (*izbach*),

---

[17] Ibid., pp. 154–5.

[18] Ibid., p. 155.

[19] 'The government of these *padishahs* was a period of maximum political peace and harmony between the various Caucasian nations, and popularity of the Soviet government among the Mountaineers.' Ibid., p. 155.

[20] Karataeva (note 4), p. 87.

who is well versed in Soviet law and politics. The young people have a great craving for knowledge, which they have no choice but to satisfy through learning Arabic. Young Chechens must be supplied with an opportunity to study in order to save them from learning the Qur'an and thus to diminish the number of opium distributors...[21]

However, the people voted with their feet. The Soviet schools were situated in 'large, bright, luminous buildings, but they were almost empty', while the 'Arabic' schools, in 'small huts [*lachuzhki*]', were 'overfilled with children who, sitting in the stuffy air on the dirty floor, were committing the *Qur'an* to memory.'[22] A song warned in 1927 the people of Urus Martan:

> *Think with your hearts...*
> *Weep with your hearts to Allah.*
> *Religion is being destroyed.*
> *The armies of Satan are undermining religion,*
> *They deny the existence of Allah the greatest.*
> *The dirty age has come!*[23]

On the tenth anniversary of the 'Great October Revolution' one of the leaders of the AO summed up the achievements of Soviet Chechnya, adding:

However, the struggle is far, far from its end. [...] The mountain poor, especially the Chechens, are still waiting for basic problems to be solved. It is enough to point to the fact that Chechnya with a population of 400,000 has only 180,000 *desiatins* of arable land which has not yet been re-allocated; that the poor are still being exploited; that the reactionary element— the block of *kulaks* and clerics—is still strong; that the co-operatives are still weak; that the roads are few; that the population suffers from terrible social diseases (syphilis, TB, malaria); that illiteracy is almost universal and the [Latin-based] alphabet has just been imposed; that women are still semi-slaves; that blood feuds have not been uprooted.[24]

---

[21] Ibid., p. 89.

[22] Ibid., p. 96.

[23] Ibid., p. 93.

[24] Eshba, *Aslanbek Sheripov* (Goznyi: Serlo, 1929), pp. 142–3. In 1928 a committee to liquidate blood feuds in Chechnya was established. However, a Soviet Chechen historian wrote in 1972: 'The relics of blood feuds and other social crimes (*kalym*, polygamy etc.) have not been overcome and therefore the struggle against them has continued to this very day.' Karataeva (note 4), pp. 105–6.

Whether it was merely a coincidence or an intentional signal, in 1928 throughout the Soviet Union a full-scale attack on religion started. In early August 1928 the *kraikom* (*kraevoi komitet*; the party *Krai* committee of the Caucasus centred in Rostov) decreed the transfer of *zakat* money from the clergy to the peasants' committees, and in 1929 the authorities started closing down mosques and 'Arabic' schools. This campaign in itself was destined to cause serious unrest. However, what made the situation explosive was combining the anti-religion campaign with the 'collectivisation' drive, which started all over the country in 1929. Thus in the autumn of 1929 representatives of the *kraikom* and the CC 'arrived in the *auls*, and proceeded to confiscate personal and real estate', labelled some peasants 'as *kulaks*', and arrested and 'deported' them 'with their families to Siberia'.[25] What finally ignited the explosion was the closing down of the mosque in Goyty and of the 'Arabic' school in Shali. Revolts broke out in both these places and in Benoy. The rebels captured all the rural and regional institutions (including the petroleum refineries in Benoy), 'burned official archives and arrested the staff of the regional government, the chief of the GPU included.'

The leader of the rebellion was Shita Istamulov from Shali, who had been a follower and comrade-in-arms of 'Ali Mitayev, the War Minister of Uzun Hajji in 1919 and later a 'red' partisan. Other leaders were Zamsi Hajjiyev from Shali, Ibrahim Hajjiyev the son of Sheikh Ibrahim Hajji, Mullah Kuriyev from Goyty, and Yaroch and Hoja from Benoy. They formed a provisional government, which sent the following demands 'directly to Moscow', 'stating that only when they were given satisfaction on all of them would they agree to disarm and recognise Soviet authority':

(1) Illegal confiscation of peasant property, i.e. 'collectivisation', must be stopped.

(2) Arbitrary arrests of peasants under the pretext of fighting *kulachestvo* must cease.

(3) The GPU chiefs must be recalled from Chechnya and replaced by elected civil officers of Chechen origin whose right to prosecute would be limited to criminal elements.

(4) The 'popular courts' imposed from above must be liquidated and the institution of *Shariat* courts, as foreseen by the constitu-

[25] Avtorkhanov (note 9), p. 157.

tional congress of the Soviet Mountain Republic in Vladikavkaz in 1921, reinstated.

(5) The intervention of regional and central authorities in the internal affairs of the 'Chechen Autonomous Region' must be stopped, and all the economic and political decisions taken by the Chechen Congress of elected representatives as presumed in the status of 'autonomy'.[26]

In order to 'peacefully liquidate' the insurrection, a high-ranking delegation from Moscow came to Groznyi and set up a 'peace commission' to negotiate with the rebels.[27] The commission conceded that 'responsibility for recent events lay with the local executives who had not acted in keeping with Party and government instructions,' and promised 'that the authorities in question would be severely punished once the fighting stopped.' Also it published a 'Declaration to the Chechen People', which stated that 'Chechnya's internal matters will in the future be settled by the Chechen people'.[28]

The rebels now returned to their homes and a special GPU detachment was sent to Shali 'to arrest and punish rural and regional leaders':

The GPU detachment completed operations against the Soviet executives in three days, and on the fourth day, towards one o'clock in the morning, it surrounded the house of the former leader of the insurgents, Shita Istamulov. He was taken by surprise, but in response to an ultimatum to surrender he and his brother Hasan opened fire. At dawn, when help came to Shita, part of his house was ablaze and Hasan was badly wounded. Some hundred Chechen horsemen surrounded the GPU detachment besieging Shita's house, and after an hour of fighting the GPU force of about 150 men was practically annihilated.[29]

Shita Istamulov now called all the Mountaineers to *gazavat* for the re-establishment of the imamate of Shamil and the eviction of the 'infidels' from the Caucasus. In response revolts flared up in Shali,

[26] Ibid., p. 158.
[27] The committee members were D. Arsanukayev, Chairman of the Chechen *obkom* (*oblastnoi komitet*, the *oblast* Party Committee); Hasman, an old Moscow Bolshevik and the *obkom* secretary; and three religious leaders—Shamsuddin Hajji, Sultan Mullah and Mullah Ahmed Tugayev.
[28] Avtorkhanov (note 9), p. 158.
[29] Ibid., p. 159.

Goity and Benoy as well as in some areas of Daghestan, Ossetia, Kabarda, Balkaria and Karachai.[30] Since 'peaceful' liquidation had failed, the *kraikom* 'decided', on 7 December 1929, to launch a 'wide-scale operation to liquidate the anti-Soviet demonstrations by the *kulaks* and the clergy in Chechnya'.[31] By the end of December 1929 four infantry divisions and one 'combat' division, the Vladikavkaz Infantry School, the Krasnodar Cavalry School, three artillery regiments, two regiments of border guards (from the Turkish and Iranian borders) and three squadrons of GPU forces[32] (from Groznyi, Vladikavkaz and Makhachkala) were concentrated in Chechnya under Belov, commander of the North Caucasus Military District. A 'series of serious joint *Chekist*-army operations were undertaken supported by artillery and the air force.'[33] By mid-January 1930 Belov conquered both Goyty and Shali, but at a terrible cost: in Goyty, where the insurgents' general staff, including Kuriyev and Ahmet Mullah', was wiped out, 'the whole 82nd Infantry Regiment was annihilated'. Near Shali the Red Army lost an entire division, only to find the *aul* empty: Istamulov's forces had retreated into the mountains of Upper Chechnya.[34] Having paused to reorganise and receive reinforcements, Belov renewed his offensive in March 1930 to capture the last fortress held by the insurgents: Benoy.

In April 1930, after two months of fierce fighting with heavy losses, Belov entered Benoy but found the place empty: all the inhabitants, women and children included, had been evacuated to remote hiding places in the mountains. The victorious Belov sent a negotiator to the insurgents offering honourable peace conditions to all who would return of their own

---

[30] They all raised similar national-religious slogans. It is difficult to establish whether there was any connection in the organisation of these uprisings, but their national and ideological bond was obvious. The slogans of *gazavat* were common to all the fighters for the Mountaineers' independence: Mansur, Gazi Muhammad, Hamza Bek and Shamil.

[31] Karataeva (note 4), p. 107.

[32] The GPU, like its successors, had military forces of its own, parallel to those of the Red Army and the Interior Commissariat (later Ministry).

[33] Report of the Section for the Special Settlement of the NKVD, 5 September 1944, published in 'Iz arkhiva Iosifa Stalina', *Nezavisimaia Gazeta*, 29 February 2000.

[34] Without the support of archival documents, Avtorkhanov's numbers of Soviet casualties, though they seem to be exaggerated, are the only ones available.

free will and surrender their weapons. The insurgents replied that they would return to their *auls* only when Belov and his army left.[35]

Meanwhile, in view of the problems created by collectivisation, Moscow executed a U-turn. The CC condemned those responsible for collectivisation as 'leftist deviators' and promised that *kolkhozes* would be set up only 'voluntarily'. In areas like Chechnya they were banned altogether as premature. Rather, TOZes (*tovarishchestva obrabotki zemli*—Associations of Land Cultivation) could be established wherever the villagers agreed. In Chechnya almost all party leaders (Arsanukayev and Hasman among them) were removed as 'leftist deviators'[36] and the policy towards the rebels changed abruptly. An amnesty was granted to them all, the troops were pulled out, and 'large quantities of industrial goods at very low prices' flooded the country. The Red Army was obviously disappointed: 'The mistakes of the first [previous] campaigns', wrote the military district staff, 'were not only repeated but intensified.... Since we learned nothing from the past, we have repeated the previous mistakes, and again have no decisive successes, allowing the bandits to get away unpunished, thereby undermining the authority of "the Red Army".'[37]

The rebels returned to their homes and Shita Istamulov was appointed president of the Rural Consumers' Cooperative in his *aul*, Shali. But the Soviets forgot nothing and forgave nothing:

In the autumn of 1931 Baklakov, chief of the regional GPU, invited Istamulov allegedly to hand him the official amnesty act from Moscow. Baklakov gave him the document with one hand while firing the entire charge of a Mauser pistol with the other. Though badly wounded, Istamulov had time to stab Baklakov to death before being killed by a guard stationed outside.[38]

This was (literally) the opening salvo in a large-scale GPU operation to 'eliminate the *kulak* counter-revolutionary elements and mullah–nationalist ideologists' in Chechnya. As many as 35,000

[35] Avtorkhanov (note 9), 'The Chechens', p. 160.

[36] Having 'displayed helplessness', 'Party and Soviet leadership in Shali and Goyty' had already been 'fully replaced' according to a *kraikom* decision of 6 February 1930. Karateva (note 4), pp. 107–8.

[37] Quoted in Valery Tishkov, *The Mind Aflame: Ethnicity, Nationalism and Conflict in and after the Soviet Union* (London: Sage, 1997), pp. 198–9.

[38] Avtorkhanov (note 9), p. 160. Istamulov's brother Hassan organised a new 'gang', which until 1935 hunted and killed *Chekists* to avenge the murder of Shita.

men were arrested and convicted by a GPU 'Extraordinary Commission of Three'. 'It is hard to determine the percentage of those who were shot,' wrote Avtorkhanov, 'but not many regained their freedom.'[39] At least in one area, the Nozhay-Yurt *raion*, more than 3,000 people offered armed resistance.[40]

In 1932 the NKVD moved from the countryside to the capital of the *oblast*. In the autumn a group of ten leading officials, civil servants and academics were arrested and charged with organising a 'counter-revolutionary national centre of Chechnya in preparation for an armed uprising' and with receiving money and weapons from the British via 'the millionaire Chermoyev'. Six of the accused were shot and the others sentenced to ten years in the GULag (*Glavnoe Upravlenie Lagerei*, that is Chief Administration of [detention] Camps). In addition, some 3,000 men were arrested in the districts of Gudermes and Nozhay-Yurt and an unknown number of them executed. 'The Chechen regional section of the NKVD', commented an eye witness, 'created this "counter-revolutionary centre" so expertly and plausibly that even many Chechens believed in its existence.'[41]

Generally, however, the early- and mid-1930s were calm. 'True, some NKVD officials were murdered, but these were generally old scores being settled. Even the guerrilla movement in the mountains took on a defensive character.'[42] On 5 January 1934 the Chechen and Ingush AOs were merged into a single Chechen-Ingush Autonomous *Oblast*, and on 5 December 1936, the day of the new constitution of the Soviet Union, the Chechen-Ingush, Kabardino-Balkar and North Ossetian AOs were promoted to the status of ASSRs. A communiqué published by *Izvestia* on 15 January 1939 glorified the Soviet achievements in Chechnya:

Under the Soviet regime the republic has been so transformed as to be unrecognisable. The *kolkhozes*, within which 92.7 per cent of all agricultural undertakings are now combined, have been accorded a perpetual

---

[39] Ibid., p. 161.

[40] Report of the Section for the Special Settlement of the NKVD, 5 September 1944, published in 'Iz arkhiva Iosifa Stalina', *Nezavisimaia Gazeta*, 29 February 2000.

[41] Avtorkhanov (note 9), p. 167.

[42] Ibid., p. 173.

grant of more than 400,000 hectares of land. An important oil industry has been created. New oilfields have been exploited and two big refineries built, as well as a machine factory. Food factories, chemical factories and other forms of local production have been brought into being or organised. Under the sun of the Stalin Constitution the culture of the Chechen-Ingush people, national in form but socialist in content, has made a great step forward. Before the Revolution there were only three schools in the whole of Checheno-Ingushetia. Today there are 341 primary and secondary schools accommodating 118,000 pupils. Hundreds of engineers and teachers emerge every year from the high schools, the technical schools and the workers' faculties.[43]

'All these brilliant results', the communiqué added, 'have been achieved in the course of a bitter struggle against the enemies of the people—Trotskyites, Bukharinites and bourgeois nationalists who have sought to rob the workers of the fruits of the great October Socialist Revolution.'[44] These words referred to the events that in 1937 had broken the relative calm in the Soviet Union in general and in the Chechen-Ingush ASSR in particular.

[43] R. Conquest, *The Nation Killers: the Soviet Deportation of Nationalities* (London: Macmillan, 1970), pp. 40–1.
[44] Ibid., p. 41.

12

FROM 'POLITICAL BANDITISM'*
TO NATIONAL LIBERATION

The night of 31 July–1 August 1937 marked the beginning of the 'General Operation for the Removal of Anti-Soviet Elements', better known in the former Soviet Union as the '*yezhovshchina*' (after Yezhov, the People's Commissar for Internal Affairs between 1936 and 1938) and in the West as the 'Purges of 1937'.[1] In the first stage of the operation—on that and the following nights—nearly 14,000 men, representing 3 per cent of the population, were arrested all over the Chechen-Ingush ASSR and sent to Groznyi. Since the number of prisoners was far beyond the capacity of the two prisons there (the 'inner prison' with 1,000 and the 'outer prison' with 5,000), men were jailed in the *militsia* (police) headquarters and in other places converted to serve the purpose, like the central garage of *Grozneft* (3,000) and a club named after Stalin (5,000). All of the arrested 'were condemned after one and the same trial' conducted by an 'extraordinary *troika*' of the NKVD. 'It is impossible to say exactly how many were shot, but every night there were mass executions in the cellars of the NKVD to the accompaniment of the roar of motorcars outside.'[2] According to an eye-witness,

As it would have been impossible to carry out the death sentences pronounced by the *troika* within the assigned time, a special 'execution hall' was established for the extermination of large groups. It was situated in the

---

* Direct translation from the Russian '*banditizm*' or '*politicheskii banditizm*'.

[1] For the purges in the Northern Caucasus in general, see Alexander Uralov, *The Reign of Stalin* (London: The Bodley Head, 1953), pp. 140–7.

[2] Avtorkhanov, 'The Chechens and the Ingush during the Soviet Period and its Antecedents' in M. Bennigsen-Broxup (ed.), *The North Caucasus Barrier: The Russian Advance towards the Muslim World* (London: Hurst, 1992), p. 175.

northern part of the NKVD building facing the Sunja river. The *Chekists* called it the 'relay chamber' because the doomed prisoners taken there were told that they were being sent to Siberia by 'relay-stages'. The relay chamber was made of reinforced concrete and hermetically sealed from the outside world. Revolving firing positions were fitted into the walls and the ceiling from the exterior. The bodies were carried off in lorries under the cover of darkness, and taken to a mass grave in a forest at the foot of the Goriachevodskaia mountain.[3]

The second stage started at the beginning of October, when Shkiriatov, Yezhov's deputy, came to Groznyi 'with a large *Chekist* staff'. On 7 October 1937 a special, enlarged plenum of the Chechen-Ingush *obkom* was convened, with the participation of leading city and *okrug* activists. At that meeting all Chechen and Ingush *obkom* members were arrested. A wave of arrests then swept the country, 'from the President of the Republic down to the president of the *selsovet*' (*sel'skoi sovet*; village council). During the following weeks and months (arrests continued until November 1938) all the *okrug* committees and the twenty-eight *okrug* EC chairmen, almost all the chairmen of the village councils, and the *kolkhoz* and Party members who had organised them were arrested. In total 137 party activists were arrested, of whom 120 stood trial at the court-martial of the North Caucasus Military District three years later (seventeen either did not survive torture or committed suicide). They were accused of belonging to a 'bourgeois-nationalist centre of Checheno-Ingushetia', which in alliance with other 'bourgeois-nationalist centres' in the Northern Caucasus aimed at establishing a 'North-Caucasian federal republic under the protection of Turkey and England'.[4] All of them disappeared into the GULag.

The composition of the arrested party activists was the same as in other parts of the Soviet Union: of the 137 charged with 'bourgeois-nationalist' activities, ninety-nine had joined the party after 1921, eight-two were under the age of thirty and fifty-two had been edu-

---

[3] Ibid., *loc. cit.*

[4] Ibid., pp. 175–6. They were prosecuted under various clauses: 'bourgeois-nationalism', 'counter-revolution', 'insurrection', 'Bukharinist-Trotskyist anti-Soviet terrorism', 'espionage' and 'sabotage'. In legal terms this meant they were tried under Article 58 of the criminal code for (1) treason to the fatherland; (2) preparation of armed uprising; (7) detrimental activity (*vreditel'stvo*); (8) terrorist acts; (9) subversion; (10) anti-Soviet propaganda; (11) membership of an anti-Soviet organisation; (14) sabotage.

cated in a Communist party VUZ (*Vysshee Uchebnoe Zavedenie,* Institution of Higher Education) and Stalin's KUTVa (*Kommunistcheskii Universitet Trudiashchikhsia Vostoka,* Communist University of the Toilers of the East). In other words, they belonged to 'Stalin's school', not to 'Lenin's guard'.[5] Consequently, their accusation of 'bourgeois nationalism' appears groundless. After all, they had barely had an opportunity to come across bourgeois persons or ideas. What they were 'guilty' of was correctly quoting Lenin's line on the national question, but in the wrong circumstances (which would in Stalin's later years be called 'talmudism'). Thus they stated openly that it was highly important to employ 'in Chechnya *and in Groznyi* [emphasis added] experienced Russian comrades with a *Leninist* attitude to the "nationals" and a Leninist ability to be assistants, not "nannies" *and definitely not "commanders"* [emphasis added].'[6] Furthermore, they maintained that 'real international solidarity and brotherly relations between the Russian workers and the Chechen toilers' required Chechen Communists 'to wage a furious, unmasking battle against "their own" nationalist prejudices.' But their Russian comrades had

...to struggle even more resolutely against Great Russian chauvinism, against any oppressive attitude to the Chechens, to strongly and openly defend the necessity of a specially sensitive, specially cautious Russian attitude to a nation that has for decades been exposed to humiliating mockery and has therefore the right to be suspicious of the smallest manifestation of a similar oppressive attitude.[7]

In the 1930s Russian chauvinism was on a steady, uninterrupted rise reaching a peak in Stalin's 1945 victory toast to the 'Great Russian people'. Consequently, 'proletarian internationalism' increasingly meant the demand from non-Russians to accept and support this trend. Views such as those quoted above were tantamount to a mortal sin and their exponents, whether *aparatchiks* or members of the *intelligentsiia,* were hunted down.

In the long run the most serious result of the purges of 1937 was the massive blow they dealt to the young Soviet-educated Chechen *intelligentsiia,* which had barely started to emerge. An entire genera-

---

[5] See table and its interpretation in Avtorkhanov (note 2), p. 177.
[6] E. Eshba, *Aslanbek Sheripuv* (Gronznyi: Serlo, 1929), p. 147.
[7] Ibid., pp. 148–9.

tion of writers, poets, artists and academics was wiped out, in some cases metaphorically, in most physically. Their *oeuvre* was banned and confiscated;[8] even where single copies survived they soon became inaccessible to practically all future readers: in 1938 the Latin-based Chechen alphabet (introduced a decade earlier) was changed to a Cyrillic-based one. In one blow all previously educated people were reduced to functional illiteracy and all the previous literary production became obsolete. As in other non-Russian, and especially Muslim, parts of the Soviet Union a new educated generation and new *intelligentsiia* had to be created from scratch. With the elimination of the government and party cadres and the liquidation of the *intelligentsiia*, 'the link between the people and the authorities was broken', especially since the arrested *aparatchiks* were replaced by 'imported officials who neither knew the language nor had any idea of the customs and history of the people entrusted to their care.'[9]

However, in the immediate outcome of the purges, and with the establishment in early 1938 of 490 *kolkhozes* in the Chechen-Ingush ASSR,[10] armed resistance to the Soviet authorities drastically increased. 'Peasant revolts in the mountains of Chechnya', wrote a high-ranking Chechen later to find refuge in Germany, 'occurred every spring as though carefully pre-planned. As to guerrilla warfare it was a permanent phenomenon.' These acts of 'political banditry', as the Soviet authorities preferred to call them, 'were induced' not as much by 'a passionate longing for freedom' as by 'provocation[s]'. In other words, 'notwithstanding the harshness of Soviet laws and the cruelty with which they were carried out', the Chechens 'might have bowed to their fate had it not been for these deliberate provocations.'[11] Examples of such provocations were the attempt to establish a pig farm in Vedeno and the treatment by the NKVD of Ibrahim Geldygenskii, a renowned Red partisan hero and a personal friend

[8] Ramazan Karcha, 'The Peoples of the North Caucasus' in *Genocide in the USSR: Studies in Group Destruction* (Munich: Institute for the Study of the USSR, 1958), p. 41.

[9] Avtorkhanov (note 2), p. 179.

[10] A. M. Nekrich, *The Punished Peoples: the Deportation and Fate of Soviet Minorities at the End of the Second World War* (New York: W. W. Norton, 1978), p. 46.

[11] Avtorkhanov (note 2), p. 165. 'It should be noted', he added, 'that it was always the NKVD officials who supplied weapons and ammunition to the guerrillas.'

of Ordzhonikidze, who was burnt alive by two NKVD officers in front of the entire *aul*.[12]

Another constant irritant was the matter of *amanats*. The Soviets, like the imperial Russian authorities before them, used to take *amanats* to force 'bandits' to surrender. But they did so with two major differences: first, they were not satisfied with only a few hostages, as their predecessors had been, but arrested entire extended families; and secondly, whereas

...the former Caucasian administration freed the *amanat* when the bandit gave himself up, there is not a single case in the history of Soviet Chechnya-Ingushetia of an *amanat* being freed after the surrender of the 'bandit'. When the latter gave himself up voluntarily, he was shot despite solemn promises to spare his life. As to the hostages they were all—men, women and children—sent to Siberia.[13]

Indeed, 'the code of deceit' was 'second nature to the Soviet administration', and gave rise to the Chechen proverb 'to lie like the Soviets'.[14]

However, one thing was common to the Soviets and their predecessors: on many occasions the *amanats* they took could not be used as leverage. A letter from a gang of 'political bandits' addressed to the GPU in Groznyi states bluntly that 'the *amanats* you have taken do not concern us at all. They are neither relations of ours nor friends.' The letter went on demand that the authorities stop 'spreading lies about us. As you know,' it stated, 'we never attack civilians. But we are responsible for the ambush of the military lorry last week and for mining the train three weeks ago.'[15]

Indeed, in accordance with their code of honour the 'bandits' refrained from hurting civilians. Major' Sa'adalla Mahomadov, their most famous leader during the 1920s and '30s, ordered his men to spare Russian civil servants, but 'show no mercy' to *Chekists* and to Chechen civil servants 'if they were Communists'. 'The Russians', he said, 'are against us because it is their duty. Honour to men engaged in service but death to scoundrels.'[16] In 1939 the NKVD attributed to his band, consisting of only six men, the killing of 'more than thirty Red Army men' and 'terrorist acts' against seven Chechen

---

[12] For details see ibid., pp. 166, 169–70 respectively.
[13] Ibid., p. 166.
[14] Ibid., p. 166.
[15] Copied by the author in May 1992 in the KGB archives in Groznyi.
[16] Avtorkhanov (note 2), p. 173.

Soviet officials 'during the last ten years'.[17] However, if the 'bandits' spared Russian officials, the NKVD did not. A famous example is that of Smoltsin, the *obkom* Secretary for Industry and Transport. In the spring of 1940 he was captured by 'band elements' in the forests between Shallazh and Yalkhoroy. The 'bandits' shot Smoltsin's Chechen guide, but freed the high-ranking Russian official. However, on his return to Groznyi Smoltsin was arrested as a 'traitor to the fatherland'.[18]

Each 'provocation', each clash with the authorities, each wave of arrests resulted in new people joining the ranks of the 'band-elements'. After the purges of 1937 thousands flocked to the mountains. The guerrilla groups thus reinforced, their operations became bolder. NKVD chiefs in the *raions* of Galanchozh, Gudermes and Kurchaloy were killed and in September 1937 a military train between Groznyi and Nazran was derailed.[19] This activity reached its peak following Soviet defeats in the 1939–40 war against Finland, when a full-fledged revolt broke out, led by Hasan Israilov (Terloyev).

Born in 1910 in Nashkhoy (in the Galanchozh *raion*), Hasan Israilov had been a member of the Communist Party since 1929 and a graduate of a party VUZ in Rostov and of KUTVa in Moscow. Originally a poet and playwright with little interest in politics, he nevertheless became involved in political affairs. In a series of articles in the Moscow *Krestianskaia Gazeta* (Peasants' Newspaper) Israilov 'expertly criticised Soviet laws while seeming to defend them from the abuses' of the local Soviet and Party leadership that 'plundered' Chechnya.[20] Consequently he was arrested in the spring of 1931 for 'counter-revolutionary slander' and having 'connections with a gang'. Released in 1934, he was once again arrested in 1937 after signing a petition to the Soviet authorities warning that 'if the government persisted in its policy in Chechnya, the unavoidable result would be a general popular uprising.'[21] Released again in 1939,

---

[17] People's Commissar for Internal Affairs of the Chechen-Ingush ASSR, Riazanov to the People's Commissar for Internal Affairs of the USSR, 25 February 1939, published in *Nezavisimaia Gazeta*, 29 February 2000.

[18] Avtorkhanov (note 2), p. 173. This was the standard accusation against Soviet prisoners of war in the Second World War.

[19] Ibid., p. 175. For an alternative view, claiming that NKVD reports of 'banditism' were grossly exaggerated, see Nekrich (note 10), pp. 43–6.

[20] Avtorkhanov (note 2), pp. 181–2.

[21] Ibid., p. 182.

he saw in the Soviet Union's preoccupation with the Second World War and its active engagement (and defeats) in the war against Finland an opportunity to regain independence. In January 1940 he published the following declaration:

For twenty years now, the Soviet authorities have been fighting my people, aiming to destroy them group by group: first the *kulaks*, then the Mullahs and the 'bandits', then the 'bourgeois-nationalists'. I am sure now that the real object of this war is the annihilation of our nation as a whole. That is why I have decided to assume the leadership of my people in their struggle for liberation. [...] I understand only too well that Chechnya-Ingushetia—indeed, the whole of the Caucasus—will find it difficult to get rid of the yoke of Red imperialism. But a passionate faith in justice and the hope that the freedom-loving people of the Caucasus and of the world will come to our assistance inspires me in this enterprise which you may consider foolhardy and senseless but which I believe to be the only possible path. The brave Finns are proving that this great empire built on slavery is devoid of strength when faced with a small freedom-loving nation. The Caucasus will be a second Finland and we will be followed by other oppressed nations.[22]

Within a month Israilov controlled the *raions* of Galanchozh, Sayasan, Chaberloy and a part of Shatoy. According to NKVD reports, he 'established a fighting group in the Galanchozh *raion* and a band in the Itum Kale *raion*. Such groups were also formed in Borzoy, Kharsinoy, Dagi Borzoy, Achekhenoy and other places.'[23] He then convened a national congress in Galanchozh, which adopted his 'provisional programme for the organisation of Checheno-Ingushetia' and established a 'provisional popular Revolutionary Government' with Israilov at its head.

Finland's defeat dealt a moral blow to Israilov and his men, but the German attack on the Soviet Union gave the rebels a boost, both moral and material. In 1941 Israilov expanded the movement's aim to the liberation of the entire Caucasus and established the OPKB (*osvoboditel'naia partiia Kavkazskikh Brat'ev*; the Liberation Party of the Caucasian Brothers), later renamed the NSKPB (*narodnaia Severo-Kavkazskaia partiia brat'ev*, the People's Northern Caucasus Party of Brothers). By 10 November 1941 Israilov had held 'meetings of illegal organisations in forty-one anti-Soviet *auls* and

---

[22] Ibid.

5,000 people joined the OPKB.'[24] On 28 January 1942 the constit-
uent assembly of the OPKB was held in Ordzhonikidze (Vladikavkaz). Representatives of seven 'neighbouring *oblasts* and eleven
sections of the OPKB' elected a thirty-three-man Executive Committee and a nine-member politburo, with Israilov as secretary-gen-
eral, and adopted a programme.[25]

If one is to believe the NKVD reports, an entire underground
organisation was established both in the countryside and in the cities of Groznyi, Gudermes and Malgobek. All in all 24,970 men were
ready to rise up at Israilov's order. Among the leaders of this organisation was the People's Commissar for Internal Affairs of the
Chechen-Ingush ASSR, Albogachiyev.[26] However, the uprising planned for 10 January 1942 was prematurely started in the mountains
in September 1941. Consequently, on 10 September 1941 Albogachiyev allegedly wrote Israilov the following letter:

I am in pain [*ogorchen*] that your Mountaineers started the revolt earlier
than planned. I am afraid that if you don't obey me we, the officials of the
republic [*rabotniki, respubliki*], shall be exposed as well... Mind you, in
Allah's name, keep your oath. Don't mention us to anyone.

You have caused yourself to be exposed. Work deeply underground.
Don't allow yourself to be arrested. Be aware that you will be shot on the
spot [*tebia budut resstrelivat*]. Keep contact with me only through my trusted
accomplices.

Send me a hostile, threatening letter and I shall also start to persecute
you. I shall burn your house, arrest some members of your family and
speak against you everywhere. You and I must prove that we are irreconcilable enemies and pursue each other.

You are not familiar with the Gestapo agents in Ordzhonikidze through
whom, as I told you, we have to send all the information about our anti-

---

[23] People's Commissar of Internal Affairs of the Georgian SSR, Karanadze to
Beria, 18 September 1943, published in *Nezavisimaia Gazeta*, 29 February 2000.
[24] Ibid.
[25] Israilov's diary, quoted in ibid.
[26] In an *obkom* meeting on 15 July, Albogachiyev was rebuked for failing 'to organise an active struggle against 'banditism' and mass desertion [*dezertirstvo*]' (strictly
secret, separate file, extract from protocol no. 124z, Bureau of the Chechen-
Ingush *oblast* committee of the VKP(b), 15 July 1941, published in *Nezvisimaia
Gazeta*, 29 February 2000). This raises the possibility that Albogachiyev had
been marked for a forthcoming 'purge' and that the letter was 'produced' by the
NKVD. On the other hand, the fact that Israilov was later joined by Sheripov
might point to the plot being real.

Soviet activity. Sum up the results of the present revolt and send them to me. I shall be able to forward them to Germany immediately.[27]

Tear my letter to pieces in the presence of my messenger. The times are dangerous and I am afraid.[28]

Whether such a plot existed or not, in February 1942 Israilov received a serious reinforcement. Mairbek Sheripov, the former republican chief prosecutor, and the brother of Aslanbek Sheripov (a famous Bolshevik hero and martyr killed in battle against the 'Whites' in 1919), led an insurrection in Shatoy and Istumkala and joined Israilov.[29] Though not a major threat, the rebels' activities, which drew a considerable Soviet force, seriously constrained and complicated the Soviet Army's efforts against the German advance into the Caucasus.[30] Nevertheless, by the end of summer 1942 the Red Army had blocked the German offensive before it could reach the Chechen-Ingush ASSR, and during the first months of 1943 it pushed the Germans out of the Caucasus.[31]

Making considerable use of their air force,[32] the Soviets crushed the rebellion and by the summer of 1942 had reoccupied most of the areas controlled by the rebels. Some of the rebels (between several dozen and several hundred, depending on the sources quoted) managed to cross the front lines to join the Germans.[33] The rest were pushed high up into the mountains, where some groups and individuals managed to survive and go on challenging Soviet power

---

[27] This sentence might be (though was not necessarily) forged. A real plotter would probably speak simply of 'German' rather than 'Gestapo' agents, and not use a Communist phrase such as 'anti-Soviet'.

[28] Published in *Nezavisimaia gazeta*, 29 February 2000.

[29] According to Sheripov's sister, he 'was sent to the mountains by the state-security organs to disrupt the functioning of a band and then "accidentally" perished in a crossfire.' Nekrich (note 10), p. 53, footnote.

[30] Ibid., pp. 54–5.

[31] Soviet historiography did not mention Israilov, or for that matter any other revolt in the Caucasus during the 'Great Patriotic War' as the Second World War is known in the former Soviet Union. And see, for example, the definitive Soviet history, A. A. Grechko, *Bitva za Kavkaz* (Moscow: Izdatel'stvo Ministerstva Oborony SSSR, 1973), pp. 83–215. Grechko was the commander-in-chief of the Caucasus front and Brezhnev his chief commissar.

[32] Following two such bombardments of the *auls* of Shatoy, Istumkala and Galanchozh, in the spring of 1942, 'the number of dead was greater than that of the living.' Avtorkhanov (note 2), p. 182.

[33] Among these was Abdurrahman Avtorkhanov.

for years and even decades. The last anti–Soviet *abrek*, Mahomadov, was killed in 1976. According to eyewitness accounts he was old and ill and came down to his native village to die. Schoolchildren found him in the graveyard and reported to their schoolmaster, who then reported to the authorities. Forces arrived in the village and surrounded the 'bandit'. He was killed in the exchange of fire, but not before taking several Soviet servicemen with him.[34]

Israilov, pursued by the NKVD, continued his activities from hiding places in the mountains. On 13 February 1944 two brothers who had given shelter to him were arrested and on the following night led an NKVD force to a cave on mount Bachi Chu in the area of Itum kale. Although no one was there,[35] the Soviets found 'a "Dektiarev" sub-machine gun with three disks, English, Iranian and Russian rifles with 200 bullets, and original documents … relating to Israilov's insurrectionary activity, weighing roughly 2 kgs.' Among these documents were 'lists of members of the insurrectionary organisation NSKPB …, altogether 6,540 people' and 'a German map of the Caucasus on which *auls* were marked both in the Chechen-Ingush ASSR and the Georgian SSR in which cells of the NSPKB existed.'[36]

The NKVD was now closing the net around Israilov, successfully surrounding him with its agents and informers. In November 1944 an NKVD agent returned from a meeting with Israilov bearing a letter to Drozdov, a senior commander of the NKVD in Chechnya. In the letter Israilov asked Drozdov to send him copying paper, pencils, 'Stalin's report of 7 November', some 'military-political brochures' and medicine for TB. Most important, Israilov asked Drozdov 'to do everything possible to get Moscow's pardon for my sins, since they are not as great as they appear.'[37] Finally, two of his bodyguards, who were on the payroll of the NKVD, killed him. On 29 December 1944 Kaku and Drozdov reported 'the task [conferred] by comrade Beria was fulfilled. Israilov Hasan was killed and his body identified and photographed. The agents have been turned towards the liquidation of the remaining heads of bands [*bandglavari*].'[38]

[34] Accounts heard in Groznyi, in May 1992.

[35] The son of one of the brothers forewarned Israilov and led him to another shelter.

[36] Secret report to Beria, February 1944, printed in *Nezavisimaia Gazeta*, 29 February 2000.

[37] Top Secret report to Leont'ev, Head of the BB *upravlenie* of the NKVD, 26 November 1944, ibid.

[38] Top secret report by Comrades Kaku and Drozdov to the deputy People's Com-

Israilov's revolt brought to the fore the gradual shift that had occurred in the leadership of the resistance to the Soviets during the 1920s and '30s. A 'new Soviet-educated generation, well able to understand the intricacies of Soviet colonial policy in the Caucasus',[39] had replaced the religious leaders and Sufi sheikhs, at least partly and at the head of the movement.[40] All of them belonged to the 'Stalin school'. Growing up under the Soviets and having been educated in the party schools, they were familiar only with 'Marxism Leninism' and the crucial importance of the (one and only) party and nothing else. This was reflected in both their ideology and their organisational work. In a Pavlovian reflex the first thing they did was organise a party of their own. Furthermore, they appeared to be typical 'Stalin School' products in another important respect. If Israilov's letter to Drozdov is genuine and not an NKVD forgery, his behaviour fits that of most—if not all—the Bolsheviks when arrested, behaviour scorned by Solzhenitsyn:

The victims of the Bolsheviks from 1918 to 1946 never conducted themselves as despicably as the leading Bolsheviks did when the lightning struck them. If you study in detail the whole history of the arrests and trials of 1936 to 1938, the principal revulsion you feel is not against Stalin and his accomplices, but against the humiliatingly repulsive defendants—nausea at their spiritual baseness after their former pride and implacability.[41]

---

missar for Internal Affairs of the USSR, Comrade Kruglov, 29 December 1944, ibid.

[39] Avtorkhanov (note 2), 'The Chechens', p. 181.

[40] This does not mean the Sufi Sheikhs stopped playing any role. As a matter of fact, some of them led their own bands and 'succeeded to hold on longer than other rebels' (Bennigsen, 'The Qadiriyah' (Kunta Hajji) Tariqah in North-East Caucacus: 1850–1987', *Islamic Culture*, LXII, 2–3 (April–July 1988), p. 71). For example, Quraysh Belkhoroyev, the last surviving son of Batal Hajji, 'lasted with his men in the higher mountains of Ingushetia and Eastern Ossetia until 1947' (that is, three years after the deportation), when he and his men were persuaded to give themselves up (Kh. M. Mamiev, *Reaktsionnaia sushchnost' miuridizma* (Groznyi: Checheno-Ingushskoe Knizhnoe Izdatel'stvo, 1966), pp. 24–8). Also, see S. Smith, *Allah's Mountains. Politics and War in the Russian Caucasus* (London: I. B. Tauris, 1998), pp. 79–80.

[41] A. Solzhenitsyn, *Arkhipelag GULag, 1918–1956. Opyt khudozhestvernogo issledovaniia*, Paris: YMCA Press, 1973), pt 1, chapter 3.

In a way this was also reflected in the survivors' emphatic denial of any connections with Nazi Germany.[42] 'My enemy's enemy is my friend' is a proverb common to all humanity and nothing is more natural than to follow it when one is at war. Germany was at war with the Soviet Union. Thus Israilov and his fellow Chechen rebels, like many other Soviet groups, including Russians, regarded Germany as their liberator.[43] They might have been suspicious of Berlin, they might have disliked the Nazi regime, but this was their only way to win. One can dispute the number of ties and the nature of the collaboration with Germany as well as the significance of their contribution to its war effort, but not deny them.

The rebels' appeal to Germany for help gave Stalin an excuse to administer a radical treatment for Russia's 'Chechen headache'. On 26 June 1946 *Izvestiia* published the following law, signed the day before:

During the Great Patriotic War, when the peoples of the USSR were heroically defending the honour and independence of the Fatherland in the struggle against the German-Fascist invaders, many Chechens and Crimean Tatars, at the instigation of German agents, joined volunteer units organized by the Germans and, together with German troops, engaged in armed struggle against units of the Red Army; also at the bidding of the Germans they formed diversionary bands for the struggle against Soviet authority in the rear; meanwhile the main mass of the population of the Chechen-Ingush and Crimean ASSRs took no counter-action against these betrayers of the Fatherland.

In connection with this, the Chechens and the Crimean Tatars were resettled in other regions of the USSR, where they were given land, together with the necessary governmental assistance for their economic establishment. On the proposal of the Presidium of the Supreme Soviet of the RSFSR the Chechen-Ingush ASSR was abolished and the Crimean ASSR was changed into the Crimean Province by decrees of the Presidium of the Supreme Soviet of the USSR.[44]

Thus Stalin carried out what so many past Russian generals and governors, from the eighteenth century onward, had suggested but never dared to do.

[42] For example, Avtorkhanov (note 2), p. 183; Uralov (note 1), pp. 153–4.

[43] So did various groups fighting British rule.

[44] R. Conquest, *The Nation Killers: The Soviet Deportation of Nationalities* (London: Macmillan, 1970), p. 47.

13

DEPORTATION AND RETURN

The actual 'deportation'—the euphemism officially used to this very day—took place almost sixteen months earlier than the date when the law was signed, on Soviet Army Day (23 February) 1944. It was a well-planned, well-prepared operation codenamed '*Chechevitsa*' (lentil). In total 459,486 Chechens and Ingush from the Chechen-Ingush ASSR, Daghestan and Vladikavkaz were on the lists to be deported. The operation was to be carried out in eight days. In the first three days the people living in the lowland, the foothills and 'several mountain populations', that is 'over 300,000 people', were to be 'evicted'. In the following days it was the turn of 'the remaining 150,000 people' living in the mountain areas-areas which were 'to be blocked in advance'.[1]

The preparations for this operation lasted several weeks.[2] Hundreds of American 'Lend Lease' Studebaker lorries and 14,200 closed carriages and 1,000 open goods wagons—that is, 235 trains—were massed in Groznyi. Almost 100,000 troops of the NKVD army and 19,000 'operative workers' of the NKVD, NKGB (*Narodnyi Kommisariat Gosudastvennoi Bezopastnosti*, People's Commissariat for State Security) and SMERSH (*Smert' Shpionam*, Death to Spies—a special unit that operated in the armed forces and in German-occupied territories), all in Red Army uniforms, were concentrated in the republic and billeted in all the villages.[3] Officially they were

---

[1] Beria to Stalin, State Defence Committee, 17 February 1944, published in *Nezavisimaia Gazeta*, 29 February 2000.
[2] However, the order to prepare the logistics in the Caucasus, on the way and in Central Asia was issued fairly late—Top Secret Decree of the State Defence Council no. 5074s, 31 January 1944, published in *Nezavisimaia Gazeta*, 29 February 2000.
[3] William Flemming, 'The Deportation of the Chechen and Ingush Peoples: A

stationed for rest, training or war-related deployment. The newspapers published statements and appeals to the population such as 'We are going to repair the roads and bridges' and 'Let us all do our best to help our beloved Red Army during its mountain manoeuvres'.[4] 'Soldiers came to live in our houses and we put them up like guests,' recounted a Chechen woman half a century later; 'they ate with us, dumped all their gear everywhere. We had about thirty in our place and they were there for more than a month.'[5] Everywhere they celebrated Soviet Army Day's eve, lit bonfires and danced with the villagers. On that night (22–23 February) the troops surrounded the villages to prevent escape.

On 20 February 1944 Lavrentii Beria, Yezhov's successor since 1938, arrived in his armoured train in Groznyi to supervise the operation personally. He immediately summoned Molayev, the chairman of the Council of People's Commissars of the Chechen-Ingush ASSR, and told him of the planned 'deportation'. Molayev 'shed tears [*proslezilsia*] but regained self-control and promised to fulfil all the tasks assigned to him.' Then all the Chechen and Ingush party functionaries were called, told the same thing and given their assignments. To minimise any possibility of resistance, Beria summoned the most influential (Naqshbandi) sheikhs—Baudin (Baha al-Din) Arsanov, Abdul Hamid Yandarov and Gaysumov—and obtained their co-operation in the forthcoming operation.[6]

Thus, in spite of fairly widespread rumours of an imminent deportation,[7] surprise was achieved. At dawn the villagers were woken and called to assemble. Once gathered, they were read the decree of their deportation (which had been kept secret and would remain so) and then given between 15 and 30 minutes to pack no more

---

Critical Examination' in Ben Fawkes (ed.). *Russia and Chechnia: The Permanent Crisis. Essays on Russo-Chechen Relations* (London: Macmillan, 1998), p. 72.

[4] A. Uralov, *The Reign of Stalin* (London: The Bodley Head, 1953), p. 152; A. Karcha, 'The Peoples of the North Caucasus' in N. K. Deker and A. Lebed (eds), *Genocide in the USSR: Studies in Group Destruction* (Munich: Institute for the Study of the USSR, 1958), p. 45.

[5] S. Smith, *Allah's Mountains: Politics and War in the Russian Caucasus* (London and New York: I. B. Tauris, 1998), p. 60.

[6] Beria to Stalin, State Defence Committee, 22 February 1944, published in *Nezavisimaia gazeta*, 29 February 2000.

[7] Uralov (note 4), p. 152; Flemming (note 3), p. 84, note 30.

than 20 kilos per family and be ready to be moved in the Studebaker lorries. The women were then sent to pack while the men
were disarmed and led to the lorries. Their shock has perhaps best
been described by the poet Abdulla Saadulayev:

> *It happened in Forty-Four*
> *at four o'clock in the morning. At four*
> *Chechnya was asleep,*
> *unaware of its guilt.*
> *Somewhere in the West*
> *thunder outlined the sky,*
> *our fathers*
> *were fighting battles, winning the war.*
> *Chechnya was asleep…*
> *And suddenly, breaking the silence,*
> *creating in the dark alleys*
> *a dreadful echo*
> *penetrating mountains,*
> *Human hearts and homes,*
> *the terrible word:*
> *Out!*
> *Out!*
> *Out!*[8]

Crammed into the lorries, the people were brought to the railway stations and packed 'like sardines' into cargo or cattle cars. 'It
was cold and pitch-black and everybody was shouting and crying
because they couldn't see or find a place to sit,' recalled a deported
woman almost half a century later.[9] According to a Russian woman
who as a girl witnessed the scene, 'people were crying out and weeping. A lot of people were from the mountains and couldn't speak a
word of Russian and they cried out in Chechen from the wagons.
The NKVD said they would take people out of the wagons and
shoot them.'[10] This was not an idle threat. In the cold, misty, short
days of February the NKVD would not be bothered with people
who slowed down the execution of the operation. In many cases
the old, the infirm and the ill, who could not be moved from their

---

[8] Quoted in Hamzat Yandarbiyev, *Prestuplenie Veka* (Groznyi: Kniga, 1992), p. 8.
[9] Smith (note 5), p. 61.
[10] Ibid., p. 65.

beds, were either killed or—even worse—left to starve unattended. Ahmed Mudarov from Tiysta in the Galanchozh *raion* was one of these. He, his mother, three sons, brother, sister and niece were in bed sick and left behind unattended. Several days after the 'deportation' soldiers came to their village, stole their belongings, dragged them all out of the house and shot them. But miraculously Ahmed survived to tell his story fifty years later. He regained consciousness in time to hear his son's last words: '*apa* [father], I'm in pain.' Having lost consciousness again, he was found and saved by relatives who had escaped deportation. For two months he stayed in a hidden cave until he could walk again and then joined the *abreks* in the mountains. A year later the Soviets sent Sheikhs Arsanov and Yandarov to convince those left behind to give themselves up. 'I had to chose between joining my family and staying alone,' recalled Ahmed. He gave himself up.[11]

In some places the entire population could not be moved. In Galanchozh heavy snow made the mountain passes inaccessible to lorries. Thus the residents of the neighbouring villages were concentrated at Lake Galanchozh and shot. For many years to come no one was allowed near the lake.[12] Beria reported to Stalin: 'Some 6,000 Chechens from several settlements in the upper Galanchozh *raion* have not been evacuated due to heavy snow and the lack of roads [*bezdorozhie*].'[13]

Moysty was the highest *aul* in the mountains of Checheno-Ingushetia. In 1909 the road leading to it collapsed in an earthquake, isolating it completely. Consequently an alpine battalion of the NKVD was used to reach it. On ropes they climbed down a 300-metre-high almost vertical slope and on arriving were asked by the *aqsaqal* (chief) about the health of the 'White Tsar'. When the sixty or so residents had been gathered, the commander of the Battalion ordered them to be shot. The soldiers of the platoon charged with the task fired into the air. The enraged *politruk* then ordered half of

[11] Said-Emin Bitsoyev, 'Ia ne dolzhen byl vyzhit', *Respublika* (Groznyi), 22 February 1992; M. Katysheva, 'Sud'ba cheloveka', *Golos Chechenskoi Respubliki* (Groznyi), 30 May 1992.

[12] Oleg Jurgayev, 'Zhutkaia taina Galanchozha', *Ekho Chechni* (Groznyi), 12 February 1992.

[13] Beria to Stalin, State Defence Committee, 1 March 1944, published in *Nezavisimaia Gazeta*, 29 February 2000. He added they would be evicted and loaded on trains within a couple of days.

the platoon's soldiers to join the villagers and another platoon shot them all.[14]

But events at Khaybakh *aul*, which has become a symbol second only to Dadi Yurt, were the most notorious. Since the road was not suitable for lorries the men were separated from their families and led down the narrow mountain track. The women, children and old people—numbering 770 altogether—were shut in the collective stable, which was then set ablaze.[15] NKVD Colonel Gveshiani, who was in charge of this operation, reported to Beria: 'In view of the impossibility of transportation and the necessity to complete fully and on schedule the goals of operation *Gory* (mountains),[16] it was necessary to liquidate more than 700 inhabitants of the village of Khaybakh.' Beria replied: 'You have been recommended for a decoration and promotion for your uncompromising activity during the evacuation of the Chechens in the area of Khaybakh. Congratulations.'[17] In the years between the declaration of independence and the war of 1994–6 an association was established to exhume and bury the remains and make Khaybakh into a national monument of remembrance.[18]

All the Chechens and Ingush were rounded up, even individuals living far away in other parts of the Soviet Union. Among them were Chechen and Ingush soldiers from the front.[19] These were in

[14] V. Tulin, 'Krasnyi "Edelweis"', *Serdalo* (Groznyi), 10 March 1992. And cf. unpublished testimony quoted in Nekrich, *The Punished Peoples: The Deportation and Fate of Soviet Minorities at the End of the Second World War*, New York: W. W. Norton, 1978, pp. 58–9.

[15] Said-Emin Bitsoyev, 'Khaibakh—aul, kotorogo net' in Yu. A. Aydayev (ed.), *Chechentsy: Istoriia i sovremennost'* (Moscow: Mir Domu Tvoemu, 1996), pp. 275–7; *Khaibakh: sledstvie prodolzhaetsia* (Groznyi, 1994).

[16] Probably the code name for the moving of people to the trains.

[17] Mahomed Jurgaev and Oleg Jurgaev, *Krugi ada* (Groznyi, 1989), front and back inner cover. Also in *Ternystyi put'k svobode* (Vilnius, 1994), pp. 27–8 as quoted in Anatol Lieven, *Chechnya: Tombstone of Russian Power* (New Haven and London: Yale University Press, 1998), p. 319.

[18] For the commemoration of the 'deportation' see Brian Glyn Williams, 'Commemorating "The Deportation": The Role of Memorialization and Collective Memory in the 1994–96 Chechen War', *Memory and History*, 12, 1 (spring/summer 2000), pp. 101–34.

[19] According to A. Avtorkhanov ('The Chechens and the Ingush during the Soviet Period and its Antecedents' in M. Bennigsen-Broxup (ed.), *The North Caucasus Barrier: The Russian Advance towards the Muslim World*, London: Hurst, 1992,

many cases sent to the GULag forced labour camps rather than to their families' places of 'resettlement'. It took them many years and enormous efforts to re-establish contact with their families, or what was left of them. Members of other nationalities living in the soon to be abolished Chechen-Ingush ASSR were left in peace. 'In the village where I was', recounted a Russian student who was sent to look after the property until new settlers arrived, 'seven or eight people from Daghestan were left behind.'[20] 'The soldiers never knocked on our door,' reminisced a Russian woman. 'They knew we were Russians, of course they did—they knew everything.'[21]

On 1 March 1944 Beria sent Stalin a preliminary summary of the operation. The operation, he reported, was carried out 'with no serious instances of resistance and other incidents'. By the evening of 29 February '478,479 people (including 91,250 Ingush) had been loaded on the trains. All in all 180 trains have been loaded, 157 of which have already been sent to the places of resettlement.' In addition, 2,016 'anti-Soviet elements' were arrested and 20,072 firearms were confiscated, including 4,868 rifles and 479 sub-machine-guns.[22] In reply Stalin expressed 'gratitude' in the name of the Communist party and the State Defence Committee to 'all the units of the Red Army and the Internal Security Forces for the successful execution

---

(pp. 179–80) the Chechens were not conscripted into the Red Army, but after the German attack on the USSR volunteer 'wild' units were raised, which were not accepted into the Red Army, and Chechens were conscripted into 'labour battalions' (*trudbatal'iony*). Nekrich, in *The Punished Peoples* (note 14), pp. 56–8, gives a more detailed picture of Chechens both volunteering and being conscripted into the Red Army and fighting with distinction. One such unit became famous for its defence to the last man of Brest-Litovsk (see Khalid Oshaev, *Brest—oreshek ognennyi. Khudozhestvenno-dokumental'naia povest'* (Groznyi, 1990)). According to a later NKVD report, obviously intended to justify the deportation, in 1942–3, 1,500 of those conscripted deserted and 2,200 dodged the draft (*Nezavisimaia Gazeta*, 29 February 2000). It seems that not all Chechen soldiers were rounded up during the deportation, because on 17 June 1944, following a query from the Interior Ministry in Groznyi, an order was given to send demobilising Chechens and Ingush 'in separate groups by civilian trains under supervision [*pod soprovozhdeniem*]' to the IM in Taldy Kurgan in the Kazakh SSR (ibid.).

[20] Uralov (note 4), p. 153.

[21] Smith (note 5), p. 65.

[22] Beria to Stalin, State Defence Committee, 1 March 1944, published in *Nezavisimaia gazeta*, 29 February 2000. Karcha's (note 4; p. 45) version of resistance is too general, without details.

of the important state task in the Northern Caucasus'.[23] On 7 March an unpublished decree dissolved the Chechen-Ingush ASSR and created in its stead the Groznyi *okrug* within the Stavropol *krai*. The decree also re-drew the administrative boundaries, granting some territories of the abolished republic to the neighbouring Georgian SSR and Daghestani and North Osset ASSRs. On 22 March 1944 the Groznyi and Kyzliar *okrugs* were united to form the Groznyi *oblast*.[24]

It is impossible to calculate the extent of Chechen losses during the deportation, because the available Soviet statistics usually bind the Chechens and Ingush together and the numbers are contradictory. The above figures quoted by Beria were not final. In a later, final report he stated that 496,480 Chechens and Ingush had been deported.[25] This number is slightly higher than that reported on the lists drawn up before the operation, 495,486,[26] but less than the number of Vaynakhs registered in the census of 1939: 499,764 (407,691 Chechens and 90,074 Ingush). Even without taking into account the natural growth between 1940 and 1943, some 3,000 people are not accounted for by Beria. Further losses are disclosed by additional Soviet reports. According to General Bochkov, the commander of the NKVD convoy, 491,768 (that is 4,692 fewer) Chechens and Ingush were 'delivered to the prescribed unloading points'.[27] According to another report, 467,768 Vaynakhs (that is 29,095 less than Beria's and 24,402 less than Bochkov's reports) were resettled in the Kazakh and Kirgiz SSRs and in the Vologda, Kostroma and Ivanovo *oblasts* of the RSFSR.[28] Finally, after Khrushchev's famous 'secret speech' at the twentieth congress of the CPSU, the figure of 400,478 Chechens and Ingush 'deported' to Kazakhstan and Kirgizia was given[29]—95,982 less than Beria's numbers.

Indeed, many died during the twenty-day-long train journey. A tiny minority of them were shot by the guards. All the others—the weak, the children and the old—were unable to survive the terrible

[23] Smith (note 5), p. 60.

[24] Text of the second decree published in *Nezavisimaia Gazeta*, 29 February 2000.

[25] Beria to Stalin, July 1944, ibid.

[26] Beria to Stalin, State Defence Committee, 22 February 1944, ibid. Beria seems to have followed here a 'standard' Soviet procedure to 'minimise' the target and thus be able to report to have achieved more than planned.

[27] Quoted in Flemming (note 3), p. 73.

[28] Ibid., p. 76.

[29] Quoted in Lieven (note 17), p. 319.

conditions. The cold, dark, unventilated cars with no sanitary facil-
ities were crammed far beyond their capacity. An official report
stated that 'given the presence of 40 to 50 per cent children', more
people were packed into each car. Also 'the fact that the deportees
have not been permitted to take heavy items with them and each
family brought its own personal things into the wagons ... allowed
us to economise significantly on the quantity of wagons' and to 'do
away with the baggage wagons'.[30] The trains stopped irregularly for
15 minutes or so, and food was delivered sporadically and in insufficient quantities. Some Chechens are adamant that chemicals and
poisons were added to the food.[31] Attempts to keep corpses of relatives in the cars for later burial—if discovered by the guards they
were thrown out 'like rubbish'—must have added to the toll. And
there were reports of a typhoid epidemic among the deportees.[32]

To this must be added the constant state of anxiety over their fate,
since no one had bothered to inform the deportees of where they
were being taken. A recurrent story told by the survivors reports
that when they crossed the river Volga and saw the water below
them,[33] they were sure the NKVD guards were going to drown
them all, so they started to say their final prayers. (Indeed, a persis-
tent rumour attributes to Beria the words 'They should all have
been dropped into the middle of the Caspian Sea.')

The frozen land of Kazakhstan and Kirgizia, where the deportees
were resettled, also took its toll in lives. Exposure to the extremes of
a climate they were not used to finished off those barely left alive
after starvation, diseases, sheer fatigue and weakness. According to
all indications the death-rate remained very high during the first
years after resettlement. Chechen sources calculate that about 60–
65 per cent of the deported died in those years,[34] for which no

---

[30] Mil'shtein, head of the Third Directorate of the NKGB to Kobulov, Beria's deputy, 18 March 1944, quoted in Flemming (note 3), p. 75.

[31] Usmanov, *Nepokorennaia Chechnia* (Moscow: Izdatel'skii dom Parus, 1997),
pp. 83–4.

[32] Mil'shtein (note 30), p. 75. Uralov (note 4), p. 153. Typhoid epidemics were not
rare in the Soviet Union during the Second World War.

[33] A statement frequently heard in testimonies of the survivors was 'We had to cut
a hole in the floor.'

[34] Ibid., p. 83; Yu. Aytbayev and A. Aytbayev, 'Tiazhki put'k millionu', in Aytbayev
(ed.), *Chechentsy: Istoriia i sovremennost* (Moscow: Mir Domu Tvoemu, 1996),

Soviet data of the Chechen losses are available. However, a report from November 1956 states that roughly 395,000 Chechens and Ingush then lived in the Kazakh and Kirgiz SSRs, that is more than 100,000 less than the number of deportees reported by Beria and about 70,000 less than the reported number of those resettled in these two republics.[35] But what demonstrates best the Chechens' demographic catastrophe is the Soviet censuses: in the thirteen-year period between the censuses of 1926 and 1939 the Chechen population grew by 28 per cent. These years were hardly an idyllic time, with the Soviet anti-religious drive, collectivisation, recurrent purges and frequent revolts. Thousands of people were killed or executed and tens of thousands died of starvation or vanished in the GULag. In the twenty years between the censuses of 1939 and 1959, the Chechen population grew by only 2.5 per cent. (In comparison, the rate of growth of the Ingush during these two periods was 24% and 15% respectively, that of the Balkars 28% and nil, and of the Karachay 37% and 8%).[36]

Therefore, it is understandable that the Chechens, like all other 'repressed' (another official euphemism) nations, consider themselves the victims of genocide. 'The scar is deep,' wrote a British journalist,

...not only on the generation which survived the train journey and the generation born in exile, but on their descendants. Because this was punishment based on race, the deportations have become part of the national identity of the Chechens, Ingush, Karachai and Balkars. Like Jewish Holocaust survivors, it is an event which quietly dominates both individuals' lives and the nation as a whole. Everyone without exception is a victim. Even for those born after, the tragedy is impossible to put aside, since their parents, relatives, village and entire people suffered.[37]

---

pp. 228–32.

[35] Report by Gromov and Chuvarev, 14 November 1956—*Nezavisimaia Gazeta*, 29 February 2000.

[36] For an analysis of the data in the two censuses and their significance, see R. Conquest, *The Nation Killers: The Soviet Deportation of Nationalities* (London: Macmillan, 1970), pp. 160–3; Nekrich (note 14), p. 138. All the available statistics have been collected and analysed by J. Otto Pohl in his *The Stalinist Penal System: A Statistical History of Soviet Repression and Terror, 1930–1953* (Jefferson, NC: McFarland, 1997), pp. 100–8, and *Ethnic Cleansing in the USSR, 1937–1949* (Westport, CT: Greenwood Press, 1999), pp. 79–86.

[37] Smith (note 5), p. 60.

Like other victims in analogous situations, the Chechens are determined never to forget. In a poet's words,

> I am PAIN
> I am thousands,
> thousands of tears
> shed to
> the sound of wheels
> in February
> Nineteen-Forty-Four...
> I am the se-e-e-e-ea,
> I am hundreds, I am thousands
> of thrown-out corpses
> of the dead
> in obscure stations...
> I am a tomb-stone.
> I am the shattered anguish
> of a mother
> with a frozen plea:
> 'Oy Dela
> sa-a-a-ave
> my last son! ...'
> I am Khaybakh,
> Khatyn and the GULag,
> the bloody thrones,
> the dictates...
> I am glasnost
> I am the poet's heart
> raging with pain,
> stuck in the throat,
> calling for freedom...
> I am a voice.
> I demand:
> 'REMEMBER!'[38]

The Chechens are also determined to make sure it never happens
again. On 23 February 1994—the fiftieth anniversary of the deportation—the president of the self-proclaimed independent Chechen
Republic, Johar Dudayev, unveiled a monument to the deportation
in the centre of Groznyi. (The monument was destroyed in the battles

---

[38] Ismail Kerimov quoted in Aytbayev (ed.) (note 34), p. 274.

of 1995, rebuilt in 1997 and destroyed again in 1999, which perhaps symbolises best the fate of the Chechens and their country.) Old gravestones, which had been used for road and house building by the Soviet authorities and the colonists they had brought to the Chechen villages, were the main component of this monument. Tables naming the places where massacres occurred ('Khaybakh, 770 killed; Urus Martan hospital, 62 killed', etc.) were engraved on the surrounding walls, as were some of the above-quoted reports made to and by Beria. In the centre of the monument were the sculptures of an open Qur'an and a huge fist holding a sword, with the inscription 'We shall not weep. We shall not weaken. We shall not forget.'[39]

The deported Chechens were moved mainly to the Kazakh and partly to the Kirgiz SSRs.[40] They were 'resettled' in 'special settlements', though in some cases they were added to existing Kazakh or Kirgiz *kolkhozes* and *sovkhozes*. Their status was that of '*spetsposelentsy*' (special settlers), which denoted that they were under a '*spetsrezhim*' (special regime). This meant they were not allowed to leave the premises without a pass from the local NKVD *spetskomendatura*, to which they had to report once a month.[41] Anyone caught outside his or her settlement without authorisation was sent to the GULag. This hampered contacts between family members who had been torn apart, of which there were plenty since the deported Chechens were resettled exactly as they were found on 23 February 1944. Thus family members who had been absent from home on that day were not deported with their families, while guests who happened to be staying overnight were 'annexed' to their host's family until quite some time after 'resettlement'. At some point during the deportation all households were meticulously registered on

[39] See B. G. Williams, 'Commemorating "The Deportation": The Role of Memorialization and Collective Memory in the 1994–96 Chechen War', *Memory and History*, 12, 1 (spring/summer 2000), pp. 101–34.

[40] 380,397 Vaynakhs were resettled in Kazakhstan and 89,617 in Kirgizia. Flemming (note 3), p. 76. Apparently, these numbers do not include those who were suspected of 'banditism' and sent directly to the GULag. And see Karcha (note 4), p. 46.

[41] In the Kazakh SSR 520 *spetskomendatury* were formed, 145 regional (*raionnye*) and 375 in each settlement (*poselkovye*) (Report to Beria on the preparations to receive the deportees, 28 February 1944—*Nezavisimaia Gazeta*, 29 February 2000). Flemming, note 3, p. 77, quotes different data: 488 *spetskomendatury* in the Kazakh SSR and 96 in the Kirgiz SSR.

20 cm × 14 cm 'cards of registration of special contingents [*kartochka po uchetu spets. kontingentov*]', which detailed all the household members. A random card found in the KGB archives in Groznyi in May 1992 had the following information:

surname/name/patronymic	nationality	age	occupation	education
Ahmedov Aki Ahmedovich	Chechen	29	agricultural worker	illiterate

			relation to head of household	
Akhmedova Maryam Yusupova	Chechen	22	wife	
Akhmedov Ibrahim Akiyevich	Chechen	9	son	
Akhmedova Sofiyat Akiyevna	Chechen	7	daughter	
Akhmedov Beybulat Akiyevich	Chechen	4	son	

Signature of head of household (in Arabic)[42]

On the back of the card the number of farm animals was registered along with any missing household member. The details and signature of the registering NKVD officer were also recorded. If the husband was absent, the wife was registered as head of the household, and if both parents were absent, then the oldest brother or sister. Guests were registered as members of the household. These cards accompanied the deported families to their places of 'resettlement'. There personal files were opened for each household head. These files included sheets with that person's signature for each time he or she reported to the *spetskomendatura,* reports—mainly from the workplace—and all the correspondence between the person and the authorities (like requests for family reunions, travel permits etc.).[43]

In these conditions an entire people had to start building their lives from scratch. First was the task of survival.[44] In many cases

---

[42] For another sample card, see Larisa Parova, 'Dokumenty svidetel'stvuiut. Istochniki istorii vyseleniia Vainakhov v 1944 godu', *Serdalo* (Groznyi), 27 February 1992, p. 3.

[43] In the early 1970s, when the KGB in Alma Ata found no more use for these files and cards, they were transferred to the KGB archives in Groznyi. The Dudayev government intended to open the archives, but did not do it. Any hope of using these and other archives was lost when they were destroyed during the battle for Groznyi in the winter of 1994–5. For the destruction of the archives, see Mahomed Movzayev, head of the Archive Department of the Moscow-Based Government, in *Prague Watchdog,* 17 July 2004.

[44] See Flemming (note 3), pp. 78–82; Nekrich (note 14), pp. 86–136.

the new arrivals were helped by earlier ones. 'When we arrived in Kazakhstan,' recalled an elderly Chechen journalist to a British colleague; 'the ground was frozen hard and we thought we would all die. It was the German exiles who helped us to survive—they had already been there for several years.'[45] 'We lived like sheep in Kazakhstan,' recounted another survivor, 'whole families in one room. But bit by bit we started to build our own houses', and when the Kazakhs saw that 'we were not bandits but hard-working people they began to help us.'[46]

Nevertheless, the Chechens more than other repressed peoples managed to 'preserve their culture, language, identity and especially spirit of independence' in a 'deeply impressive' way. 'Ethnic solidarity and kinship-based mutual support, as well as a sheer determination to survive' played a major role in this.'[47] So did the Sufi orders, first and foremost the Qadiriyya. These became 'not only the very symbol' of the Chechens' 'nationhood', but also 'very efficient organizers ensuring their survival'.[48] Thus, despite all the restrictions they managed to stay in touch, organise themselves and resist the deportation. Many people moved without permission from one settlement to another and a few tried to return to their ancestral homes. Consequently, in 1948 the CC of the CPSU decreed that the 'resettlement' to remote regions of the Soviet Union of the Chechens (and other nationalities) was 'for ever, without the right to return to their previous places of residence'. Ordering greater vigilance of the NKVD and NKGB forces, it ruled that 'persons guilty of unauthorised exit (escape) [*samovol'nyi vyezd (pobeg)*]' would be punished with 'twenty years' hard labour'. Persons guilty of 'sheltering escaping *spetsposelentsy*', facilitating their escape, and 'delivering to settlers permits to return to their previous places of residence' would be liable to 'five years' hard labour'.[49]

[45] Lieven (note 17), p. 320.
[46] Smith (note 5), p. 61. And see Michaela Pohl, '"It Cannot be that our Graves will be Here": The Survival of Chechen and Ingush Deportees in Kazakhstan, 1944–1957', *Journal of Genocide Research*, 4, 2 (September 2002).
[47] Lieven (note 17), p. 321. And see Birgit B. Brauer, 'Chechens and the Survival of their Cultural Identity in Exile', *Journal of Genocide Research*, 4, 3 (September 2002).
[48] Bennigsen, 'The Qadiriyah', pp. 71–2.
[49] Highly secret 'to be returned' excerpt from protocol no. 66, 1948 published in *Nezavisimaia Gazeta*, 29 February 2000.

'From the moment we arrived', an 'elderly Chechen journalist' related to a British colleague,

...people were writing to the Central Committee in Moscow, saying that we had been deported unjustly, and from 1953—Stalin's death[50]—we secretly began to send back individual men, who came to Chechnya with false papers, and acted as scouts. Of course, some were caught, and at first they were severely punished; later not.

In 1956, when they opened the camps,[51] there was a big push to return—by arrangement some families assembled in Akmolinsk, just bought tickets and went—thirteen wagons full, with five to seven families in each... Of course it wasn't that simple—we'd planned it carefully, collected money from the whole Chechen community and we paid huge bribes to the police, the KGB and the railway authorities. We were acting as an advance guard for the rest of the nation.

They didn't finally stop us until we reached Mozdok. They held us there for several weeks, then by order of Khrushchev they let us go, and the next year the rest of the people followed. You have to grant it to Khrushchev, he didn't follow the old Russian policy of force, there was a real move at that time to get rid of the memory of Stalin, and we exploited that.[52]

Indeed, it was Khrushchev who 'rehabilitated' the Chechens and other 'repressed' peoples as part of his de-Stalinisation drive. In his famous secret speech at the twentieth party congress in February 1956 he defined the 'mass deportations from their native places of whole nations, together with all Communists and *Komsomol* members' as 'monstrous acts' and 'crude violations of the basic Leninist principles of the nationality policy of the Soviet state'. In that speech Khrushchev announced that 'practical measures for the restoration of the national autonomy of these peoples' would be taken.[53] Following that, on 9 January 1957 a decree by the Presidium of the Supreme Soviet of the USSR recommended the Presidium of the Supreme Soviet of the RSFSR to 'examine the question and take

[50] In April 1953, that is about a month after Stalin's death, a group of Politburo members had already recommended removing the restrictions from the *spetsposelentsy* (text in ibid).

[51] On 16 July 1956 a decree of the Supreme Soviet of the USSR removed the deported nationalities from the status of '*spetsposelentsy*', but without returning to them their property confiscated during the deportation and with no right 'to return to the places from which they were deported' (text in ibid.).

[52] Lieven (note 17), p. 320.

[53] Conquest (note 36), pp. 144, 146.

decisions' on the restoration of several autonomies including the Chechen-Ingush ASSR within the RSFSR. On 7 March 1957 the Presidium of the Supreme Soviet of the RSFSR passed several decrees supporting this suggestion.[54]

In principle the Chechens were now allowed to return. In practice 'the resettlement of citizens of the stated nationalities', Khrushchev asserted, 'requires a certain amount of time' and 'much organisational work'. Therefore, he 'proposed' carrying out the repatriation of the Chechens and Ingush and restoring their autonomy over a period of three years, from 1957 to 1960.[55] But the Chechens, like the other deported peoples, were not prepared to wait. By September 1957 140,000 Chechens and Ingush had returned,[56] and by the beginning of 1958 some 200,000 more (instead of the 100,000 scheduled) had arrived.[57] And by the end of that year almost all the Vaynakhs had returned to their republic.[58] An entire generation was now for the second time in its lifetime going to start rebuilding its life. And a new generation of Chechens, born in exile, were now to see their ancestral homeland of which they had been told by their parents. None would find it as remembered or imagined.

Their return created some problems and clashes, since the land to which they returned had not remained empty. With the deportation all the students of the institutes of higher education in Groznyi, their teachers, and 'all housewives who were not working in factories' were mobilised 'to collect and look after the cattle, and list the crops and equipment'.[59] They were soon relieved when settlers were

[54] Ibid., pp. 145, 147.

[55] Ibid., pp. 146–7.

[56] Komarov, Secretary of the Organising Committee of the Chechen-Ingush ASSR, to Cherkevich, secretary of the Chechen-Ingush *obkom* of the CPSU, 25 September 1957. Groznyi Radio of 29 October 1957 stated 142,000 Chechens and Ingush had 'so far settled in the autonomous republic' (as quoted in Conquest (note 36), p. 155).

[57] *Groznenskii Rabochii*, 12 January 1958 as quoted in Conquest (note 36), p. 155.

[58] The massive flow of the Chechens (and Ingush) created quite a few problems. At first, the authorities tried to prevent them from boarding trains. However, this led to a rather explosive situation in the railway stations, where great numbers of idle, workless families with their luggage were concentrated. For this and the (relatively) few incidents that followed see Vladimir A. Kozlov, *Mass Uprisings in the USSR: Protests and Rebellion in the Post-Stalin Years* (Armonk, NY: M. E. Sharpe, 2002), pp. 72–9.

[59] Uralov (note 4), p. 153.

brought in from Russia and the Ukraine, and in a some cases from Georgia, Daghestan and Ossetia. 'Masses of new people arrived,' recalled a Russian woman native to Groznyi. 'They were simply thrown together from everywhere. No one knew anyone else.'[60]

When the Chechens returned to claim their homes, conflicts developed. Many colonists opposed the repatriation of the Chechens and Ingush, and their claims to their ancestral homes. They might have been encouraged in this by the local party and state authorities who also resisted repatriation.[61] The Russians 'living in our old house', a Chechen woman recounted, 'refused to leave and said "we're not afraid of you, go away." We had some money left so we went and bought another house.' Indeed, 'a lot of people had no choice but to use the money they'd saved and buy back their own houses.' In other cases the returning families threatened to use force and sometimes did. 'My aunt', related another witness 'was very fierce and said to the people in her house: "If you don't get out, I'll kill you tomorrow, I'll cut your heads off." They left. Many of us gave ultimatums like that—we're a warlike people, you see.'[62]

The conflict reached its peak on 24–27 August 1958. Riots broke out in Groznyi in which some elements within the local authorities were probably involved.[63] On 23 August a drunken brawl resulted in the murder of a Russian by a Chechen. Three days later, following the funeral, several thousand people, including workers of several factories who had called a strike, marched on the central square, beating up anyone who looked like a Chechen. Demanding that the local party be cleansed of 'false Communists', the demonstrators stormed and sacked the Communist party headquarters, and then phoned the Central Committee of the CPSU in Moscow, demanding its intervention. Another crowd occupied the railway station,

---

[60] Lieven (note 17), pp. 321–2. Documents relating to the collection of the property left behind and the colonisation were published in *Nezavisimaia Gazeta*, 29 February 2000 and Larisa Parova, 'Dokumenty svidetel'stvuiut'.

[61] Report by Gromov and Chuvarev, 14 November 1956—*Nezavisimaia Gazeta*, 29 February 2000; Nekrich (note 14), pp. 148–9, 150–1.

[62] Smith (note 5), p. 66. And see Kozlov (note 58), pp. 87–94.

[63] According to Kozlov (who has provided the most detailed description of the events so far—pp. 95–109) 'it is impossible to get rid of the thought that someone, "for a reason known only to himself" as is written in police protocols, helped the disturbances to reach full force' (p. 103), and hints that the KGB (or elements within it) were that 'someone' (pp. 103, 109).

blocking the tracks so that trains bringing in returning Chechens and Ingush would not be able to enter.[64] The following petition to the CC enumerated the demonstrators' demands:

Due to the savage treatment by the Chechen-Ingush population of other nationalities, expressed in butchery, murder, rape and insults, the labourers of the city of Grozny in the name of the majority of the population propose:

1. To rename, beginning on August 27, the Chechen-Ingush ASSR either Grozny *oblast* or a multinational Soviet socialist republic.
2. The Chechen-Ingush population in Grozny *oblast* must not be more than 10 per cent of the general population.
3. All privileges of the Chechen-Ingush population relative to other nationalities must be revoked.[65]

The local authorities lost control and army units had to be deployed. The riots were suppressed and a large-scale 'screening' of the population was undertaken. It resulted in the 'removal' from the city of some 365 'persons who are not engaged in socially useful labour, who lead parasitic ways of life and who are inclined to carry out criminal acts'.[66] All this seems to have broken the colonists' spirits and they soon started to leave. 'They seemed to be afraid of us and perhaps they even had a bad conscience,' reported a German who had married a Chechen woman and become a Chechen. 'Most slipped away in the night, and the local authorities lent them lorries. Within a few months they had all gone.'[67]

Those Chechens who had lived up in the mountains found their 'mountain hamlets and farmhouses' in ruins. 'After the cattle had been removed,' reported the above-mentioned Russian student, the buildings 'were burnt, so that the "bandits" should not be able to make use of them. We watched them burning for several days.'[68] Wherever they returned, the Chechens discovered that everything had been done to obliterate their memory from those places. Mosques, monuments, inscriptions and, worst of all, graveyards had been destroyed.

---

[64] Nekrich (note 14), pp. 151–4, 183–4; *'Punished Peoples' of the Soviet Union: The Continuing Legacy of Stalin's Deportations,* Helsinki Watch report, September 1991, p. 24.

[65] Kozlov (note 58), p. 106.

[66] Ibid., p. 109.

[67] Lieven (note 17), p. 322.

[68] Uralov (note 4), p. 153.

'When Stalin deported us', Shamil Basayev begins, 'the Russians took over our empty homes and they ripped the stones of our graveyards, then they used them to make roads, bridges, pigsties.' His voice is quiet but filled with hatred. Of course. What could be more loathsome to a people who consider ancestors as important as the living, who still rise out of their car seats in respect as they drive past cemeteries?[69]

[69] Smith (note 5), pp. 1–2.

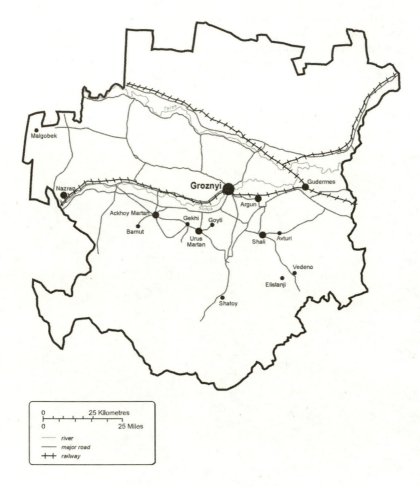

The Chechen–Ingush ASSR after 1958.

14

REHABILITATION

In 1991 a Karachai leader had the following to say about 'rehabilitation':

It's not like in the United States where the Japanese-Americans who were put in camps during World War II were apologized to and given financial compensation. Or look at the Germans, the way they have apologized to the Jews and banned anything anti-Jewish.

Instead, our repressed peoples came back in the late 1950s either to have their oil exploited in the case of the Chechens, their best lands taken away in the case of the Ingush, their autonomous status removed in the case of the Karachai and, again, a loss of territory in the case of the Balkars.[1]

Indeed 'the deportations were considered non-events. No memorial monuments were erected and there was certainly no mention of what had happened. [...] The punished peoples carried their pain in silence.'[2] In a way this symbolised the half-heartedness of Khrushchev's 'thaw' in many, if not all, spheres. In the case of the Chechens and Ingush the lack of enthusiasm in executing their rehabilitation—to a great degree the people themselves had forced rehabilitation on Moscow[3]—had *inter alia* three sources: opposition

---

[1] S. Smith, *Allah's Mountains. Politics and War in the Russian Caucasus* (London and New York: I. B. Tauris, 1998), p. 91.

[2] Ibid., p. 67. 'People kept quiet,' wrote a distinguished Russian anthropologist, 'as if the tragedy were some sort of collective stigma for which they had to pay.' Furthermore, 'middle-aged Chechens, particularly those who had attained prominent administrative posts, curiously referred to their exile period as work on the "virgin lands".' (Valery Tishkov, *Chechnya: Life in a War-Torn Society* (Berkeley: University of California Press, 2004), pp. 25, 26).

[3] 'Most impressive, too, was the way in which, after Stalin's death in 1953, the Chechens organised their own return. As described above ..., they and other deported peoples effectively forced the Soviet government's hand over the issue.'

by the party and state bureaucracy, both in the Caucasus[4] and in Moscow; the importance to Moscow of the smooth continuance of economic activities, first and foremost the uninterrupted production of oil;[5] and Moscow's lingering suspicion and belief in the 'guilt' of the deported peoples, and the Chechens in particular, and thus the need to keep them under tight control.[6] Hence the republic and its indigenous population were indeed put under the direct strict control of Moscow.

Many of the returning Chechens and Ingush 'were not getting their own homes and villages back'. This is especially true of the mountain villagers, most of whom were not allowed to return to their former districts. Rather, they were 'being directed where the State desired'—that is Groznyi and the lowlands, including 'the hitherto non-Chechen area' to the north of the Terek—where 'thousands' of houses were built. In this way Moscow tried to kill two birds with one stone: the returning Chechens were settled in the centres of economic production 'to provide a reserve of labour for the industries of Groznyi';[7] and they were kept away from the

---

A. Lieven, *Chechnya: Tombstone of Russian Power* (New Haven and London: Yale University Press, 1998), p. 321.

[4] The *obkoms* of the Groznyi *oblast* and of the Daghestan and North Osset ASSRs responded 'negatively' (*otritsatel'no*) to the new policy of allowing the Vaynakhs to return 'to their places of former residence'. According to the local party leadership a 'certain part' of the Chechens and Ingush 'has made a bad impression' in the present no less than in the past. Another argument was that 'the economic possibilities of the *raions* of the previous Chechen-Ingush ASSR do not allow for them working places [*trudoustroit'*] and re-settlement [*rasselit'*].' (Report by Gromov and Churaev, 14 November 1956 published in *Nezavisimaia Gazeta*, 29 February 2000).

[5] For oil production during the Soviet period, see van der Leeuw, *Oil and Gas in the Caucasus and Carpian* (London: Curzon Press, 2000), pp. 101–18.

[6] The Chechens alone of the many peoples of the Caucasus have become infamous to generations of Russian pupils who memorised rhymes by Pushkin and Lermontov such as 'Run, oh Russian maidens/Hurry beauties home/Across the Terek Chechens roam' (Alexander Pushkin, 'Cherkesskaia pesnia') or 'Terek flows among the mountains/With a roaring sound;/In the night the evil Chechen/Steals along the ground' ('Cossack Cradlesong' in Mikhail Lermontov, *The Demon and Other Poems*, transl. Eugene M. Kayden (Yellow Springs, Ohio: Antioch Press, 1965), p. 65). In the original the 'evil Chechen' is 'crawling to the bank sharpening his dagger'. These and other negative images must have influenced Russian attitudes to the Chechens.

[7] R. Conquest, *The Nation Killers: The Soviet Deportation of Nationalities* (London:

mountains, where topography complicated control and anti-Soviet bands were still active. In 1957 'systematic liquidation of the last *khutor* settlements of the Chechens' resumed and continued until 1963, which 'may be regarded with some justification from the historical point of view as the completion of "the conquest of the Caucasus".'[8]

To facilitate control the boundaries of the restored Chechen-Ingush ASSR were modified, in an obvious attempt both to 'divide and rule' and to 'dilute Chechnya ethnically'.[9] In the west the Prigirodnyi *raion*, immediately east of Vladikavkaz, was not returned to the restored republic. It remained part of the North Osset ASSR, and its Ingush inhabitants were legally not allowed to return to their homes, which had been occupied by Ossets. This unresolved problem would burst into an armed conflict between the Ingush and the Ossets in the 1990s.[10] By way of compensation—or so it was presented—the republic's northern boundary was moved far beyond the Terek to include two traditionally Cossack *raions,* Naurskii and Shelkovskii,[11] which had been part of the Stavropol *krai,* and Chechens were resettled there, as noted above.

Macmillan, 1970), pp. 156–7, quoting Groznyi Radio of 29 October 1957 and *Groznenskii Rabochii* 12 January 1958, which reported 20,500 houses built in Groznyi and 15,000 in the country. Yet homes and work for the repatriates and schools for their children were not available. Nekrich, *The Punished Peoples: The Deportation and Fate of Soviet Minorities at the End of the Second World War,* New York: W. W. Norton, 1978, p. 156.

[8] Ibid., pp. 155–6; Tishkov (note 2), p. 33. Still, in later years many Chechens ignored the prohibition and resettled in the high mountains, and the Soviet authorities did very little to prevent them from doing so. I am grateful to Anatoly Khazanov for this information. During the years 1992–4 (that is after the proclamation of independence) a great number of people started to build houses in their ancestral villages in the mountains.

[9] Lieven (note 3), p. 322. Another reason for the annexation of the two *raions* north of the Terek to the Chechen-Ingush ASSR was economic—to provide the republic with agricultural land and bread-producing capability. Anna Matveeva, 'Daghestan: Inter-ethnic Tensions and Cross-border Implications' in Moshe Gammer (ed.), *The Caspian Region,* vol. II: *The Caucasus* (London: Routledge, 2004), p. 144, note 54.

[10] For the Ingush-Osset war, see Julian Birch, 'Ossetia: A Caucasian Bosnia in Microcosm', *Central Asian Survey,* 14, 1 (1995), pp. 43–74; Human Rights Watch, *The Ingush-Ossetian Conflict in the Prigorodnyi Region* (New York and London, 1993); Tishkov, *The Mind Aflame: Ethnicity, Nationalism and Conflict in and after the Soviet Union* (London: Sage, 1997), pp. 155–82.

The combined effect of these border changes was above all to drive a new wedge between the Ingush and the Chechens, whose common encounter with deportation would otherwise have brought them closer together. Secondly it changed the demographic balance in the republic in favour of the Russians, or rather 'Russophones' (*ruskogovoriashchie*).[12] The importance of this imbalance was demonstrated by the fact that for many years to come the Soviet authorities made efforts to retain it. A general feeling among the Chechens, echoed in conversations with foreigners, is that the authorities tried to increase the number of Russophones by offering preferential jobs, salaries and accommodation to 'Russian' immigrants at the expense of the Chechens who were denied these opportunities.[13]

Keeping this demographic balance was obviously in the interest of the Russophone population of the Chechen-Ingush ASSR, but it was in the Kremlin's interest as well. After all, the Russians were the element deemed most loyal to the Soviet Union, if not the only one. Therefore they were the mainstay of Soviet control in the non-Russian areas of the USSR. With the Chechens and Ingush considered 'pardoned rather than politically rehabilitated',[14] Russian dominance in the republic was much stronger and more manifest. Thus, for example, in contradiction to the usual Soviet practice, the first secretary of the republican party *obkom* had for thirty-two years always been a Russian.[15] Only towards the end of Gorbachev's rule, in 1989, and after strong Chechen pressure, was a Chechen, Doku Zavgayev, nominated as First Secretary.

The turning-point came with the mass demonstrations of 23 February 1973 in the midst of the 'era of stagnation' (*zastoi*). Beginning

---

[11] In fact, a third *raion*—Kargalinskii—was included in the republic, but was later divided between the other two.

[12] 'Russophones', or 'Russophone population' (*russkogovoriashchee nasselenie*), was a term coined in the 1970s–80s to augment the numbers of Russians in the non-Russian units of the Soviet Union.

[13] A 'fact', repeated frequently in conversations with Chechens, is that the (Russian) secretary of the Chechen-Ingush *obkom* had on his office wall a demographic chart of the republic's population, with the 25 per cent line marked in red next to the Russians.

[14] Jabrail Gakayev, *Ocherki politicheskoi istorii Chechni (XX vek)* (Moscow: Chechenskii Kul'turnyi Tsentr, 1997), p. 107 as quoted in Tishkov (note 2), p. 34.

[15] The usual Soviet practice was to have a member of the titular nationality as a figurehead First Secretary, while a Russian was the Second Secretary who held real power. For details, see Tishkov (note 2), pp. 35–40.

as a demand for the return of the Prigorodnyi *raion*, these demonstrations rapidly came to include demands for a larger share of official positions.[16] Surprisingly, although the immediate reaction of the Soviet authorities was to launch a campaign 'to combat the cult of "the land of our forefathers"',[17] in the long run the requests were largely, though not fully, granted. From such a beginning, 'by the advent of Gorbachev' the Chechens were 'effectively in control … in most fields'[18] (although it would take sixteen years and a major shift of policy in Moscow for a Chechen to become the First Secretary.) This was when the Russian population began to feel uncomfortable and started to leave the republic. 'By the 1970s', recounted a Russian native of Groznyi, 'the Chechens got the upper hand.…

We had always been frightened of them—in school, they always stuck together and made us feel like foreigners. Unlike us Russians, they have tremendously strong family and clan links. Every Chechen is a member of a clan [*te'ip*], it helps him and he is completely loyal to it. Also they soon began to outnumber us. For Chechens in those days it was common to have six or more children—we heard that their elders went round encouraging them to do this—whereas for Russians to have more than three was already uncommon, and since then of course it has dropped even further.

But what really gave the Chechens their chance was the decay of the Soviet organs of power. As the Soviet state became more and more corrupt under Brezhnev, and the police got weaker, the Chechens moved into the cracks. Soon several powerful Chechen criminal clans had a strong presence in Moscow, with influence in central ministries, and after that there was nothing anyone locally could do to stop them. When I returned home to Grozny in 1974 from my military service, I saw how powerful the Chechens had become, and I decided to leave. It was already clear that there was nothing there for Russians.[19]

A Western observer admired 'the Chechen success, through what can only be called an exercise in sheer national willpower, in gaining the psychological, economic and finally even political ascen-

---

[16] Nekrich (note 7), pp. 158–61, 184–5. Apparently the demonstrations were covertly encouraged, and perhaps even instigated by leading Chechen Communist party officials (Lieven (note 3), p. 56, quoting *Nezavisimaia Gazeta*, 2 December 1992).

[17] Nekrich (note 7), pp. 161–6.

[18] Lieven (note 3), p. 322.

[19] Ibid., p. 323.

dancy over the Russian population in the region.'[20] However, there was more behind the Chechen success story than 'sheer national willpower'. Complex processes affecting Chechen society during the thirty-odd years between repatriation and '*glasnost*' had much to do with it, most notably Chechen responses to Sovietisation, Russification and Modernisation.[21]

The Soviet authorities tried their best to modernise the population. This was part of the effort to build a communist society in which all citizens would be equal, modern, economically efficient and productive atheists and materialists. In other words, they expended a lot of effort to 'Sovietise'—as it was called in the West— their people. As has until recently been the case in the West, the Soviets believed that 'modernity' was diametrically opposed to tradition, and therefore everything that related to national (especially non-Russian) traditions was condemned as 'reactionary'. Unlike in the West, however, religion was also regarded as a relic of the past that contradicted modernity and had therefore to be eliminated.[22] Thus repeated campaigns were launched throughout the 1950s–80s to eradicate such 'vestiges' and 'prejudices' of the 'reactionary' past.

Since modernisation/Sovietisation was served through the vehicle of the Russian language and via the prism of Russian culture, it necessarily entailed Russification of all the non-Russian nationalities. The policy of Russification had already started under Stalin in the 1930s. Khrushchev reinforced it under the slogan of 'getting together [*sblizhenie*] the peoples of the Soviet Union'. Under Brezhnev it was further intensified under the slogan 'the merging [*sliianie*] of the Soviet peoples'.

In the case of the Chechens, the first step towards Russification was the introduction of the Cyrillic alphabet in the second half of the 1930s.[23] After the deportation it was decided that the deported children would be taught in Russian because it was 'impossible' to teach them in their native language 'due to the lack of suitably

[20] Ibid., p. 322.
[21] For changes in Chechen society in the 1960s–80s, see Tishkov (note 10), pp. 196–8.
[22] The belief that religion contradicts modernity is also fairly widespread in the West.
[23] The immediate reason for the change of alphabets from Latin- to Cyrillic-based orthography seems to be Atatürk's change of the Turkish alphabet to a Latin-based one in 1927.

[security-] cleared pedagogical cadres'.[24] After the Chechens' return no Chechen-language schools were established and all the pupils had to study in Russian schools. Even Chechen literature was taught in Russian translation. Only in 1990, 'in keeping with *perestroika*', was Chechen introduced as a 'foreign language' into the curriculum of elementary schools (grades 1–4).[25] Thus although a newspaper and books were published in Chechen and a national theatre performed in the language, for the generations educated after the deportation Russian had become the primary language, both written and spoken, while Chechen had been reduced to merely 'a household language [*na bytovom urovne*]'. And even then, 'when we begin to talk about politics, say, half the words are Russian.'[26] This is especially true of the better-educated strata residing in Groznyi. Many of these people, who wanted their children to learn their native language, had to send them for several years to relatives in the villages.

This seemed to be the Soviets' most clear-cut success. In all other spheres the repeated campaigns against the 'vestiges of religion and clericalism', 'chauvinistic bourgeois nationalism' etc. only underlined, as Western 'Sovietologists' were quick to point out, the Soviets' failures.[27] This impression is supported by a study based on Soviet archives.[28] According to Soviet statistics, in 1970 about 90 per cent

---

[24] *Izvestia sovetov deputatov trudiashchikhsua SSSR*, 1946, p. 5 published in *Nezavisimaia Gazeta*, 29 February 2000.

[25] Helsinki Watch Report, p. 25. For further details of the education system and its standards, see Tishkov (note 2), pp. 45–7.

[26] Helsinki Watch Report, p. 25. And cf. Tishkov (note 2), pp. 47–8.

[27] For example, Fanny E. B. Bryan, 'Internationalism, Nationalism and Islam' in Marie Bennigsen-Broxup (ed.), *The North Caucasus Barrier: The Russian Advance towards the Muslim World* (London: Hurst, 1992), pp. 195–218; Fanny E. B. Bryan, 'Anti-Religious Activities in the Chechen-Ingush Republic of the USSR and the Survival of Islam', *Central Asian Survey*, 3, 2 (1984), pp. 99–116; Alexandre Bennigsen and Chantal Lemercier-Quelquejay, '"L'Islam parallèle" en Union Soviétique. Les organisations soufies dans la République tchétcheno-inguche', *Cahiers du Monde Russe et Soviétique*, XXI, 1 (January–March 1980), pp. 49–63; Michael Rywkin, 'The Communist Party and the Sufi Tarikat in the Checheno-Ingush Republic', *Central Asian Survey*, 10, 1–2 (1991), pp. 133–46; Michael Rywkin, 'Power and Ethnicity: Party Stuffing in the Autonomous Republics of the Caucasus in the Middle 1980s', *Central Asian Survey*, 12, 3 (1993), pp. 347–64.

[28] Yaacov Ro'i, *Islam in the Soviet Union: From World War II to Gorbachev* (London: Hurst, 2000).

of the Chechens married according to Muslim rituals, 99 per cent of the dead were given religious funerals, and 98 per cent circumcised their sons.[29] Religious holidays were celebrated *en masse*—in 1959, for example, 'over 44,000 beasts were slaughtered on *Qurban Bayram* (*'Id al-Adha*), as against a figure of less than 30,000 slaughtered for meat consumption in two regular months', while during the *Uraz Bayram* (*'Id al-Fitr*) 'no work was done in many *kolkhozes* and *sovkhozes* for three or four days' and 'so many pupils failed to attend school that in some places classes were called off.'[30] In the late 1960s in two *raions* 80 per cent of the pupils fasted during Ramadan 'from three to six days and missed school into the bargain', while surveys made in a few schools in the early 1970s 'revealed that no less than 40–50 per cent of the pupils were believers'.[31]

In 1966 the Chechen-Ingush *oblast* party conference was told:

> The mysterious shortcoming in the struggle against survivals and prejudices of the past is passivity on the part of the party and Soviet *aktiv*, connivance, softness and even personal participation by certain leading comrades in religious rites. In some places in *raions* of Checheno-Ingushetia there are still cases of polygamy,[32] forcing women into marriage, kidnapping of girls, encouragement of bride-money, and other feudal survivals.[33] We must create circumstances of intolerance toward these shameful phenomena.[34]

Indeed, Soviet documents reveal that already after the return of the deportees 'the local organs of government seemed to identify totally with the believer population.' In one case both the first and second *raikom* secretaries refused to speak at a citizens' meeting against a number of 'parasites', including several 'illegal' Muslim preachers.

---

[29] Ibid., pp. 81–2.

[30] Ibid., pp. 495, 501 respectively.

[31] Ibid., pp. 478, 98 respectively.

[32] 'In 1953 what was described as a partial enquiry revealed 800 instances of polygamy, some of the men concerned having as many as five wives.' (Ibid., p. 539.) According to an article published in *Groznenskii Rabochii*, 31 January 1958, 'There had been a revival of polygamy—one man being mentioned as having five wives. This may, as Kolarz has suggested, reflect the extent of the number of Chechen males to have perished—just as in Paraguay, after the wars of the dictator Lopez that had almost exterminated the male population, polygamy had to be introduced.' Conquest (note 7), p. 155.

[33] And see above, chapter 11, note 23.

[34] *Partiinaia Zhizn*, 6 March 1966, quoted in Conquest (note 7), p. 157.

In another, the deputy chairman of the republican council of ministers, who 'bravely suggested at the *obkom* to bring pigs to those places where Muslims met for prayers so "they will never gather there again"', refused 'to speak before the local population on the unjustifiability and harmfulness of Islamic "vestiges"'.[35] In every *raion*, Soviet reports stated,

...private homes were given over to *murids* to use for clandestine prayer-meetings. The *raiispolkoms* knew this but neither provided the central authorities with any information whatsoever of goings-on nor conducted any struggle of their own against violations of the law. Some *selsovet* chairmen consciously endeavoured to conceal the true state of affairs in their localities.[36]

A report by the KGB chairman to the CC of the CPSU on 30 April 1966 noted an increase in 'nationalistic and chauvinistic manifestations' and in 'cases of inter-ethnic dissent which frequently grew into group incidents and excesses'.[37] Among the causes behind this phenomenon, it was stated, were 'the harmful activity of "people of the older generation"', 'religious and clan memories' and 'individual [religious] authorities' who 'preach hatred to the "unbelievers"', prophesy the destruction of Soviet power, exert harmful influence on believers, incite fanaticism, and attempt to preserve and support obsolete traditions and morals.'[38] No less significant, Chechens and Ingush occupied, as they had during Tsarist rule, the prime place in violent crime. According to a report by the Interior Minister of the USSR on 7 May 1971, 'for a long time criminal gangs from among the Chechens and Ingush have continued to operate in the territories of Checheno-Ingushetia, North Ossetia, Daghestan, Kazakhstan and Kirgizia. In a number of regions they have carried out robberies of banks, cash boxes and stores as well as terrorizing the population and stealing livestock.'[39]

---

[35] Ro'i (note 28), p. 663.
[36] Ibid., p. 647.
[37] Tishkov (note 10), 194–5. According to official reports sixteen 'group clashes' took place in 1965, resulting in 185 'severe bodily injuries', sixteen of them 'fatal'. During fourteen weeks in 1966 twenty-six murders and sixty 'severe physical injuries were recorded' (ibid., p. 195). And cf. Tishkov (note 2), pp. 41–4.
[38] Tishkov (note 10), p. 195.
[39] Ibid., p. 196.

Clearly 'the Chechens were un–co–operative, addicted to ideological, social and economic practices disliked by the regime, and in
general still possessed by a desire not to be under their present rulers.'[40] However, this does not mean that they resisted modernisation
per se. The Chechen attitude to the Soviet campaigns was perhaps
best phrased by a *kolkhoznik* who insisted 'there was nothing negative in religion's struggle for the preservation of old traditions and
customs: "If we repudiate old traditions, how will the Chechen
nation's specificity be given expression?"'[41] Indeed, recent studies
dismiss the bipolar, black–and–white contraposition of traditional-
ism and modernity. They reject the ahistorical view of tradition as
something static and unchanging and convincingly demonstrate
that both traditional and modern elements converge in various forms
and combinations peculiar to each society.[42] Also, in the case of the
Chechens modern and Soviet elements were combined with traditional ones. As with other peoples, the Chechens adopted modern,
Soviet and Russian elements compatible with their traditions, while
traditional elements had to adapt to the realities of the modern
world in its Soviet version.

At the forefront of the struggle against 'Sovietisation' were the
Sufi *ta'ifas,* first and foremost the various branches of the Qadiriyya.
The 'deportation' propelled the Sufi *ta'ifas* into the centre of the
Chechens' national life and identity, a process that continued to
gather momentum after 'rehabilitation'. Since deportation, explained
a Western expert on Islam in the Soviet Union,

...the social structure of the Chechens and Ingush has been deeply modified. The clan system in particular, which had been before 1943 the very
basis of Chechen and Ingush communities, has been, if not completely
destroyed, at least seriously disturbed. Moreover, during the deportation all
the mosques in the Chechen-Ingush republic had been destroyed. More
than ever before, the *tariqa*, especially the Qadiriyya, appeared as the only

---

[40] Conquest (note 7), p. 157.

[41] Ro'i (note 28), pp. 704–5.

[42] See, for example, Vladimir (Ze'ev) Khanin, 'Clientelism, Corruption and Struggle for Power in Central Asia: The Case of Kyrgyzstan' in Moshe Gammer (ed.),
The Caspian: vol. 1: *A Re-Emerging Region* (London: Routledge, 2004), pp. 181–
202, and Paul Georg Geiss, 'The Problems of Political Order in Contemporary
Kazakhstan and Turkmenistan' in ibid., pp. 203–27.

centre around which the surviving Mountaineers could organize their national and spiritual life.[43]

In the absence of religious life they did indeed fill the vacuum. To the Sufi adepts, who had always been a minority within the population,[44] the *dhikr* 'formed an unbreakable shield' around their 'sense of identity and self-confidence' and 'reinforced' their 'feelings of ethnic brotherhood and religious purity'.[45] But after deportation, with no 'official' mosque open until 1987,[46] the *ziyarts* and other places used by the Sufis for prayer and *dhikr* ceremonies[47] provided people with almost the only opportunity to worship. Among the many old and new *ziyarts*[48] the most popular were the house of Kunta Hajji in Eliskhan-Yurt and his mother's tomb in Hajji-Aul:

One of the very first reports from the republic related that pilgrims visited it [Hajji-Aul] every week in order to pray, the ceremony entailing collective incantation and stamping of feet. Here, too, although the tomb was officially closed off by the local authorities in the early 1960s, pilgrimages continued; in 1962 'fanatics' broke the lock and no less than 500 pilgrims gathered to celebrate the *Mavlud* [*Mawlid*]. Every year in the month of

---

[43] Bennigsen, 'The Qadiriyyah (Kunta Hajji) Tariqah in North-East Caucasus: 1850–1987', *Islamic Culture*, LXII, 2–3 (April–July 1988), p. 72.

[44] In the late 1960s 300 Sufi groups were reported in the Chechen-Ingush ASSR with a membership of 15,000 and more than 500 Mullahs, Tamadas and Turkhs Ro'i (note 28), p. 92.

[45] Smith (note 1), p. 40.

[46] In the Chechen-Ingush ASSR 'in the period following the return of the deportees as of 1957, three churches operated officially and, until 1978, not a single Mosque. [...] Consequently, it was hardly surprising that the 200 or so "religious authorities", who in the early years after the return directed their activity to the reconstruction of mosques that prior to the deportation had existed in every *aul*, were reportedly inciting national animosity and dissension in the process. [...] According to all accounts, the issue there became a national, not just a religious, one, questions being posed at public lectures and written and oral statements put out by intelligentsia and young people calling on the authorities to open mosques or to prohibit the activities of Christian religious societies. The editor of a local Komsomol paper received a letter asking why a church operated in the centre of Groznyi, whereas mosques constructed with the miserable kopecks of old people were pulled down. Was this not reminiscent of the Russian colonisation of the Chechen and Ingush in the previous century?' (Ro'i (note 28), pp. 704–5)

[47] According to Soviet reports, Sufis used structures for funeral equipment in cemeteries for prayer (ibid., p. 301).

[48] For new *ziyarts* in Chechnya see ibid. p. 374.

May thousands of pilgrims came here not only from the Chechen-Ingush ASSR, but also from Daghestan, North Ossetia and Georgia. In 1970 their number was reportedly about 10,000 and they came in a variety of vehicles, from tour buses to racing cars, and even a helicopter. (The appearance of pilgrims descending from the sky caused no little sensation.)[49]

The activity of the *ta'ifas* was not limited to prayer. They ran a clandestine education system, in which children and adults were taught the essentials of Islam, prayer, the Qur'an and some Arabic. They established their own *samizdats, magnitizdats* and even a 'primitive radio network', which distributed underground Qur'ans, religious literature in Arabic, instruction books in Russian and Chechen, and recordings of *dhikr* ceremonies, sermons, recitation of the Qur'an etc.[50] Furthermore, the *ta'ifas* engaged in an active propaganda war against state sponsored atheism, in which they attacked verbally, and sometimes even physically, Chechen 'traitors' who came out against religion.[51] According to a Soviet report, the *ta'ifas* were 'engaged in instigating national [i.e. anti-Russian] hatred and disagreements and in deflecting young people from communist influences and participation in public life.'[52]

More important, they successfully established what might be termed 'parallel communities' with a flourishing parallel (in Soviet vernacular, 'left') economy, which maintained as little contact as possible with the Soviet state, society and economy. In large parts of the Chechen-Ingush ASSR (as well as in neighbouring republics) the Sufi sheikhs and elders regulated life according to *shari'a* and the *'adat*, not the Soviet legal system. In the words of an English ethnographer, 'there seemed to be three legal systems in force—Soviet law, local Party extortion and the old customary law.'[53]

Thus the *ta'ifas* had become an unprecedented challenge: they were both an alternative to the Soviet system, and a constant reminder of its failure, in every sphere of life. No wonder the authorities reacted with repeated and escalating campaigns (the repetition

---

[49] Ibid.
[50] Ibid., p. 421.
[51] For examples see ibid., p. 415.
[52] Ibid., p. 414.
[53] Robert Chenciner, *Daghestan: Tradition and Survival* (London: Curzon Press, 1997), p. 237. And cf. Anna Zelkina, 'Islam and Politics in the North Caucasus', *Religion, State and Society*, 21, 1 (1993), p. 120.

of which *ipso facto* proved their failure) against the 'vestiges of religion and clericalism' and of 'chauvinistic bourgeois nationalism'. Sufis were arrested for a variety of offences such as 'hostile' or 'reactionary propaganda', 'parasitism', 'economic sabotage', 'banditism' and 'terrorism', and were given severe sentences.[54] But the greatest challenge to the Soviet authorities—and in the long run probably the most important process—was what the Soviets termed the 'convergence of religion and nationalism'. In other words, the Qadiriyya became the focus and the standard-bearer of national identity. In practical terms both sides had a lot to gain: the national movement obtained an organisational infrastructure and the Qadiriyya won a clear and modern political goal, which it had lacked throughout its resistance to Soviet rule. In a broader sense the alliance between religion and nationalism is part of a process shared by many other societies, Muslim and non-Muslim alike.[55]

The erosion of the clan system is part of modernisation, which many, if not all, traditional societies have experienced. For the Chechens the deportation may have accelerated it, but was neither its cause nor its starting-point. As in many similar Islamic societies, where Sufi *ta'ifas* had been an integral part of the community long before modernisation, they have become alternative foci of group identification. Moreover, for such societies going through the pains of modernisation the *ta'ifas* have become alternative, non-Western (in this case non-Soviet) agents of modernisation. In terms of political modernisation they have become the agents of modern nationalism. Thus the *ta'ifas* provided both the organisational and the conceptual/attitudinal framework for the Chechen dominance of their republic. The expression of this dominance was in the main 'unofficial, informal and in large part illegal'.[56] This suited both the Chechens and the Soviet authorities. Like other citizens of the Soviet Union, and perhaps more so, the Chechens lived in two parallel worlds—the 'official' one of the regime's public reports and statistics and the 'real' one of a 'left' economy and society. Thus in the 'official' world the economic situation of the Chechens in 1990 was described as 'very bad', with '80 per cent' of the Chechen pop-

---

[54] For examples see Ro'i (note 28), pp. 349–50, 580.

[55] Irish and Polish nationalisms are two prominent European examples.

[56] Lieven (note 3), p. 322. And cf. Tishkov (note 2), pp. 40–2.

ulation 'living below the official Soviet poverty line'. Housing was 'still in critically short supply' and 'severe unemployment' forced many 'to leave their own republic to seek summer agricultural employment in Siberia and other parts of the Soviet Union, a second exile without kin and in a foreign language environment.'[57] In the 'real' world things were different:

Officially, there used to be 200,000 unemployed Chechens before 1990. In fact, all of us were working, but none of us was registered with the authorities. We never lived from the state. We always lived on the side, unofficially. We made money, and we also always helped each other in time of need. That is why other peoples hate us so much, but that is why we are a strong people, and why so far we have been able to beat this Russian blockade, for example.[58]

However, there was a major drawback to the 'unofficial, informal and in large part illegal' nature of this Chechen dominance of their republic. No Chechen political or economic élites (other than a few individuals) capable of running the country were created. The detrimental consequences of this lack of experienced élites would be revealed in the post-Soviet period.

---

[57] Helsinki Watch report, p. 24. 'Soviet official statistics showed Chechnya close to the bottom of the list of Russian autonomous republics and regions in most socio-economic and educational indicators—though as in Georgia and elsewhere, this of course ignored the huge unofficial, black market sources of income. What undoubtedly has been of great importance however—and could be a great danger in nature, not just to Russia, but to Chechen governments themselves—is that the high birthrate produced large numbers of unemployed young men. [...] In the 1970s, an estimated 25,000 young men left Chechnya for other regions each spring to work as part-time labour, mostly in building.' (Lieven, *Chechnya*, p. 57).

[58] Shamil Basayev, quoted in ibid., p. 36.

Part V POST-SOVIET DISORDER

Do you know the land where tears are shed?
Where smoke scatters over the houses?
Where aeroplanes overhead are loaded with bombs?
Where these bombs fall on the people's heads?
This land is called Chechnya.

There the houses lie in ruins,
There war thunders twinkle,
There both day and night are hell,
There it is cold, people are starving.
This land is called Chechnya.

(Khizar Ahmadov[1])

Well, two-headed eagle,
Into what have you flown
In a new shameful fame
Into the Chechen snow-storm?

There, in the heights
The eagle's two heads
Will not look into each other's eyes.
They are full of shame and dread.

High above the ruins and ashes
Your feathers were ripped
Because you had to make an infamous choice
Between shame and dread.

(Yevgenii Yevtushenko[2])

---

[1] Khizar Ahmadov, quoted in L. Usmanov, *Nepokorennaia Chechnia* (Moscow: Izdatel'skii dom Parus, 1997), p. 168.
[2] Yevgenii Yevtushenko, 'Mezhdu stydom i strakhom', December 1994.

15

FROM CHECHEN REVOLUTION
TO *JIHAD*

As in the rest of the periphery of the Soviet Union, Gorbachev's policies of '*glasnost*' and '*perestroika*' reached the Chechen-Ingush ASSR after a few years' delay. By the end of 1988 a 'Chechen-Ingush Popular Front in Support of Perestroika' (Checheno-Ingushskii Narodnyi Front Sodeistviia Perestroike; ChINFSP) was founded.[3] Like similar 'Popular Fronts' all over the Soviet Union, the ChINFSP's membership came mainly from the *intelligentsiia*, and included a considerable number of local Russians. The front's aims were moderate: it came out strongly against plans to build a biochemical plant in Gudermes; it demanded religious freedom and protection for the Chechen and Ingush languages and culture; it insisted on the commemoration of the deportation and on full rehabilitation of the deportees and compensation for them; and finally it demanded an end to the use of politically dictated historical formulae, like the one claiming that the Chechens and Ingush 'joined' Russia 'voluntarily'.[4]

The protests organised by the ChINFSP were supported by Chechen party officials and KGB and *militsiia* officers who wanted a Chechen appointed First Secretary of the *obkom*. Indeed Doku Zavgayev, a former *kolkhoz* chairman who had risen to become a member of the *obkom*, soon became the first Chechen to be appointed First Secretary since the reinstatement of the Chechen-Ingush ASSR. Using the continuing protests against unpopular officials and ethnic Russians, Zavgayev replaced them with his own men.

---

[3] For its charter and programme see *Spravedlivost'*, 1 (January 1989).

[4] Ibid. For the formula, see L. R. Tillet, *The Great Friendship: Soviet Historians on the Non-Russian Nationalities* (Chapel Hill: University of North Carolina Press, 2004).

Furthermore, he acquired 'considerable control' over the ChINFSP, which then became a major cause of its collapse.

In November 1990 more radical members of the ChINFSP and nationalist elements, who had not entered politics before, established the All-National Congress of the Chechen People (Obshchenatsional'nyi Kongress Chechnskogo Naroda; OKChN). Among the major instigators and leaders of the new movement was Zelimkhan Yandarbiyev, a nationalist poet and ideologue and leader of the Bart (Harmony) Party, which in 1990 was renamed the 'Vaynakh Democratic Party'. Yandarbiyev was among the very first to come out publicly against Zavgayev's government and be arrested. The OKChN elected Major-General Dudayev chairman of its EC and commander of its 'national guard'.

Johar Dudayev was born in January 1944, just before the deportation. He spent his first seven years with his family in Kazakhstan, and returning with them to Chechnya in 1957, he soon left to study at the military flying school in Tambov. Between 1966 and 1990 he served in the Soviet air force. He was the first Chechen to reach the rank of major-general, and commanded a division of strategic bombers stationed in Tartu in Estonia, the targets of which were in Britain. In this capacity he prevented Soviet military intervention against Estonian demonstrators.

The OKChN was more nationalist and radical than the ChINFSP, at least on two counts: first, it demanded that the Chechen-Ingush ASSR become an SSR (that is, a fully fledged Union republic equal to and not part of the RSFSR). Second—and more important—it did not recognise the existing Soviet authorities of the republic. Thus the OKChN called for the dissolution of the Supreme Soviet of the Chechen-Ingush ASSR, elected in 1990, and for new and free elections. In reaction Zavgayev banned all opposition activity, arrested some of the OKChN's leaders and curbed opposition propaganda and meetings. The OKChN had to carry on its activities outside the Chechen-Ingush ASSR, mainly in the Baltic republics.[5]

The anti-Gorbachev putsch of 19 August 1991, which proved to be the first step towards the dissolution of the Soviet Union, turned the tables on Zavgayev. Like many other Communist 'bosses' from the periphery, he remained (wisely from his point of view) uncom-

[5] For a somewhat different description of events, see V. A. Tishkov, *Chechnya: Life in a War-Torn Society*, Berkeley: University of California Press, 1969, pp. 57–60.

mitted until it was clear that the putsch had failed. Then he denounced the putschists. However, it was too late. While Zavgayev became 'conspicuous by his silence',[6] Dudayev spoke out on the first day of the putsch, denouncing it as 'criminal' and calling for a mass movement of resistance. He then denounced the government of the Chechen-Ingush ASSR for supporting the putsch and demanded its resignation, the dissolution of the republic's Supreme Soviet, and the transfer of power to the EC of the OKChN.

A general strike was proclaimed by the OKChN, coupled with a mass *miting* (non-stop demonstration) in the central square of Groznyi which went on for several weeks, ignoring the state of emergency proclaimed by Zavgayev.[7] On 22 August 'the demonstrators seized the Television building and Dudayev went on the air to proclaim "the Chechen Revolution".'[8] Zavgayev's reaction was constrained by Yeltsin and Khasbulatov, then still partners, who regarded Dudayev and the OKChN as allies in 'getting rid of the remaining pro-Gorbachev elements in the administration'. Thus 'presumably on their orders ... the highest Chechen within the Russian administration, Police Major-General (and RSFSR parliamentary Deputy) Aslanbek Aslakhanov, visited Groznyi at the end of August [and] gave a strong warning to Zavgayev not to use force to crush the protests.'[9]

On 6 September 1991 the National Guard (whose ranks had swelled with released criminals) stormed the Supreme Soviet headquarters, and during this action the Russian head of the Groznyi *gorkom* either fell or was pushed out of a window to his death; he seems to have been the only casualty of 'the Chechen Revolution'. Later, when circumstances changed, Yeltsin would accuse Dudayev of seizing power by an 'illegal coup d'état'; however, at the time he

---

[6] S. Smith, *Allah's Mountains: Politics and War in the Russian Caucasus* (London: I. B. Tauris, 1998), p. 126.

[7] See Tishkov (note 5), pp. 60–3. The most detailed contemporary accounts of the events in Groznyi are to be found in *Komsomol'skaia Pravda*, which had a team of correspondents there and published their reports daily.

[8] Smith (note 6), p. 126; Jabrail Gakayev, 'Put' k chechnskoi revoliutsii' in Dmitrii Furman (ed.), *Rossiia i Chechnia. Obschestva i gosudarstva* (Moscow: Sakharov Foundation, 1999); Georgii Derluguian, 'Chechnskaia revoliutsiia i chechenskaia istoriia' in ibid., pp. 197–222.

[9] A. Lieven, *Chechnya: Tombstone of Russian Power* (New Haven: Yale University Press, 1998), p. 60.

put pressure on Zavgayev to quit and on the Supreme Soviet of the Chechen-Ingush ASSR to dissolve. On 15 September the latter held its last session in Groznyi, surrounded by the National Guard. It voted to accept Zavgayev's resignation and to dissolve itself. Power was officially transferred to a provisional supreme council headed by a neutral personality—Professor Huseyn Ahmadov. However, Dudayev and his men 'never allowed Ahmadov to assume even the appearance of power. On 5 October the National Guard dissolved the provisional council and occupied its building.'[10] The negative reactions in Moscow—expressed by various spokesmen, Parliament and, finally, Yeltsin himself—only served to increase Dudayev's popularity and strengthen his position.

On 27 October presidential and parliamentary elections were held in Chechnya in which Dudayev won 90 per cent of the vote[11] and the nationalists captured all the parliamentary seats. Despite allegations of 'numerous irregularities, including intimidation of the local Russian population', 'the results seem to have reflected fairly enough the Chechen national mood at that time.'[12] On 2 November 1991 (that is, almost two months before the official dissolution of the Soviet Union) the newly-elected parliament held its inaugural session, in which the full independence of 'the Chechen Republic of Ichkeria' (*Noxciyin Respublika Noxciyico* in Chechen; *Chechenskaia Respublia Ichkeriia* in Russian) was declared[13] and Dudayev was sworn in on the Qur'an as its first president.

In response to the Chechen declaration of independence Yeltsin declared on 8 November a state of emergency in Chechnya, and threatened to restore order by force. Indeed two days later, on 10 November, 600 Interior Ministry troops landed at the airport of Groznyi, where they were surrounded by vastly larger numbers of the National Guard and armed civilians.[14] Yeltsin's moves met with

[10] Ibid., p. 61.

[11] Out of 638,608 eligible voters 458,144 (71.74 per cent) cast their vote, of whom 412,671 (90 per cent of the votes, 64.62 per cent of the electorate) voted for Dudayev.

[12] Lieven (note 9), p. 63.

[13] On 15 September 1991, when it had become clear that the OKChN was aiming at Chechen independence, an Ingush congress declared Ingushetia a separate Autonomous Republic *within* the Russian Federation. This was formalised by the Ingush parliament several months later.

[14] Yeltsin could not use the (still) Soviet Army because it was under the command of Gorbachev.

strong criticism from both Gorbachev, then still President of the Soviet Union, and the Supreme Soviet of the RSFSR, which on 11 November annulled the state of emergency. In the first of many changes of direction over Chechnya, Yeltsin backed off. An agreement was reached with the Chechens, whereby the Interior Ministry troops were escorted out of Chechnya by the Chechen National Guard. By June 1992 all (ex-)Soviet forces had left Chechnya, leaving a great part of their arms and equipment to the Chechens.[15] The 'Chechen Revolution' had won its first battle, but was far from winning the war. Russia was not ready to accept Chechen independence, and in the Nadterechnyi *raion* (Zavgayev's native district over which he retained control) Zavgayev and his comrades started to organise an armed opposition. The countdown to the first Russo-Chechen war of 1994–6 had started.[16]

The events of the 1990s and the turn of the millennium have been narrated and recounted again and again,[17] and there is there-

[15] According to the report of the Duma (Russian Parliament's Lower House) commission of investigation into the Chechen war, chaired by Stanislav Govorukhin, the Chechens either seized or were given in those months 42 tanks, 56 armoured personnel carriers, 139 artillery systems and 24,737 automatic weapons (Lieven (note 9), pp. 64–5).

[16] For a concise analysis, see Anatoly Khazanov, 'A Last-Minute Postscript: The Chechen Crisis (as of May 21, 1995)' in Anatoly Khazanov, *After the USSR: Ethnicity, Nationalism and Politics in the Commonwealth of Independent States* (Madison: University of Wisconsin Press, 1995), pp. 212–29.

[17] The most detailed study of the events and origins of the first Russo–Chechen war is Tracey C. German, *Russia's Chechen War* (London: Routledge Curzon, 2003). For an interesting analysis by a senior Russian scholar and politician of the war's origins, see V. A. Tishkov, *The Mind Aflame: Ethnicity, Nationalism and Conflict in and after the Soviet Union* (London: Sage, 1997), pp. 198–227, and *Chechnya* (note 5), pp. 63–74. The first war was described both in journalistic and academic publications. In addition to the books quoted here, the following sample (in English only) should be mentioned: John B. Dunlop, *Russia Confronts Chechnya: Roots of a Separatist Conflict* (Cambridge University Press, 1998); Reza Shah-Kazemi, *Crisis in Chechnia: Russian Imperialism, Chechen Nationalism, Militant Sufism* (London: Islamic World Report, 1995); Carlotta Gall and Thomas de Waal, *Chechnya: Calamity in the Caucasus* (New York University Press, 1998); Lena Jonson and Murad Esenov (eds), *Chechnya: the International Community and Strategies for Peace and Stability* (Stockholm: Swedish Institute of International Affairs, 2000). The inter-war period and the second Russo-Chechen war have so far been described only in accounts by journalists and human rights organisations. For example: Anne Nivat, *Chienne de Guerre: a Woman Reporter Behind the Lines of the War in Chechnya* (New York: Public Affairs, 2001); Anna Politkovskaya,

fore no need to repeat them in detail here. In many ways Chechnya under Dudayev shared the experiences of the rest of the former Soviet Union (FSU): a deteriorating economy and standard of living; collapsing state services; massive corruption and creeping 'mafia-isation' of large political, economic and social sectors; an influx of Chechens from other parts of the FSU and emigration of Russians; and a political power struggle to shape the new regime, the climax of which was the confrontation between parliament and president. Like Yeltsin in Russia and Akayev in Kyrgyzstan, Dudayev also used tanks to disperse a defiant parliament.[18]

Yet Chechnya between 1992 and 1994 was also an anomaly. The issue of sovereignty had not been solved—Moscow neither recognised Chechnya's independence nor made a serious effort to re-annex it—and this fact had several consequences. The first was that Ichkeria became a 'grey zone', a no-man's-land, and thus a paradise and haven for smugglers and other criminal elements, though far from the 'criminal state' of Russian propaganda. In fact, if Chechnya was criminal, Russia was its partner. Not only was the official economic blockade on Chechnya a 'virtual' one—Daghestan, Ingushetia and the Stavropol *krai* ignored it—but elements in the Russian establishment, not merely the underworld, were full partners in the uninterrupted export of oil, the continuing flights of Aeroflot, the sale of weapons to Chechnya, and so on.

Second, although Dudayev derived some benefits from Moscow's hostility and his claims of its subversion of his authority, on the whole Moscow's non-recognition denied him legitimacy and support and thus encouraged the growing opposition to his regime.

Third, Moscow indeed tried to get rid of Dudayev and his regime, and the widening circles that became increasingly alienated from him encouraged the Kremlin. Eventually the efforts deteriorated into

---

A Dirty War: A Russian Reporter in Chechnya (London: Harvill Press, 2001); Human Rights Watch, *Russia/Chechnya: the "Dirty War" in Chechnya: Forced Disappearances, Torture, and Summary Executions* (New York: Human Rights Watch, 2001); Human Rights Watch, *Russia: Last Seen: Continued "Disappearances" in Chechnya* (New York: Human Rights Watch, 2002). See also the special issue dedicated to Chechnya of *Central Asian Survey*, 22, 4 (December 2003). For a study emphasising the oil factor in the conflict, see Sanobar Shematova, 'The War for Chechen Oil', *Capitalism, Nature, Socialism*, 14, 1 (March 2003).

[18] See Taymaz Abubakarov, 'Mezhdu avtoritarnostiu i anarkhiei (Politicheskie dilemmy prezidenta Dudayeva)' in D. Furman (ed.), *Rossiia i Chechnia* (note 8).

full-scale war. 'The immediate response of the Russian government' to Chechnya's declaration of independence, wrote a Western researcher,

...was to crush the rebellion with armed force, but owing to the political chaos that accompanied the break-up of the USSR and the opposition of the military establishment, the Chechen Republic was not invaded in 1991. In the years that followed, the Russian government (in collusion with various opposition groups) tried to de-stabilize Dudayev's regime through covert operations in an attempt to restore Moscow's authority in the republic. As the initial attempts failed, Russia increased its military role in the secret operations and began to deploy Russian servicemen and 'mercenaries' and supply heavy equipment to the opposition forces in an effort to shift the balance in the republic. Altogether five covert operations against Dudayev's regime were orchestrated by the Federal Counter Intelligence Service. The battle for Groznyi was *the unintended consequence* of one such operation [emphasis added].[19]

And yet the answer to the question whether the first Russo-Chechen war was inevitable is necessarily a negative one. To start with, the Chechens' definition of independence (this included members of the OKChN leadership) was a 'negative' one. In other words, to them independence meant being left alone, living no more under the *diktat* of the 'godless' (*bezbozhniki*) Soviet authorities. None of them had a 'positive' definition of the independence they had declared. When asked how they envisioned their future relations with Russia, the answer was always 'as they used to be'. No one thought in terms of border control, visas, a separate currency etc.[20] Moscow, for its part, was not averse to a compromise as long as Chechnya would remain a member ('subject'—*sub'ekt*—in Russian legal terminology) of the Russian Federation. 'Creative diplomacy' (to borrow a phrase of Kissinger) could have reached such a compromise. Tatarstan is an example.[21]

---

[19] Pontus Siren, 'The Battle for Grozny: The Russian Invasion of Chechnia, December 1994–December 1996' in Ben Fowkes (ed.), *Russia and Chechnia: The Permanent Crisis: Essays on Russo-Chechen Relations* (London: Macmillan, 1998), p. 96.

[20] This was true in May 1992. Later an attempt was made and immediately abandoned to introduce a Chechen currency. For Chechen separatism, see German, *Russia's Chechen War*, and Viktor Kogan Iasnyi and Diana Zisserman-Brodsky, 'Chechen Separatism' in Metta Spencer (ed.), *Separatism, Democracy and Disintegration* (Lanham, MD: Rowman and Littlefield, 1998), pp. 205–26.

[21] On 15 February 1994 a treaty was signed between Tatarstan and the Russian

The failure to reach a compromise is usually explained by the conflict between Yeltsin's and Dudayev's clashing personalities. Dudayev's weakness, arrogance and lack of tact (and of political experience) soon alienated not only Moscow, but also most Chechens—including many of his closest erstwhile allies. According to a Western journalist,

Dudayev, with his macho fantasies and total disregard for democracy, bore a particular guilt for what was about to happen. When there were chances for negotiations, he baited the Russian bear; when compromise might have kept peace, he threatened war. He began his rule with a threat, in November 1992, to blow up Russian nuclear power stations, and on the eve of war in December 1994 he threatened to kill prisoners, and his foreign minister repeated the threat about nuclear stations. A showdown, to Dudayev, was a self-fulfilling prophecy.[22]

Yeltsin's weakness, vanity and 'ruthless determination to keep power' resulted in erratic changes of policy (which, in turn, confused the Chechen leadership) and a refusal to meet Dudayev personally because of his insults. These personal aspects added to the structural causes of the failure to reach a compromise. On the Russian side the zigzagging policies were not merely the result of Yeltsin's weakness. The dissolution of the Soviet Union left post-Soviet Russia weakened territorially and demographically, in the throes of an economic crisis and, most important, in a state of disorientation. Russia was left without a clear vision of itself and of its place in the world and had to find a new definition of itself, its borders, its relationship with its neighbours and with the rest of the world, its interests and aims, and its policies. And while this painful process was (and perhaps still is) going on, numerous state agencies and various levels within each of them defined and carried out their own policies. An

---

Federation, which gave Tatarstan a special status compared to, and more powers than, any other 'subject' of the Federation. For the text of the treaty, see Aleksandr Arinin and Mikhail N. Guboglo (eds), *Federalizm vlasti i vlast' federalizma* (Moscow: Intel Telsh, 1997), pp. 247–52. For interpretations, see Oktay F. Tanrisever, 'The Impact of the 1994 Russian-Tatar Power-Sharing Treaty on the Post-Soviet Tatar National Identity', *Slovo*, 13, 1 (2001), pp. 43–60; B. L. Zheleznov, *Pravovoi status Respubliki Tatarstan* (Kazan: Tatarskoe Knizhnoe Izdatel'stvo, 1996).

[22] Smith (note 6), p. 142. For a detailed analysis of Dudayev and his role, see Tishkov (note 5), pp. 77–89.

inconsistent policy is the worst possible policy. In the case of Che-chnya, the indecision between reaching a compromise with the Dudayev regime and trying to replace it ultimately resulted in war.

No less important was the lack of an experienced political élite on the Chechen side. In many of the post-Soviet states the ex-Communist political élite (based on the Soviet *nomenklatura* and known as *partokratiia* in the post-Soviet space) were replaced by nationalists. The inexperience of the new leadership resulted in considerable damage to their countries, and they were sooner or later replaced by the *partokratiia*. This did not happen in Chechnya because there was no Chechen *partokratiia*. The consequences of the half-hearted rehabilitation combined with Soviet policies of the 1950s–80s, which prevented the formation of a Chechen political élite, now emerged with a vengeance. As well as lacking experience the new Chechen leadership also lacked a common language with the Russian (ex-*nomenklatura*) leadership. Political experience and possession of a common language were two important components of the successful efforts of the *partokratiia* of Tatarstan to reach a compromise with Moscow.

Finally, the growing opposition to Dudayev created a temptation to replace him that Moscow could hardly resist. However, in this the Russian security services seem to have over-played their hand, and once Russian assistance to the opposition became obvious, its lead-ers were marked out as 'traitors' and 'collaborators'. As soon as cap-tured Russian servicemen were displayed on Chechen television, war was almost inevitable, and the Chechens rallied to defend their coun-try and homes. Dudayev was resurrected as the symbol of Chechen independence and resistance. Yet his death from a Russian air-to-ground missile on 21 April 1996 probably removed a major obstacle to negotiations. Indeed his deputy and temporary successor, Yandar-biyev, met Yeltsin in Moscow five weeks later, on 27 May 1996.

However, the major reason for negotiations was the Chechen military victory in the war. In its attempt to capture Groznyi, the Russian army encountered a modern version of the traditional Chechen forest warfare. The attempt to capture the city on New Year's Eve 1995 ended in disaster as two Russian brigades were wiped out, and it took the Russian army three months of intensive fighting and heavy shelling and bombardment to conquer the ruins of Groznyi. But this was only the prelude to the war over each town and each village. The Chechen *boyeviki* (fighters in Russian) did not merely succeed in maintaining resistance,[23] but won the war in at least two respects. First, they achieved their prime objective: to turn the war into a war between equals, and—more important—to portray it as such: state against state and army against army, and not skirmishes between an army and 'gangs of bandits' as Moscow claimed.[24] Second, they succeeded time and again in bursting the balloon of the Russian official version of 'victory', the greatest and most shocking occasion being Shamil Basayev's raid on Budennovsk on 14 June 1996. But all attempts at negotiations were merely tactical manoeuvres to win a respite in the fighting. An agreement was reached only after the final Chechen success—the recapture of Groznyi on 6 August 1996.

The Khasav Yurt agreement of 31 August 1996 (see Appendix 1) and the Moscow peace accord of 12 May 1997 (see Appendix 2) symbolised the Chechen victory, especially as on the latter occasion Yeltsin stated: 'We have signed a peace deal of historic dimensions, putting an end to 400 years of history'[25]—something the Chechen leadership had consistently been insisting on.[26] However, they were also compromises. Both agreements, especially the one signed in Moscow, came close to recognising Chechen independence *de facto*. However, the *de jure* status of Chechnya was left for future negotiations to be concluded within five years, by 31 December 2001. The agreements also stipulated co-operation in various fields and Russian assistance for the reconstruction of Chechnya.

In the presidential elections of 27 January 1997 Aslan (Khalid) Maskhadov won by a large margin over eight other candidates, including the acting president Yandarbiyev.[27] Maskhadov was the real architect and hero of the Chechen victory. Born in Kazakhstan in

---

[23] For a study of the *boyeviki*, see Tishkov (note 5), pp. 90–196.

[24] For a military analysis of the war from this viewpoint see Yagil Henkin, 'Lo Gerila: haMilhamma haChechenit haRishona veTe'oriyot "haMilhama heHadasaha"' (Jerusalem, 2003).

[25] *Monitor*, 3, 94 (13 May 1997).

[26] See, for example, 'Doklad predsedatelia ispolkama obshchenatsional'nogo s'ezda chechenskogo naroda, generala Dzhokhara Dudaeva, g. Groznyi, 8 iiun' 1991 g.', *Bart* (Groznyi), 6 (010), June 1991, p. 3.

[27] Of 513,585 registered voters 407,699 (79.38 per cent) cast their vote. Of these 241,765 (59.3 per cent of the vote and 47 per cent of the electorate) voted for Maskhadov. Lieven (*Chechnya* (note 9), p. 145) gives another figure—64.8 per cent. According to Lieven, Yandarbiyev received only 10.2 per cent of the vote.

1951, he returned with his family to Chechnya in 1958. In 1972 he graduated from the Tbilisi Artillery School and in 1982 from the Kalinin Leningrad Military Academy. He served as an artillery officer in the Soviet Far East, Hungary and the Baltic republics, was considered a brilliant commander by his superiors and admired by his soldiers.[28] In 1992 he retired from the Russian army with the rank of colonel to become First Deputy Chief of Staff of the Chechen Armed Forces; in 1994 he was made Chief of Staff and promoted general. In this capacity Maskhadov proved a brilliant and innovative military leader; the way he conducted the war, and especially the innovative and (until then) unthinkable way he reconquered Groznyi, will for many years to come be the subject of study in military academies worldwide.[29] Now as president of Ichkeria he had to tackle the immense price of the Chechen victory and its consequences.

Of a population of roughly 1,000,000 before the war, between 40,000 and 100,000 perished and some 3–400,000 became refugees,[30] mainly in camps in neighbouring Daghestan and Ingushetia. According to an OSCE diplomat, 'the human and physical toll for such a small place was, proportionally, equivalent to the ghastly Soviet losses during World War II.'[31] Figures for Russian casualties were contradictory. According to a Defence Ministry source, 'who was in a position to know the truth', 5,620 army soldiers were killed and roughly three times that number wounded; the Interior Ministry lost between 1,800 and 2,500 men; the FSB, border guards and other branches of the security forces lost a few hundred more—all in all more than 25,000 killed, wounded and missing in action.[32]

As for the country, it was in ruins. Second World War veterans compared Groznyi to Stalingrad. Many other towns and villages were reduced to rubble and became uninhabitable. 'That first winter of peace', observed a Western journalist, 'brought remembrance ceremonies for the dead, snow falling through smashed roofs, cold winds funnelling across the jagged walls, and ice over fields which

---

[28] Henkin, 'Lo Gerila'.
[29] Ibid.
[30] This number includes the many Russians who left before the war during the Dudayev regime.
[31] Smith (note 6), p. 261.
[32] Ibid., p. 261.

no one crossed for fear of landmines.'[33] These mines prevented cultivation of the land, while other employment was also scarce. Ruined Chechnya desperately needed Russian aid, but it failed to arrive, despite Moscow's promises. The reasons for this failure are a matter of debate. Some observers maintain that it was due to lack of money,[34] others that Russia intended to 'bleed' Chechnya 'to death'.[35] Whatever the reason—it may well have been a combination of both—the results for Chechnya and for Maskhadov were disastrous.

Many of the *boyeviki* found neither houses nor jobs to return to. The young, unmarried ones 'who long ago had cut themselves off entirely from mundane responsibilities, were especially adrift. A few became bodyguards to the warlords or the ministers in the new ruling élite. Others turned to crime or sought more war to fill the gap.'[36] Indeed, in the following couple of years Chechnya would become a dangerous place to visit owing to the spate of kidnappings of foreigners, and Chechens would become 'heavily involved both in bomb attacks and ambushes on Russian forces, and in kidnappings and other criminal activities beyond Chechnya's borders, mainly in Daghestan'.[37] Maskhadov, without Russian aid, was unable to solve the economic problems, rebuild a state structure and maintain order. Rather, he followed Dudayev and accused the FSB (Federal'naia Sluzhba Bezopasnosti—Federal Security Service) in all such incidents, especially kidnappings of foreigners.[38] But his major problem

---

[33] Ibid., p. 260. For life in Chechnya after the war, see Tishkov (note 5), pp. 180–95; Zura Al'tamirova, 'Zhizn' v poslevoennoi Chechne' in Furman (ed.), *Rossiia i Chechnia.*

[34] Lieven (note 8), p. 146.

[35] Smith (note 6), p. 260. In fact, some funds were allocated by Moscow, but were embezzled by Russian and Chechen officials. I am grateful to Anatoly Khazanov for this information.

[36] Ibid., p. 263. For the collapse of social and moral norms, see Tishkov (note 5), pp. 151–63; Zalpa Bersanova, 'Sistema tsennostei sovremennykh chechentsev (po materialam oprpsov)' in Furman (ed.), *Rossiia i Chechnia* (note 8), pp. 223–49.

[37] Lieven (note 9), *Chechnya*, p. 146. And see Tishkov (note 5), pp. 107–26.

[38] Whether he was right or not is irrelevant. However, one cannot ignore information connecting some of the Chechen warlords, who were involved more than others in the 'slave trade', to Russian intelligence services. Furthermore, it may be assumed that a certain instability in Chechnya, as long as it did not slip out of control, was not necessarily against Russia's interests. Indeed, there have been

was inability to control the 'field commanders'—the warlords who had become, more or less, the independent rulers of their own areas during the war. Many, if not all, of them were now unwilling to relinquish their powers and independence. Some of them defied Maskhadov openly, carried out their own policies and were even engaged in the criminal activities referred to above. The most noticeable among them was Shamil Basayev.

Born in 1965 in Vedeno, Basayev started his career very ordinarily. He finished high school, served as a private in the Soviet air force, failed three times to enter the Law Faculty of the Moscow State University, and having been accepted at the Moscow Institute of Agricultural Engineering (Moskovskii Institut Inzhenerov Zemleusrtoistva) was dismissed the following year for poor academic performance. He found work in Moscow and during the 1991 putsch was among the defenders of the 'White House'. His name first came to the world's attention on 9 November 1991 when he was among the hijackers of a TU-154 passenger aircraft flying to Turkey. His career as a war leader started in the 1992–3 war in Abkhazia where he commanded the 'Chechen Battalion'. The battle experience in Abkhazia made Basayev's battalion one of the most efficient Chechen forces in the 1994–6 war, during which he also commanded the central sector, centred on his native Vedeno. His raid on Budennovsk on 14 June 1996 catapulted him to international fame, on to the Russian list of most wanted terrorists and into the Chechen pantheon of super-heroes.

Despite his popularity, Basayev failed to be elected President in January 1997.[39] Although he accused both Maskhadov and Yandarbiyev of election fraud,[40] he joined the Maskhadov administration as Prime Minister, but not for long. Both he and Movladi Udugov—the Information Minister under Dudayev and during the war, another presidential candidate in 1997 and Maskhadov's first Vice-

---

indications that Russian servicemen have been involved in covert operations there—see for example, Igor' L'ianov, 'Ofitserov GRU podozrevaiut v organizatsii teraktov', *Kommersant*, 4 June 1999, p. 1 and reaction to it in Genadii Alekhin and Anatolii Borovikov, 'Sgusili kraski', *Krasnaia Zvezda*, 9 June 1999, p. 1.

[39] According to Lieven (note 9) (p. 145), Basayev came second to Maskhadov with 22.7 per cent of the votes.

[40] The OSCE stated the elections were 'free and fair'.

Premier and Foreign Minister—pursued their own aggressive anti-Russian policy of 'decolonisation' of the Northern Caucasus and especially Daghestan.[41] In June 1998 Basayev resigned and two months later joined the 'Field Commanders' defying Maskhadov, and eventually became their leader. On 9 February 1999 they established a '*Shura*' (Council) chaired by Basayev, which rivalled the authority of Maskhadov.

Whether Moscow had intended to keep its promise and cooperate with Maskhadov, but was disappointed by his inability to control the country, or had from the start seen the agreements as a tactical truce until an opportunity arose to take control of Chechnya again, the anarchy in Chechnya drew the Russians back in. In August and again in September 1999 Basayev (and his partner Khattab) invaded Daghestan to assist their allies there. Moscow, with a new leader now in the Kremlin, reacted with a full-scale military operation, with the intention of taking control of the country, deposing the Maskhadov regime and re-annexing it to the Russian Federation. A major Russian excuse, or perhaps a genuine concern, which triggered the military operation was the Islamisation of Chechnya and the growing strength there of Islamic 'fundamentalists' following what throughout the post-Soviet space was dubbed 'Wahhabism'.[42]

Being Chechen has always *ipso facto* meant being (Sunni) Muslim. Even the most secularised and Westernised nationalists have always regarded Islam as one of the principal components of Chechen

---

[41] Udugov established and led the 'Islamic *Umma* Congress', which officially aimed at 'the creation of a single Islamic nation' and the reinstatement of 'Islam in its previous historical borders' (RIA-Novosti, 24 August 1997). According to Russian media, the 'Islamic *Umma*' also aimed at uniting Daghestan and Chechnya in a 'kind of state emulating Shamil's Imamate' (*Nezavisimaia Gazeta*, 17 September 1997). Basayev, for his part, established and led the 'Congress of the Peoples of Daghestan and Ichkeria', the declared goal of which was to unite 'the Muslim peoples of Daghestan and Chechnya in one free state' and by that achieve 'peace and stability in the region' (ITAR-TASS, 26 April; *Kommersant-Daily*, 28 April 1998). For that purpose the Congress established a 'Peacekeeping Brigade', which in July 1998 conducted manoeuvres near the Daghestani border (Interfax, 6 July 1998). And see also Tishkov (note 5), pp. 196–209; Lema Vakhayev, 'Politicheskie fantazii v sovremennoi Chechnskoi respublike' in Furman (ed.), *Rossiia i Chechnia* (note 8), pp. 324–34.

[42] Tishkov (note 5), pp. 165–79; Sanobar Shermatova, 'Tak nazyvaemye vakhkhabity' in Furman (ed.), *Rossiia i Chechnia* (note 8).

identity, tradition and culture. Furthermore, as mentioned above, the deportation enhanced the Chechens' national consciousness and their negative attitude to Russian/Soviet rule. Islam thus became the antithesis of everything Marxist and Soviet. The Islamic alternatives to the Soviet state and code of law, so deeply engraved in national history and tradition, are the *imama* and the *shari'a* respectively.[43] Therefore it was natural that Dudayev took his oath as President on the Qur'an and that the republic was termed 'Islamic' (with no definition of this term).

The war of 1994–6 strengthened the Islamic dimension of Chechen identity and brought to the fore memories of the Islamic resistance to Russia in the eighteenth and nineteenth centuries. It also became an opportunity to enhance Dudayev's leadership by putting him on an equal footing with past leaders of the *gazavat* and other heroes in the nation's pantheon.[44] Furthermore, Islam proved the strongest rallying call inside Chechnya and more effective than secular ideologies in calling for unity and mobilising support among other North Caucasian nationalities, first and foremost the Daghestanis. In addition, the war was a catalyst for importing ideologies, trends and fashions from the wider Islamic world which, as already mentioned, were commonly labelled in the ex-Soviet Union as 'Wahhabism'.

Originally the 'Wahhabis' arrived in Chechnya during the 1994–6 war as 'volunteers ... from the Arab countries'.[45] Many if not all of them were veterans of the Afghanistan war, where they fought against the Soviets. They were led by Samir Salih 'Abdalla al-Suwaylim who adopted the *nom de guerre* 'Emir Khattab' after the second Caliph, 'Umar ibn al-Khattab. Al-Suwaylim was born in 1969 in Ar'ar, in the north-east of Saudi Arabia, into a well-to-do family. He was described as a brilliant student, who after graduating from secondary school joined a training course given by ARAMCO,

---

[43] The *shari'a* is the only alternative state legal system to the Soviet one, as opposed to the *'adat* which is the traditional tribal law. The *shari'a* was also the legal system of Shamil's Imamate in the nineteenth century.

[44] For further details, see Moshe Gammer, 'Nationalism and History: Rewriting the Chechen National Past' in Bruno Coppieters and Michel Huysseune (eds), *Social Knowledge and Secession* (VUB Brussels University Press, 2002), pp. 117–40.

[45] Ahmad-Hajji Kadyrov, then Chief Mufti of Ichkeria, in *Nezavisimaia Gazeta*, 11 August 1998.

intending to study in the United States. Instead, in 1987 he joined the Arabs fighting the Soviets in Afghanistan. He fought there until 1992, following which he joined the Islamic forces in the civil war in Tajikistan. In 1995 he arrived in Chechnya and during the first Russo-Chechen war was a junior commander of a group of volunteers. After the war he decided to stay, believing 'the fight should not end until the enemies' threat was totally removed'.[46] He married a woman from the village of Karamakhi in Daghestan and established himself in the area of Serzhen Yurt. At the end of April 2002 Russian media reported that Khattab had been killed by the FSB in a special operation.

Being Islamic 'fundamentalists' and in many cases of the strict Saudi-'Wahhabi' background, these volunteers called for the establishment of an Islamic order, social as well as political. Furthermore, they publicly criticised Sufism and the traditional leadership—sanctified, in believers' eyes, by seventy years of Soviet anti-religious persecution—for 'deviations' from 'pure' Islam. They 'endeavoured to teach us', the Chief Mufti complained, 'claiming that we distorted Islam.'[47] Thus the 'Wahhabis' antagonised both the political and the traditional religious leadership and caused resentment and animosity among the adherents of the Sufi sheikhs. Nevertheless, the 'Wahhabis' contributed to the diffusion, legitimation and popularisation of Islamic language in politics and more particularly to demands for an Islamic state (*imama*) based on the *shari'a*. Thus Islam seemed to the war-ravaged people the only answer to the anarchy prevailing in the country. 'People are fed up with the disorder all around them,' explained a professor at the University of Groznyi to a Western reporter. 'They think that introducing the *shari'a* will bring an immediate halt to crime.'[48] Hence practically all presidential candidates in the January 1997 elections pledged to establish 'an Islamic order'. After the elections both Maskhadov and his rivals—Basayev, Udugov, Salman Raduyev (a maverick field commander who after the death of Dudayev had acknowledged no authority) and other 'field commanders'—competed intensely over who was more 'Islamic'. This competition, which started with Maskhadov's

[46] Suwaylim's elder brother, Mansur, to *al-Sharq al-Awsat* (London), 5 May 2002.
[47] Rotar, *Nezavisimaia Gazeta*, 11 August 1998.
[48] Reuters, 20 January 1997.

establishment of the 'Supreme *Shari'a* Court',[49] ended with his imposition of the *shari'a* on 3 February 1999.[50]

The post-war conditions supplied the 'Wahhabis' with ample opportunities to grow in numbers and power. Although initially Chechnya 'proved a less fertile ground for their activities than Daghestan', because the Chechens were 'intoxicated with nationalism',[51] a growing number of young Chechens now found the 'Wahhabis' attractive. These foreigners had money, weapons, battle experience and simple answers to the problems faced by young alienated *boyeviki: jihad*, the (re-)establishment of the Imamate and the enforcement of the *shari'a*. The religious leadership pressed Maskhadov to confront them. 'For a long time', explained the Chief Mufti to a Russian journalist, 'we have tried to reach an amicable agreement with the "Wahhabis". Alas, the dialogue failed.'[52] Indeed, clashes took place in Urus Martan in January 1999,[53] but Maskhadov failed to suppress the 'Wahhabis' who had by now become allied to Basayev and other 'field commanders'.[54]

This seems to have signalled the end of the partnership between the Qadiriyya and the national movement. The Qadiriyya—which in the main had supported Dudayev and later Maskhadov, support

[49] Its rulings were not necessarily according to the *shari'a*. See e.g. Evgenii Krutikov, 'Shariatskogo suda v Chechne net. To, chto proiskhodit, osnovano na "zakony gor"', *Segodnia*, 20 September 1997, pp. 1, 3.

[50] AP, 4 February 1999; RFE/RL *Caucasus Report*, 2, 6, 9 February 1999. What was meant by *shari'a* can be seen from the draft of the new '*shari'a*' constitution. According to the secretary of the state committee for drafting the new constitution, Dolkhan Khozhayev, it 'draws on the Qur'an, the *shari'a*, the *sunna* of the Prophet, Chechen customs and traditions and the constitutions of several Islamic states, including Pakistan, Egypt, Iran and Syria.' (*Nezavisimaia Gazeta*, and *Izvestiia*, 7 May 1999)

[51] Sergei Ivanov and Vakhtang Shelia, 'Talebany idut!', *Kommersant*, 31, 1997 as quoted in Zulfiye Kadir, 'The Rise of Political Islam in Russia' (unpublished paper), p. 6.

[52] *Nezavisimaia Gazeta*, 11 August 1998.

[53] In a press conference on 23 January Maskhadov called it a coup attempt and accused Russia of provoking it (RFE/RL, *Caucasus Report*, 2, 4, 26 January 1999).

[54] For an analysis of the spread of 'Wahhabism' in the Caucasus see Anna Zelkina, 'The "Wahhabis" of the Northern Caucasus vis-à-vis State and Society: The Case of Daghestan' in Moshe Gammer (ed.), *The Caspian Region*, vol. II: *The Caucasus* (London: Routledge, 2004), pp. 146–78. For its appeal to Basayev and others, see Georgi M. Derluguian, 'Che Guevaras in Turbans', *New Left Review*, 237 (September–October 1999), pp. 3–27.

that seems to have secured their electoral victories and in crucial moments had mobilised dozens of thousands of demonstrators into the central square of Groznyi—now changed course. Following the Russian military conquest of the country it, or at least parts of it, seemed to co-operate with the Russian authorities, and Kadyrov became head of the Chechen administration under Moscow. Thus the Russians gained a great advantage. According to a Chechen historian, the great conceptual failure of the Russians in the first Russo-Chechen war was their attempt to play 'divide and rule' with the *te'ips*. These, he argued, were not as strong as they used to be in previous decades. Had the Russians played 'divide and rule' with the Sufi *ta'ifas*, he added, they might have been successful.[55]

Although at the time of this writing the second Russo-Chechen war seems a long way from a conclusion and Moscow's control of Chechnya far from complete, Russia seems to have succeeded in reducing the nationalist element. The resistance to Russia seems more and more to be an Islamic, moreover a 'Wahhabi' one. A journalist who had covered the first war visited Chechnya in the summer of 2003.

Here in the mountains, to an increasing extent, the atmosphere is becoming influenced by radical religious doctrine. […] In other words, 'Wahhabism'—although the *mujahedin* don't like the word—is becoming the dominant ideology, not only of the war, but of peacetime. I ask the traditional journalist's question: 'Why are you here?' In the first war, the answer was no less traditional: 'for independence', they would say, 'for freedom'. The answer meant: we are fighting for our own independent state, separate from Russia—although few of the people who pronounced those words knew what that exactly meant. Today the Chechens in the mountains have a completely different answer.

Dyshna, the 23-year-old Chechen *mujahed*, told [me] why he fights: 'Today, if you bear arms, the main thing is to consider the word of Allah to be above everything else. That is the main thing. After that, there are some other things, such as freeing the people from occupation, from laws we do not need.'

Another fighter, Abdurakhman, put it this way: 'Simply, we want the word of the Prophet and the word of God to be the main arbiter in Chechnya. Today, Allah requires us to establish *shari'a* law. We want this law.'[56]

[55] Private conversation in June 1997.
[56] Jeremy Bransten 'Chechnya: Babitskii Says Rebels Better Armed, Leaning Toward Fundamentalism', RFE/RL, Prague, 14 August 2003.

If this account reflects the real situation in Chechnya and the nationalist elements have been losing ground to the 'Islamists', then a circle in the spiral seems to have been completed: having moved from Islamic resistance to national liberation, Chechens are fighting a 'Holy War' again. This time, however, it is the new, modern, 'fundamentalist' *jihad* of the 'Wahhabis', not the traditional *gazavat*.[57]

---

[57] Although this was written before the assassinations of Kadyrov and Maskhadov (by the 'separatists' and the Russians respectively), the situation in Chechnya seems not to have changed significantly.

POSTSCRIPT

In one of his punch-lines Karl Marx stated that history repeats itself twice: the first time as tragedy and the second time as farce. Winston Churchill, who shared Marx's belief that history repeats itself, differed on a major point: each time history repeats itself, he said, it does so with more catastrophic results. Although Russia adopted Marxism as its dogma in the twentieth century, its history in general and that of Russo-Chechen relations in particular could serve as evidence to support Churchill's thesis. One can easily exchange past events—be they from the eighteenth, the nineteenth or the twentieth century—for contemporary ones. All one has to do is change personal names and dates. The places are the same. The follies are the same. Only the results are far more catastrophic.

Is there a way out of this vicious circle? To a great extent the answer depends on Russia. After all, it is Russia as the great power, neighbour to a small people, that has dictated the events and the agenda for more than three centuries. The Chechens have mainly reacted to Russia's moves and policies, not initiated their own. Russia is at a crossroads and the direction it chooses will affect many issues, including the future of Chechnya and the relationship between them. The magnitude of the choice may perhaps only be compared to two previous junctures in Russian history.

In the late fifteenth century Russia faced a choice comparable to that of Germany three centuries later, between two routes of development, two diametrically opposed structures of state and society. On the one hand was Novgorod—a merchants' republic not unlike the many city-states in Western Europe, which contributed to the republican and (ultimately) democratic tradition in the West. On the other hand was the Muscovite state—an autocracy that had combined the Mongol and Byzantine traditions to make its ruler omnipotent. Moscow won, conquering its rival (just as in Germany

Prussia prevailed over Hanover and eventually swallowed it and all the other independent kingdoms and principalities). The Westernisation or Europeanisation of imperial Russia served to enhance the autocrat's power and control over the populace.

In 1917 Russia again faced such a choice, and again the Muscovite tradition, or model, won with the victory of the Bolsheviks. In the Soviet Union, especially under Stalin, the ruler reached an unprecedented level of control over the life of his subjects. Again, as in Germany, there was nothing inevitable in either choice.[1] The deeds and misdeeds, action and inaction of specific individuals and groups at specific times decided the outcome.

Having completed the 'reunification' of Russia, Moscow's rulers took the title 'Tsar of all the Russias'.[2] From the present juncture one of the roads available to Russia leads once again to becoming 'Russias'—not in the simplistic geographical sense but in the sense of a pluralistic society. If Russia chooses to go down that road, if the Russian state accepts as legitimate the many faces of Russian society rather than trying to impose uniformity; if the populace become citizens, not subjects; then there is hope that the Chechens, like other non-Russians and the Russians themselves, will be treated according to Lenin's original promises (which he probably never intended to keep):

Moslems of Russia, Tatars of the Volga and the Crimea, Kirgiz and Sarts of Siberia and Turkestan, Turks and Tatars of Transcaucasia, Chechens and mountain Cossacks! All you, whose mosques and shrines have been destroyed, whose faith and customs have been violated by the Tsars and oppressors of Russia! Henceforward your beliefs and customs, your national and cultural institutions are declared free and inviolable! Build your national life freely and without hindrance. It is your right.[3]

---

[1] A. J. P. Taylor's determinism—in *The Course of German History: A Survey of the Development of German History since 1815* (London: Hamish Hamilton, 1948)—is, of course, unacceptable from a humanistic point of view.

[2] This is the official though imprecise French translation ('*Tsar* de toutes les Russies') of the Russian title *vserossiiskii* ('all-Russian').

[3] 'Appeal to the Muslims of Russia', quoted in R. Conquest, *The Nation Killers: The Soviet Deportation of Nationalities* (London: Macmillan, 1970), p. 32.

APPENDIX A

THE KHASAV YURT TRUCE AGREEMENT BETWEEN THE RUSSIAN FEDERATION AND THE GOVERNMENT OF THE CHECHEN REPUBLIC, 25 AUGUST 1996[1]

JOINT STATEMENT

We, the undersigned,

taking into account the progress achieved towards the ending of the warfare;

endeavouring to create [a] mutually acceptable basis for [a] political solution of the armed conflict;

recognizing that it is prohibited to use armed forces or to threaten the use of force as a means towards the resolution of [the] issue under dispute;

embarking upon the universally recognized right of nations to self-determination, upon the principles of equality, freedom of choice, free expression of will, strengthening of international accord and security of all nations;

exercising the will towards the defence of human and civil rights regardless of his or her nationality, religious affiliation, place of residence and other differences, towards the ending of acts of violence in the relations of political adversaries, while at the same time

embarking upon the Universal Declaration of Human Rights of 1949 and upon the International Pact on Civil and Political Rights of 1966,

---

[1] As published in the Chechnya Official Home Page, http://www.chechnya.org/current/truce.html (no longer available at website—copy in possession of author).

221

have jointly worked out the Rules for Clarifying the Basis for Mutual Relations between the Russian Federation and the Chechen Republic according to which the further peace process shall be developed:

RULES FOR CLARIFYING THE BASIS FOR MUTUAL RELATIONS BETWEEN THE RUSSIAN FEDERATION AND THE CHECHEN REPUBLIC

1. The treaty regulating the basis for mutual relations between the Russian Federation and the Chechen Republic, to be governed by the universally accepted principles and norms of the international law, shall have been reached prior to 31 December 2001.

2. No later than on 1 October 1996, a Joint Commission shall have been formed, constituted by the representatives of the state authorities of the Russian Federation and of the Chechen Republic, the duties of which shall be as follows:

— to assume control over the implementation of the Decree of the President of the Russian Federation issued on 25 June 1996, under no. 985, and to prepare proposals concerning the completion of the withdrawal of the armed forces;

— to initiate joint undertakings directed towards the combat of crime, terrorism and nationalistic and religious prejudices, and to control their implementation;

— to prepare proposals for the reconstruction of currency, fiscal and budgetary mutual relations;

— to prepare for the enactment by the Government of the Russian Federation of the programmes for the rebuilding of the socio-economic infrastructure of the Chechen Republic;

— to control over [sic!] the agreed forms of cooperation of the state authorities and other relevant organizations concerning the supply and distribution of food and medical aid among the population.

3. The legal system of the Chechen Republic is based upon the respect for human and civil rights, upon the right of nations towards self-determination, upon the principles of equal rights of nations, of the priority for civil accord, international peace and security for citizens residing on the territory of the Chechen Republic regardless of their nationality, religious identity and other differences.

4. The Joint Commission shall end its work upon mutual agreement of the parties.

Signed by
A. Lebed
A. Maskhadov
S. Kharlamov
S-Kh. Abumuslirnov

Date of signing 25.08.1996
Place of signing Khasavyurt, Republic of Dagestan

In the presence of the Head of the Special Task Group of the OSCE for Chechnya, Mr T. Guildemann

PEACE TREATY AND PRINCIPLES OF INTERRELATION BETWEEN THE RUSSIAN FEDERATION AND THE CHECHEN REPUBLIC OF ICHKERIA

12 MAY 1997[1]

The esteemed parties to the agreement, desiring to end their centuries-long antagonism and striving to establish firm, equal and mutually beneficial relations, hereby agree

1 to reject forever the use of force or threat of force in resolving all matters of dispute.
2 to develop their relations on generally recognized principles and norms of international law. In doing so, the sides shall inter-act on the basis of specific concrete agreements.
3 This treaty shall serve as the basis for concluding further agreements and accords on the full range of relations.
4 This treaty is written in two copies and both have equal legal power.
5 This treaty is active from the day of signing.

Moscow, 12 May 1997

signed
B. Yeltsin
President of the Russian
Federation

A. Maskhadov
President of the Chechen
Republic of Ichkeria

---

[1] http://www.chechnya-mfa.info/legal/1.htm.

SOURCES

Abdullaev, M. A., *Deiatel'nost'i vozzreniia sheikha Abdurakhmana-Khadzhi i ego rodosloviia*, Makhachkala: Iupiter, 1998.

Abu Manneh, Butrus, 'The Naqshbandiyya-Mujaddidiyya in the Ottoman Lands in the Early 19th Century', *Die Welt des Islams,* XII (1982), pp. 1–12.

Abubakarov, Taymaz, 'Mezhdu avtoritarnostiu i anarkhiei. (Politicheskie dilemmy prezidenta Dudayeva)' in Dmitrii Furman (ed.), *Rossiia i Chechnia. Obschestva i gosudarstva*, Moscow: Sakharov Foundation, 1999.

Aglarov, M. A., *Sel'skaia Obshchina v Nagornom Dagestane v XVII—Nachale XIX v,* Moscow: 'Nauka', 1988.

Ahmadov, Sharpudin, *Imam Mansur. (Norodno-osvoboditel'noe dvizhenie v Chechne i na Severnom Kavkaze v kontse XVIII v.)*, Groznyi: Kniga, 1991.

Ahmadov, Yavus, 'Dvizhenie Kunta Khadzhi', paper delivered at the First International Conference on Shamil and the Anti-Colonial Struggle in the Caucasus, Oxford, March 1991.

————, *Istoriia Chechni s drevneishikh vremen do kontsa XVIII veka,* Moscow: Mir Domu Tvoemu, 2001.

Akademiia Nauk SSSR, Institut Arkheologii and Checheno-Ingushskii Nauchno-Issledovatelskii Institut Istorii, Iazyka i Literatury, *Drevnosti Checheno-Ingushetii*, Moscow: Izdatel'stvo Akademii Nauk SSSR, 1963.

Akayev, Vahit, *Sheikh Kunta Khadzhi: Zhizn' i uchenie*, Groznyi: Nauchno-Issledovatel'skii Institut Gumanitarnykh Nauk Chechenskoi Respubliki, 1994.

Alekhin, Genadii and Anatolii Borovikov, 'Sgusili kraski', *Krasnaia Zvezda*, 9 June 1999, p. 1.

Algar, Hamid, 'A Brief History of the Naqshbandi Order' in Marc Gaborieu, Alexandre Popovic and Thierry Zarcone (eds), *Naqshbandis. Cheminements et situation actuelle d'un ordre mystique musulman*, Istanbul and Paris: ISIS Press, 1990, pp. 3–44.

Allen, William Edward David and Paul Muratoff, *Caucasian Battlefields: A History of the Wars on the Turco-Caucasian Border, 1828–1921*, Cambridge University Press, 1953.

Al'tamirova, Zura, 'Zhizn' v poslevoennoi Chechne' in Dmitrii Furman (ed.), *Rossiia i Chechnia. Obschestva i gosudarstva*, Moscow: Sakharov Foundation, 1999.

Altunay, Ahmet Rafik, *Kafkas Yollarinda* [On the Roads of the Caucasus], Yunus Zeyrek (Hazırlayan), Ankara: Kültür Bakanlığı Yayınları, 1981.

Anchabadze, Georgy, 'The Caucasian Culture of Conduct at War (Traditions and Modernity)', *Caucasian Knot*, 2003.

Anderson, Matthew Smith, *The Eastern Question, 1774–1923: A Study in International Politics*, London: Macmillan, 1966.

Andreev, A. P., 'Vosstanie v Dagestane v 1877 godu', *Istoricheskii Vestnik*, 1903, 11, pp. 548–53.

Arinin, Aleksandr and Mikhail N. Guboglo (eds), *Federalizm vlasti i vlast' federalizma*, Moscow: IntelTekh, 1997.

Avtorkhanov, Abdurakhman, 'The Chechens and the Ingush during the Soviet Period and its Antecedents' in Marie Bennigsen-Broxup (ed.), *The North Caucasus Barrier: The Russian Advance towards the Muslim World*, London: Hurst, 1992, pp. 146–94.

————, *Memuary*, Frankfurt/Main: Posev, 1983.

Aydamirov, Abuzar, *Khronologiia istorii Checheno-Ingushetii*, Groznyi: Kniga, 1991.

Aytbayev, Yu. A. (ed.), *Chechentsy: Istoriia i sovremennost*, Moscow: Mir Domu Tvoemu, 1996.

Baddeley, John Frederick, *The Rugged Flanks of the Caucasus*, Oxford University Press, 1940, 2 vols.

————, *The Russian Conquest of the Caucasus*, London: Longmans, Green, 1908 (reprint London: Curzon Press, 1998).

Barrett, Thomas M., *At the Edge of Empire: The Terek Cossacks and the North Caucasus Frontier, 1700–1860*, Boulder, CO: Westview Press, 1999.

Bennigsen, Alexandre, 'The Qadiriyyah (Kunta Hajji) Tariqah in North-East Caucasus: 1850–1987', *Islamic Culture*, LXII, 2–3 (April–July 1988), pp. 63–78.

————, 'Un mouvement populaire au Caucase du XVIIIe siècle: la "guerre sainte" de Sheikh Mansur (1785–1794). Page mal connue et controversée des relations russo-turques', *Cahiers du Monde Russe et Soviétique*, V, 2 (April–June 1964), pp. 175–9.

Bennigsen, Alexandre and Chantal Lemercier-Quelquejay, '"L'Islam parallèle" en Union Soviétique. Les organisations soufies dans la République tchétcheno-inguche', *Cahiers du Monde Russe et Soviétique*, XXI, 1 (January–March 1980), pp. 49–63.

————, *Le sufi et le commissaire. Les confréries musulmanes en URSS*, Paris: Seuil, 1986.

Bennigsen, Alexandre and S. Enders Wimbush, *Muslims of the Soviet Empire: A Guide*, London: Hurst, 1985.

Bennigsen-Broxup, Marie, 'After the Putsch, 1991' in Marie Bennigsen-Broxup (ed.), *The North Caucasus Barrier: The Russian Advance towards the Muslim World*, London: Hurst, 1992, pp. 219–40.

————, 'The Last *Ghazawat*: the 1920–1921 Uprising' in Marie Bennigsen-Broxup (ed.), *The North Caucasus Barrier: The Russian Advance towards the Muslim World*, London: Hurst, 1992, pp. 112–45.

Berreby, Jean-Jacques, *Histoire mondiale du pétrole*, Paris: Éditions du Pont Royal, 1957.

Bersanova, Zalpa, 'Sistema tsennostei sovremennykh chechentsev (po materialam oprosov)' in Dmitrii Furman (ed.), *Rossiia i Chechnia. Obschestva i gosudarstva*, Moscow: Sakharov Foundation, 1999, pp. 223–49.

Berzhe, Adol'f Petrovich *et al.* (eds), *Akty Sobrannye Kavkazskoi Arkheografìcheskoi Kommissiei. (Arkhiv glavnogo upravleniia namestnika kavkazskogo)*, Tbilisi: Tipografìia Kantselarii Glavnonachal'stvuiushchedo Grazhdanskoi Chast'iu na Kavkaze, 1866–1904, 12 vols.

Birch, Julian, 'Ossetia: A Caucasian Bosnia in Microcosm', *Central Asian Survey*, 14, 1 (1995), pp. 43–74.

Bitsoyev, Said-Emin, 'Ia ne dolzhen byl vyzhit', *Respublika* (Groznyi), 22 February 1992.

Bitsoyev, Said-Emin Bitsoyev, 'Khaibakh—aul, kotorogo net,' in Yu. A Aydayev (ed.), *Chechentsy: Istoriia i sovremennost'*, Moscow: Mir Domu Tvoemu, 1996, pp. 275–7.

———— *Khaibakh: Sledtsvie prodolzhaetsia*, Groznyl (n.p.), 1994.

Blanch, Leslie, *The Sabres of Paradise*, London: John Murray, 1960.

Blank, Stephen, 'The Formation of the Soviet North Caucasus, 1918–1924', *Central Asian Survey*, 12, 1 (March 1993), pp. 13–32.

Bobrovnikov, Vladimir Olegovich, 'Voenno-narodnoe upravlenie v Dagestane i Chechne: istoriia i sovremennost' in Galina Georgievna Lisitsyna and Ia. A. Gordin (eds), *Rossiia i Kavkaz skvoz' dva veka*, St Petersburg: Zhurnal 'Zvezda', 2001, pp. 91–107.

Brauer, Birgit B., 'Chechens and the Survival of their Cultural Identity in Exile', *Journal of Genocide Research*, 4, 3 (September 2002), pp. 387–400.

Brooks, Willis, 'Russia's Conquest and Pacification of the Caucasus: Relocation Becomes a Pogrom in the post-Crimean War Period', *Nationalities Papers*, 23, 4 (1995), pp. 675–86.

Brown, John Porter, *The Dervishes: or, Oriental Spiritualism*, London: Trübner & Co., 1868.

Brown, Sarah, 'Modern Tales of the Russian Army', *World Policy*, 14, 2 (January 1997), pp. 61–71.

Bryan, Fanny E. B., 'Anti-Religious Activities in the Chechen-Ingush Republic of the USSR and the Survival of Islam', *Central Asian Survey*, 3, 2 (1984), pp. 99–116.

————, 'Internationalism, Nationalism and Islam' in Marie Bennigsen-Broxup (ed.), *The North Caucasus Barrier: The Russian Advance towards the Muslim World*, London: Hurst, 1992, pp. 195–218.

Bubakhin L. O., and Dolkhan A.-A. Khozhayev, 'Potomki Nefertiti', *Komsomol'skoe plemia* (Groznyi), 11 February 1989, p. 10.

Bugai, N. F., *The Deportation of Peoples in the Soviet Union*, New York: Nova Science, 1996.

———, *Iosif Stalin-Lavrentiiu Berii: 'ikh nado deprtirovat'*, Moscow: 'Druzhba Narodov', 1992.

———, L. *Beriia-I. Stalinu: 'Soglasno Vashemu ukazaniiu'*, Moscow: AIRO XX, 1995.

———, '"Pogruzheny v eshelony i otpravleny k mestam poselenii." L. Beriia-I. Stalinu', *Istoria SSSR*, 1991, 1, pp. 143–60.

———, 'Pravda o deportatsii chechnskogo i ingushskogo narodov', *Voprosy Istorii*, 1990, 7, pp. 32–44.

———, '40–50e gody: posledstviia deportatsii narodov. (Svidel'stvuiut arkhivy NKVD-MVD SSSR)', *Istoria SSSR*, 1992, 1, pp. 122–43.

Bunich, Igor L'vovich, *Khronika chechenskoi boini i shest' dnei v Budennovske*, St Petersburg: Oblik, 1995.

Butbay, Mustafa, *Vospominanina o Kavkaze. Zametki turetskogo razvedchika*, transl. Z. A. Buniatov, Makhachkala: Biblioteka zhurnala 'Nash Dagestan', 1993.

Campbell, Robert W., *The Economics of Soviet Oil and Gas*, Baltimore: Johns Hopkins University Press, 1968.

Checheno-Ingushskaia ASSR za 50 let. Statistitechskii sbornik, Groznyi: Checheno-Ingushskoe Knizhnoe Izdatel'stvo, 1967.

Chenciner, Robert, *Daghestan: Tradition and Survival*, London: Curzon Press, 1997.

Chesnov, Ian V., 'Byt' Chechentsem. Lichnost' i etnicheskie identifikatsii naroda' in Dmitrii Furman (ed.), *Rossiia i Chechnia. Obschestva i gosudarstva*, Moscow: Sakharov Foundation, 1999, pp. 63–101.

———, 'Civilization and the Chechen', *Anthropology and Archaeology of Eurasia*, 34, 3 (winter 1995–6), pp. 28–40.

———, 'Zikr na ploshchadi svobody' in *K novym podkhodam v otechestvennoi etnologii. Reziume dokladov i vystuplenii*, Groznyi: Nauchno-Issledovatel'skii Institut Gumanitarnykh Nauk Chechenskoi Respubliki, 1992, pp. 54–6.

Conquest, Robert, *The Nation Killers: The Soviet Deportation of Nationalities*, London: Macmillan, 1970.

Denikin, A., *The White Army*, transl. Catherine Zvegintzov, Gulf Breeze, FL: Academic International Press, 1973.

Derluguian, Georgi M., *Bourdieu's Secret Admirer in the Caucasus*, London: Verso, 2004.

———, 'Che Guevaras in Turbans', *New Left Review*, 237 (September–October 1999), pp. 3–27.

————, 'Chechnskaia revoliutsiia i chechenskaia istoriia' in Dmitrii Furman (ed.), *Rossiia i Chechnia. Obschestva i gosudarstva*, Moscow: The Sakharov Foundation, 1999, pp. 197–222.

Djilas, Milovan, *Conversations with Stalin*, transl. Michael B. Petrovich, London: Hart-Davis, 1962.

Donogo, Hajji Murad, 'Slovo o Nazhmudine Gotsinskom', *Akhul'go*, 3 (March 1999), pp. 4–6.

Drozdov, I., 'Nachalo deiatel'nosti Shamilia (1834–1836 g.)', *Kavkazskii Sbornik*, XX (1899), pp. 250–98.

Dubrovin, N. F., *Istoriia voiny i vladychestra russkikh na Kavkaze*, St Petersburg: Tipografiia Departmenta Udelov, 1871–88.

Dudayev, Johar, 'Doklad predsedatelia ispolkama obshchenatsional'nogo s'ezda chechenskogo naroda, generala Dzhokhara Dudaeva, g. Groznyi, 8 iiun' 1991 g.', *Bart* (Groznyi), 6 (010), June 1991, p. 3.

Dunlop, John B., *Russia Confronts Chechnya: Roots of a Separatist Conflict*, Cambridge University Press, 1998.

Dunsterville, L. C., *The Adventures of Dunsterforce*, London: Edward Arnold, 1920 (2nd impression).

Eremenko, I. N. and Iu. D. Novikov (eds), *Rossiia i Chechnia, 1990–1997. Dokumenty svidetel'stvuiut*, Moscow: Vserossiiskoe obshchestverno-politicheskoe dvizhenie 'Dukhovnoe nasledie', 1997.

Ermolov, N. P. (ed.), *Zapiski Alekseia Petrovicha Ermolova*, Moscow: Universitetskaia tipografiia, 1865–8.

Esadze, Semen, *Istoricheskaia zapiska ob upravlenii Kavkazom*, Tbilisi: Tipografiia Gutenberg, 1907.

Eshba, E., *Aslanbek Sheripov. (Opyt kharakteristiki lichnosti i deiatel'nosti A. Sheripova v sviazi s narodno-revoliutsionnym dvizheniem v Chechne)*, Groznyi: Serlo, 1929 (2nd edn, corrected and enlarged).

Essad Bey (pseud. of Leo Noussimbaum), *L'épopée du pétrole*, transl. Maurice Ténine, Paris: Payot, 1934.

Fadeev, Rostislav Andreevich, 'Pis'ma Rostislava Andreevicha Fadeeva k rodnym', *Ruskii Vestnik*, 1897, 8, pp. 1–14; 9, pp. 1–17; 10, pp. 63–9; 11, pp. 88–96.

Flemming, William, 'The Deportation of the Chechen and Ingush Peoples: A Critical Examination' in Ben Fawkes (ed.), *Russia and Chechnia: the Permanent Crisis: Essays on Russo-Chechen Relations.* London: Macmillan, 1998, pp. 65–86.

Gaborieu, Marc, Alexandre Popvic and Thierry Zarcone (eds), *Naqshbandis. Cheminements et situation actuelle d'un ordre mystique musulman*, Istanbul and Paris: Isis Press, 1990.

Gabrichidze M. M. *et al.* (eds), *Shamil—stavlennik sultanskoi Turtsii i angliiskikh kolonizatorov*, Tbilisi: Gosizdat Gruzinskoi SSR—Sektor Politicheskoi Literatury, 1953.

Gadzhiev, V. G. and Kh. Kh. Ramazanov (eds), *Dvizhenie gortsevv severo-vostochnogo Kavkaza v 20–50 gg. XIX v. Sbornik dokumentov,* Makhachkala: Dagestanskoe Kniznoe Izdatel'stvo, 1959.

Gagarin, A. I., 'Zapiski o Kavkaze', *Voennyi Sbornik,* 1906, 2, pp. 25–38; 3, pp. 15–32; 4, pp. 13–32.

Gakayev, Jabrail, *Ocherki Politicheskoi Istorii Chechni (XX vek),* Moscow: Chechenskii Kul'turnyi Tsentr, 1997.

———, 'Put' k chechnskoi revoliutsii' in Dmitrii Furman (ed.), *Rossiia i Chechnia. Obschestva i gosudarstva,* Moscow: Sakharov Foundation, 1999.

Gall, Carlotta and Thomas de Waal, *Chechnya: Calamity in the Caucasus,* New York University Press, 1998.

Gammer, Moshe, 'Shamil's Most Successful Offensive: Daghestan 1843', *Journal of the Institute of Muslim Minority Affairs* (King Abdul Aziz University, Jeddah), 12, 1 (January 1991), pp. 41–54.

———, 'The Siege of Akhulgoh: A Reconstruction and Reinterpretation', *Asian and African Studies* (Haifa), 25, 2 (July 1991), pp. 103–18.

———, 'A Switzer in the Caucasus: Faesy's Campaigns in Chechnia and Daghestan', *Middle Eastern Studies,* 30, 3 (July 1994), pp. 668–82.

———, 'Russian Strategies in the Conquest of Chechnia and Daghestan, 1825–1859' in Marie Bennigsen-Broxup (ed.), *The North Caucasus Barrier: The Russian Advance towards the Muslim World,* London: Hurst, 1992, pp. 45–61.

———, 'A Forgotten Hero of the Caucasian War—General Freytag', *Annual of the Society for the Study of Caucasia,* 4–5 (1992–3), pp. 33–43.

———, *Muslim Resistance to the Tsar: Shamil and the Conquest of Chechnia and Daghestan,* London: Frank Cass, 1994.

———, 'A Preliminary to Decolonizing the Historiography of Shaykh Mansur', *Middle Eastern Studies,* 32, 1 (January 1996), pp. 191–202.

———, 'The Qadiriyya in the Northern Caucasus', *Journal of the History of Sufism,* 1–2 (April–May 2000), pp. 275–94.

———, 'Nationalism and History: Rewriting the Chechen National Past' in Bruno Coppieters and Michel Huysseune (eds), *Secession, History and the Social Sciences,* VUB Brussels University Press, 2002, pp. 117–40.

———, 'Vorontsov's 1845 Campaign: A Reconstruction and Reinterpretation' in Moshe Gammer (ed.), *Political Thought and Political History: Studies in Memory of Elie Kedourie,* London: Frank Cass, 2003, pp. 71–90.

———, '"Proconsul of the Caucasus": A Re-examination of Yermolov', *Social Evolution and History,* 2, 1 (March 2003), pp. 166–84.

———, 'The Beginnings of the Naqshbandiyya in Daghestan and the Russian Conquest of the Caucasus', *Die Welt des Islams,* 34 (1994), pp. 204–17.

————, 'Between Mecca and Moscow: Islam, Politics and Political Islam in Chechnya and Daghestan', *Middle East Studies* (due 2006).

Gatagova, Liudmila Sultanovna, 'Kavkaz posle kavkazskoi voiny: etnopoliticheskii aspekt' in Galina Georgievna Lisitsyna and Ia. A. Gordin (eds), *Rossiia i Kavkaz skvoz' dva veka*, St Petersburg: Zhurnal 'Zvezda', 2001, pp. 47–57.

Geiss, Paul Georg, 'The Problems of Political Order in Contemporary Kazakhstan and Turkmenistan' in Moshe Gammer (ed.), *The Caspian Region*, vol. I: *A Re-emerging Region*, London: Routledge, 2004, pp. 203–27.

German, Tracey C., *Russia's Chechen War*, London: Routledge Curzon, 2003.

Golovin, Evgenii Aleksandrovich 'Ocherk polozheniia voennykh del na kavkaze s nachala 1838 do kontsa 1842 goda', *Kavkazskii Sbornik*, II (1877), pp. 1–74.

Goytakin Rasu of Benoy, 'Istoriia o tom kak Albik–Khadzhi stal imamom', *Respublika*, 8 August 1991, pp. 6–7. Transl. from Arabic into Chechen A. Nazhaev (in 1928); transl. from Chechen into Russian D. Khozhaev.

Grechko, Andrei Antonovich, *Bitva za Kavkaz*, Moscow: Izdatel'stvo Ministerstva Oborony SSSR, 1973 (2nd edn).

Helsinki Watch, *'Punished Peoples' of the Soviet Union: The Continuing Legacy of Stalin's Deportations*, A Helsinki Watch Report, New York, and Washington, DC: Human Rights Watch, September 1991.

Henkin, Yagil, 'Tsalafim bShetah 'Ironi: Dugmat Chechnya [Snipers in Urban Area: the Example of Chechnya]', *Ma'arakhot*, 384 (July 2002), pp. 50–61.

————, 'Lo Gerila: haMilhamma haChechenit haRishona veTe'oriyot "haMilhama heHadasaha" [Not Guerrilla: The First Chechen War and the "New Wars" Theories]', Jerusalem, 2003 (MA thesis).

Henze, Paul B., 'Circassian Resistance to Russia' in Marie Bennigsen-Broxup (ed.), *The North Caucasus Barrier: The Russian Advance towards the Muslim World*, London: Hurst, 1992, pp. 99–105.

Hobsbawm, E. J., *Primitive Rebels: Studies in Archaic Forms of Social Movement in the 19th and 20th Centuries*, New York: W. W. Norton, 1959.

Hourani, Albert, 'Sufism and Modern Islam: Maulana Khalid and the Naqshbandi Order' in Albert Hourani, *The Emergence of the Middle East*, London: Macmillan, 1981, pp. 75–89.

Human Rights Watch, *The Ingush-Ossetian Conflict in the Prigorodnyi Region*, New York and London: Human Rights Watch, 1993.

————, *Russia: Last Seen: Continued "Disappearances" in Chechnya*, New York: Human Rights Watch, 2002.

————, *Russia/Chechnya: the "Dirty War" in Chechnya: Forced Disappearances, Torture, and Summary Executions*, New York: Human Rights Watch, 2001.

Inalchic, Halil, "Cerkes", *EI 2*, vol. II, Leiden: E. J. Brill, 1983, pp. 21–5.

International Alert, Fact-Finding Mission to Chechnia (24 September–3 October 1992), *Report*, London: International Alert, n.d. (1993)

Iasnyi, Viktor Kogan and Diana Zisserman-Brodsky, 'Chechen Separatism' in Metta Spencer (ed.), *Separatism, Democracy and Disintegration*, Lanham, MD: Rowman and Littlefield, 1998, pp. 205–26.

Isayev, E., 'Iz 'osoboi papki Stalina.' O deportatsii Chechentsev i Ingushei' in Yu. A. Aytbayev (ed.), *Chechentsy: Istoriia i Sovremennost*, Moscow: Mir Domu Tvoemu, 1996, pp. 261–74.

Ismail-Zade, Daliara Ibrahimovna, 'I. I. Vorontsov-Dashkov, namestnik kavkazskii' in Galina Georgievna Lisitsyna and Ia. A. Gordin (eds), *Rossiia i Kavkaz skvoz' dva veka*, St Petersburg: Zhurnal 'Zvezda', 2001, pp. 138–49.

———, 'Zemli… budut otdany vam v vechnoe vladenie…' in Galina Georgievna Lisitsyna and Ia. A. Gordin (eds), *Rossiia i Kavkaz skvoz' dva veka*, St Petersburg: Zhurnal 'Zvezda', 2001, pp. 357–68.

Iurov, A., '1844-i god na Kavakaze', *Kavkazskii Sbornik*, VII (1883), pp. 157–382.

Iurov, A. and N. V., '1840, 1841 i 1842-i gody na Kavkaze', *Kavkazskii Sbornik*, X (1886), pp. 205–404; XI (1887), pp. 187–301; XII (1888), pp. 217–344; XIII (1889), pp. 335–424; XIV (1890), 303–444.

Ivanenkov, N. S., *Gornye Chechentsy. Kul'turno-ekonomicheskoe issledovanie Chechenskogo raiona Nagornoi polosy Terskoi oblasti*, Vladikavkaz: Terskoe Oblastnoe Pravlenie, 1910.

Ivanov, A. I., 'Natsional'no-osvoboditel'noe dvizhenie v Chechne i Dagestane v 60–70 kh gg. XIX v.', *Istoricheskie Zapiski*, 12 (1941), pp. 165–99.

———, 'Vosstanie v Chechne v 1877 g.', *Istoricheskie Zapiski*, 10 (1941), pp. 280–94.

Ivanov, Sergei and Vakhtang Shelia, 'Talebany idut!', *Kommersant*, 31, 1997.

'Iz arkhiva Iosifa Stalina', *Nezavisimaia Gazeta*, 29 February 2000.

Jersild, Austin Lee, 'Imperial Russification: Dagestani Mountaineers in Russian Exile, 1877–83', *Central Asian Survey*, 19, 1 (March 2000), pp. 5–16.

———, 'From Savagery to Citizenship: Caucasian Mountaineers and Muslims in the Russian Empire' in Daniel R. Brower and Edward J. Lazzerini (eds), *Russia's Orient: Imperial Boundaries and Peoples, 1700–1917*, Bloomington: Indiana University Press, 1976, pp. 101–14.

Jonson, Lena and Esenov Murad (eds), *Chechnya: the International Community and Strategies for Peace and Stability*, Stockholm: Swedish Institute of International Affairs, 2000.

Jurgaev, Mahomed and Oleg Jurgaev, *Krugi ada*, Groznyi, n.p., 1989.

Jurgayev, Oleg, 'Zhutkaia taina Galanchozha', *Ekho Chechni* (Groznyi), 12 February 1992.

K., 'Levyi flang Kavkazskoi linii v 1848 godu', *Kavkazskii Sbornik,* IX (1885), pp. 368–475; X (1886), pp. 405–96; XI (1887), pp. 303–463.

Kadir, Zulfiye, 'The Rise of Political Islam in Russia' (unpublished paper in author's possession).

Kakahasanov, G. I., A.-H. S. Hajiev, S. Ch. Asil'darov, L. G. Kaimarazova and I. M. Musaev (eds), *Soiuz Ob"edinenykh Gortsev Severnogo Kavkaza i Dagestana (1917–1918 gg.), Gorskaia Respublika (1918–1920 gg.). (Dokumenty i materialy),* Makhachkala: Dagestanskii Nauchnyi Tsentr Rossiiskoi Akademii Nauk, Institut Istorii, Arkheologii i Etnografii, 1994.

Kamaisky, Alex, 'Ha Tmurot bHitpathut haHevra ha'Azerit tahat haHashpa'a haRusit veHishtaqfutan baHistoriografiya ha'Azerit haModernit [The Changes in the Development of Azeri Society under Russian Influence and their Reflection in Modern Azeri Historiography]', Tel Aviv, 1997 (MA thesis).

Karataeva, M. A., 'Reaktsionnaia ideologiia musul'manskogo dukhovenstva Checheno-Ingushetii i bor'ba s nei v 1920–1931 gg.', *Sotsiologiia, Ateizm, Religiia* (Groznyi), I, 1 (1972), pp. 93–112.

Karcha, Ramazan, 'The Peoples of the North Caucasus' in Nikolai K. Deker and Andrei Lebed (eds), *Genocide in the USSR: Studies in Group Destruction,* Munich: Institute for the Study of the USSR, 1958, pp. 36–48.

Karpat, Kemal, 'The Hijra from Russia and the Caucasus' in D. F. Eickelman and J. Piscatori (eds), *Muslim Travellers: Pilgrimage, Migration, and the Religious Imagination,* London: Routledge, 1990, pp. 132–5.

Katysheva, M., 'Sud'ba cheloveka', *Golos Chechenskoi Respubliki* (Groznyi), 30 May 1992.

Kazemzadeh, Firuz, *The Struggle for Transcaucasia (1917–1921),* Oxford: George Ronald and New York: Philosophical Library, 1951.

Kemper, Michael, 'Daghestani Shaykhs and Scholars in Russian Exile: Networks of Sufism, Fatwas and Poetry' in Moshe Gammer and David J. Wasserstein (eds), *Daghestan in the World of Islam,* Helsinki: Finnish Academy of Sciences, forthcoming.

Kenez, Peter, *Civil War in South Russia, 1918: The First Year of the Volunteer Army,* Berkeley: University of California Press, 1971.

———, *Civil War in South Russia, 1919–1920: The Defeat of the Whites,* Berkeley: University of California Press, 1977.

Khanin, Vladimir (Ze'ev), 'Clientalism, Corruption and Struggle for Power in Central Asia: The Case of Kyrgyzstan' in Moshe Gammer (ed.), *The Caspian Region,* vol. I: *A Re-emerging Region,* London: Routledge, 2004, pp. 181–202.

Khazanov, Anatoly, 'A Last-Minute Postscript: The Chechen Crisis (as of May 21, 1995)' in Anatoly Khazanov, *After the USSR: Ethnicity, National-*

ism and Politics in the Commonwealth of Independent States, Madison: University of Wisconsin Press, 1995, pp. 212–29.

————, *Nomads and the Outside World,* transl. Julia Crookenden, Cambridge University Press, 1983.

Khozhayev, Dolkhan, 'Chechnia v russko-kavkazskoi voine', S'olzhe Qala, 1991 (book MS. in author's possession).

'Khronika chechenskogo vosstaniia 1877 g.', *Terskii Sbornik,* I, 1, pp. 1–92.

Kolosov, Leonid Nikolaevich, *Slavnyi Beibulat. Istoriko-biograficheskii ocherk,* Groznyi: Kniga, 1991.

Korol'kov, M. Ia., 'Sheikh Mansur anapskii. (Epizod iz pervykh let zavoevaniia Kavkaza)', *Russkaia Starina,* 1914, 5, pp. 410–17.

Kovalevskii, G. I., *Vosstanie v Chechne i Dagestane v 1877–1878 godakh,* St Petersburg, 1912.

Kozlov, Vladimir A., *Mass Uprisings in the USSR. Protests and Rebellion in the Post-Stalin Years,* Armonk, NY: M. E. Sharpe, 2002.

Krivenko, Vasilii S., 'Vosstanie v Dagestane v 1877 godu', *Russkii Vestnik,* 1892, 3, pp. 167–84.

Krutikov, Evgenii, 'Shariatskogo suda v Chechne net. To, chto proiskhodit, osnovano na "zakony gor"', *Segodnia,* 20 September 1997, pp. 1, 3.

Kudriavtsev, Alexei, "Democratic Values and Political Reality in Chechnya, 1991–1999" in Yaacov Ro'i (ed.), *Democracy and Pluralism in Muslim Eurasia,* London: Frank Cass, 2004, pp. 359–73.

Kusheva, E. N., *Russko-Chechenskie Otnosheniia. Vtoraia polovina XVI–XVII v. Sbornik Dokumentov,* Rossiiskaia Akademiia Nauk, Institut Etnologii i Antropologii im. N. N. Miklukho-Maklaia and Rossiiskii Gosudarstvennyi Arkhiv Drevnikh Aktov, Moscow: Vostochnaia Literatura-RAN, 1997.

Lanskoy, Miriam, 'Daghestan and Chechnya: the Wahhabi Challenge to the State', *SAIS Review,* 22, 2 (2002), pp. 167–92.

Layton, Susan, 'Nineteenth Century Russian Mythology of Caucasian Savagery' in Daniel R. Brower and Edward J. Lazzerini (eds), *Russia's Orient: Imperial Boundaries and Peoples, 1700–1917,* Bloomington: Indiana University Press, 1976, pp. 80–99.

————, *Russian Literature and Empire: Conquest of the Caucasus from Pushkin to Tolstoy,* Cambridge University Press, 1994.

Leeuw, Charles van der, *Oil and Gas in the Caucasus and Caspian: A History,* London: Curzon Press, 2000.

Lermontov, Mikhail, *The Demon and Other Poems,* transl. Eugene M. Kayden, Yellow Springs, OH: Antioch Press, 1965.

Lermontov, Mikhail Iur'evich, 'Izmail Bey', transl. Susan Layton, *Russian Literature and Empire: Conquest of the Caucasus from Pushkin to Tolstoy,* Cambridge University Press, 1994, p. 142.

Lewis, Bernard, *The Middle East and the West*, New York: Harper and Row, 1966.

L'ianov, Igor', 'Ofitserov GRU podozrevaiut v organizatsii teraktov', *Kommersant*, 4 June 1999, p. 1.

Lieven, Anatol, *Chechnya: Tombstone of Russian Power*, New Haven and London: Yale University Press, 1998.

Lisitsyna, Galina Georgievna, 'Dva dokumenta o polozhenii na Kavkaze' in Galina Georgievna Lisitsyna and Ia. A. Gordin (eds), *Rossiia i Kavkaz skvoz' dva veka*, St Petersburg: Zhurnal 'Zvezda', 2001, pp. 287–339.

————, 'Kavkazskii komitet—vysshee gosudarstvennoe uchrezhdenie dlia upravleniia Kavkazom (1845–1882)' in Galina Georgievna Lisitsyna and Ia. A. Gordin (eds), *Rossiia i Kavkaz skvoz' dva veka*, St Petersburg: Zhurnal 'Zvezda', 2001, pp. 154–68.

Luzbetac, Lewis J., *Marriage and Family in Caucasia: A Contribution to the Study of North Caucasian Ethnology and Customary Law*, Vienna-Mödling: St Gabriel's Mission Press, 1951.

Mahomeddadayev, Amirkhan, 'Dagestanskaia diaspora v Turtsii i Sirii. Genezis i problemy assimiliatsii', Makhachkala, 1996 (candidate dissertation).

Mahomedov, M., 'Nota Nazhmudina Gotsinskogo Sovetskomu pravitel'stvu', *Akhul'go*, 3 (November 1999), pp. 7–9.

Mahomedov, R. M., *Vosstanie gortsev Dagestana v 1877 g.*, Makhachkala: Dagestanskoe Knizhnoe Izdatel'stvo, 1940.

Mamiev, Kh. M., *Reaktsionnaia sushchnost' miuridizma*, Groznyi: Checheno-Ingushskoe Knizhnoe Izdatel'stvo, 1966.

Mankiev, A. A., 'Iz istorii musul'mansko-klerikal'noi mysli v Checheno-Ingushetii', *Sotsiologiia, Ateizm, Religiia* (Groznyi), I, 1 (1972), pp. 36–62.

Markelov, N. V., 'Where Martial Plunder Prowls the Mountains (Prisoners of the Caucasus)', *Russian Social Science Review*, 44, 2 (March/April 2003), pp. 9–26.

Matveeva, Anna, 'Daghestan: Inter-ethnic Tensions and Cross-border Implications' in Moshe Gammer (ed.), *The Caspian Region*, vol. II: *The Caucasus*, London: Routledge, 2004, pp. 122–45.

Meskhidze, Julietta, 'Die Role des Islams beim Kampf um die staatliche Eigenständigkeit Tschetscheniens und Inguschetiens, 1917–1925' in Anke von Kügelgen, Michael Kemper and Allen J. Frank (eds), *Muslim Culture in Russia and Central Asia from the 18th to the Early 20th Centuries*, vol. II: *Inter-Regional and Inter-Ethnic Relations*, Berlin: Klaus Schwarz, 1998, pp. 457–81.

————, 'Imam Shaykh Mansur: a Few Stanzas to a Familiar Portrait', *Central Asian Survey*, 21, 3 (September 2002), pp. 301–24.

————, 'Ob idee Kavkazskoy Konfederazii (1918–1921)', *Istoricheskaia Psikhologiia i Mental'nost'*. *Epokhi*. *Sotsiumi*. *Etnosi*. *Liudi*, St Petersburg: Institut Sotsial'noi Pedagogiki i Psikhologii, 1999, pp. 217–24.

Mitzakis, John, *The Russian Oil Fields and Petroleum Industry*, London: Pall Mall Press, 1911.

Mukhtarov, Uzunhaji, 'Predaniia o Najmudine Gotsinskom v Chechne', *Akhul'go*, 3 (November 1999), p. 18.

Murzayev, Nurdin, *Prodolzhenie Pesni*, transl. into Russian Anisim Krongauz, Moscow: n.p., 1967.

Mutaliev, T., 'Total'naia deportatsiia—zakliuchitel'nyi akt istoricheskoi tragedii narodov', *Serdalo* (Groznyi), 30 May 1992.

Nart (pseud.), 'The Life of Mansur, Great Independence Fighter of the Caucasian Mountain People,' *Central Asian Survey*, vol. 10, no. 1–2 (March–June 1991), p. 83.

Nekrich, Alexandre M., *The Punished Peoples: The Deportation and Fate of Soviet Minorities at the End of the Second World War*, New York: W. W. Norton, 1978.

Nivat, Anne, *Chienne de Guerre: a Woman Reporter Behind the Lines of the War in Chechnya*, transl. Susan Darnton, New York: Public Affairs, 2001.

'Nokhchalla', *The Chechen Times*, 14 April 2003.

'O zhitele Ichkerinskogo okruga Terskoi oblasti aula Kharachoi, Taze Ekmirzaeve', *Sbornik Svedenii o Kavkazskikh Gortsakh*, IV, 4 (1870), pp. 55–62.

Ölçen, Mehmet Ârif, *Vetluga Memoir: A Turkish Prisoner of War in Russia, 1916–1918*, ed. Ali Nejat Ölcen, transl. Gary Leiser, Gainesville: University of Florida Press, 1995.

Omarov, Kh. Kh., 'Vospominaniia Abdurazaka Sogratlinskogo o vosstanii 1877 g.' in D. Kh. Hajieva (ed.), *Izuchenie istorii i kul'tury Dagestana: arkheograficheskii aspekt*. *Sbornik stat'ei*, Makhachkala: Dagestanskii Filiial AN SSSR, Institut Istorii, Iazyka i Literatury im, G. Tsadasy, 1988, pp. 88–100.

Ordzhonikidze, G. K., *Stat'i i rechi v dvukh tomakh*, Institut marksizmaleninizma pri TsK KPSS, Moscow: Gosudarstennoe Izdatel'stvo Politicheskoi Literatury, 1956.

Oshaev, Khalid, *Brest—oreshek ognennyi*. *Khudozhestvenno-dokumental'naia povest'*, Groznyi: n.p., 1990.

P....v, P., 'Chechentsy vne Chechni', *Sbornik svedenii o terskoi oblasti*, 1878, I.

Parova, Larisa, 'Dokumenty svidetel'stvuiut: Istochniki istorii vyseleniia Vainakhov v 1944 godu.', *Serdalo* (Groznyi), 22, 25, 27 February 1992.

50 let avtonomii Checheno-Ingushetii. *Statisticheskii sbornik*, Groznyi: Checheno-Ingushskoe Knizhnoe Izdatel'stvo, 1967.

Pogodin, M., *Aleksei Petrovich Ermolov. Materialy dlia ego biografii*, Moscow: Universitetskaia Tipografiia, 1863.

Pohl, J. Otto, *Ethnic Cleansing in the USSR, 1937–1949*, Westport, CT: Greenwood Press, 1999.

———, *The Stalinist Penal System. A Statistical History of Soviet Repression and Terror, 1930–1953*, Jefferson, NC: McFarland, 1997.

Pohl, Michaela, "'It Cannot Be that Our Graves Will Be There:" The Survival of Chechen and Ingush Deportees in Kazakhstan, 1944–1957', *Journal of Genocide Research*, 4, 3 (September 2002), pp. 401–30.

Politkovskaya, Anna, *A Dirty War: A Russian Reporter in Chechnya*, transl. and ed. John Crowfoot; intr. Thomas de Waal, London: Harvill Press, 2001.

Potto, Vasilii Aleksandrovich, *Kavkazskaia voina v otdel'nykh ocherkakh, epizodakh, legendakh i biografiiakh*, St Petersburg: Tipografiia R. Golike, 1885–7.

Pushkin, Alexandr Sergeevich, 'Kavkazskii plennik,' transl. Susan Layton in *Russian Literature and Empire: Conquest of the Caucasus from Pushkin to Tolstoy*, Cambridge University Press, 1994, p. 101.

———, *The Poems, Prose and Plays of Alexander Pushkin*, ed. Avraham Yarmolinsky, transl. Babette Deutsch, New York: The Modern Library, 1936.

Raynolds, Michael, 'The Ottoman-Russian Struggle for Eastern Anatolia and the Caucasus, 1908–1918: Identity, Ideology and the Geopolitical World Order', PhD dissertation, Princeton University, 2003.

Represirovannye narody: Istoriia i sovremennost'. (Tezisy dokladov i soobshchenii Rossiiskoi nauchno-prakticheskoi konferentsii, 28–29 maia 1992 g.), Elista, 1992.

Rhinelander, Laurence Hamilton, *Prince Michael Vorontsov, Viceroy to the Tsar*, Montreal: McGill-Queen's University Press, 1990.

Ro'i, Yaacov, *Islam in the Soviet Union: From World War II to Gorbachev*, London: Hurst, 2000.

Rywkin, Michael 'The Communist Party and the Sufi Tarikat in the Checheno-Ingush Republic', *Central Asian Survey*, 10, 1–2 (1991), pp. 133–46.

———, 'Power and Ethnicity: Party Stuffing in the Autonomous Republics of the Caucasus in the Middle 1980s', *Central Asian Survey*, 12, 3 (1993), pp. 347–64.

Salibi, Kemal S., *A House of Many Mansions: The History of Lebanon Reconsidered*, London: I. B. Tauris, 1988.

Samih, Aziz, *Büyük Harpte Kafkas Cephesi Hattralan* (Memoirs of the Caucasus Front in the Great War), Ankara (?): Büyük Erkanı Harbiye Matbaası, 1934.

Samurskii, N., *Dagestan*, Moscow and Leningrad: Gospolitizdat, 1925.

Seely, Robert, *Russo-Chechen Conflict, 1800–2000: a Deadly Embrace*, London: Frank Cass, 2001.

Semenov, N., 'Khronika Chechenskogo vosstaniia 1877 goda,' Appendix to *Terskii sbornik*, Vypusk I, Vladikavkaz, 1891.

Shah-Kazemi, Reza, *Crisis in Chechnia: Russian Imperialism, Chechen Nationalism, Militant Sufism*, London: Islamic World Report, 1995.

Shematova, Sanobar, 'Tak nazyvaemye vakhkhabity' in Dmitrii Furman (ed.), *Rossiia i Chechnia. Obschestva i gosudarstva*, Moscow: Sakharov Foundation, 1999.

———, 'The War for Chechen Oil', *Capitalism, Nature, Socialism*, 14, 1 (March 2003), pp. 113–23.

Sheripov, A., 'Revoliutsiia v Chechne', *Narodnaia Vlast*, 3 August 1918.

Siren, Pontus, 'The Battle for Grozny: The Russian Invasion of Chechnia, December 1994–December 1996' in Ben Fowkes (ed.), *Russia and Chechnia: The Permanent Crisis: Essays on Russo-Chechen Relations*, London: Macmillan Press and New York: St Martin's Press, 1998, pp. 87–169.

Skobtsov, D. E., *Tri goda revoliutsii i grazhdanskoi voiny na Kubani*, Paris: n.p., n.d.

'Slovo o Nazhmudine Gotsinskom', *Akhul'go* (Makhachkala), 3 (November 1999), pp. 4–35.

Smith, Sebastian, *Allah's Mountains. Politics and War in the Russian Caucasus*, London and New York: I. B. Tauris, 1998.

Solzhenitsyn, Aleksandr, *Arkhipelag GULag, 1918–1956. Opyt khudozhestvennogo issledovaniia*, Paris: YMCA Press, 1973.

Swietochowski, Tadeusz, *Russian Azerbaijan, 1905–1920: The Shaping of National Identity in a Muslim Community*, Cambridge University Press, 1985.

Tainy natsional'noi politiki TsK RKP. Stenograficheskii otchet sekretnogo IV soveshchania TsK RKP, 1923 g., Moscow: INSAN, 1992.

Takho-Godi A. A., 'Vosstanie Chechni i Dagestana v 1877 g.', *Sovetskii Dagestan*, 1990, 1 (147), pp. 31–45; 2 (148), pp. 30–8 (reprint from *Krasnyi Dagestan*, 1925, nos 215, 252, 254, 257, 259–262, 269).

———, *Revoliutsiia i kontr-revoliutsiia v Dagestane*. Makhachkala: Nauchno-issledovatel'skii Institut, 1927.

Tanrisever, Oktay F., 'The Impact of the 1994 Russian-Tatar Power-Sharing Treaty on the Post-Soviet Tatar National Identity', *Slovo*, 13, 1 (2001), pp. 43–60.

Taylor, A. J. P., *The Course of German History: A Survey of the Development of German History since 1815*, London: Hamish Hamilton, 1945.

Tereshchenko, A., 'Lzheprorok Mansur,' *Syn otechestva*, 1856, Nos. 15–16.

Thomas, Timothy L., 'Fault Lines and Fractions in the Russian Army', *Orbis* (Philadelphia), 39, 4 (Fall 1995), pp. 531–49.

Tillet, Lowel R., *The Great Friendship: Soviet Historians on the Non-Russian Nationalities*, Chapel Hill: University of North Carolina Press, 1969.

Tishkov, V. A., *Chechnya: Life in a War-Torn Society*, Berkeley: University of California Press, 2004 (shortened English version of *Obshchestvo v vooruzhennom konflikte. Etnografiia chechenskoi voiny*, Moscow: Nauka, 2001).

—————, *The Mind Aflame: Ethnicity, Nationalism and Conflict in and after the Soviet Union*, London: Sage, 1997.

Tkachev, G. A., *Ingushi i Chechentsy v sem'e narodnostei terskoi oblasti*, Vladikavkaz (n.p.), 1911.

Tolstoy, Leo, *Short Novels: Stories of God, Sex and Death*, vol. II, selected and introduced by Ernest J. Simmons, transl. (of *Hadji Murád*) Louise and Aylmer Maude, New York: The Modern Library, 1962.

—————, *The Cossacks and the Raid*. transl. Andrew R. MacAndrew, New York: Signet Books, 1961.

Toltz, Vera, 'New Information about the Deportation of Ethnic Groups in the USSR during World War Two' in J. Garrard and C. Garrard (eds), *World War 2 and the Soviet People*, London: Macmillan, 1993, pp. 161–80.

—————, 'New Information about the Deportation of Ethnic Groups under Stalin', *Report on the USSR*, 16 April 1991, pp. 16–20.

Tsaroeva, Marel, 'Anciennes croyances des Ingouches et des Tchétchènes (peuples du Caucase du Nord)', Paris, 2002 (PhD dissertation).

Tsetkin, Klara [Clara Zetkin], *Kavkaz v ogne*, transl. Shulem and Davydova, Moscow: Moskovskii Rabochii, 1925.

Tuchman, Barbara, *The March of Folly: From Troy to Vietnam*, New York: Knopf, 1984.

Tulin, V., 'Krasnyi "Edelweis"', *Serdalo* (Groznyi), 10 March 1992.

Turgey, A. Uner, 'Circassian Immigration into the Ottoman Empire, 1856–1878' in W. B. Hallaq and D. P. Little (eds), *Islamic Studies Presented to Charles J. Adams*, Leiden: E. J. Brill, 1991, pp. 193–217.

Uralov, Aleksandr [pseud. of A. Avtorkhanov], *Narodoubiistvo v SSSR: Ubiistvo Checheno-Ingushskogo naroda*, Moscow, 1991 (reprint).

—————, *The Reign of Stalin*, transl. I. J. Smith, London: The Bodley Head, 1953.

Usmanov, Lema, *Nepokorennaia Chechnia*, Moscow: Izdatel'skii dom Parus, 1997.

Vachagayev, Mayrbek, 'Chechnia v kavkazskoi voine, 1816–1859', Moscow, 1995 (candidate dissertation).

Vagapov, Yakub, *Vainakhi i Sarmaty. Nakhskii plast v Sarmatskoi onomastike*, Groznyi: Kniga, 1990.

Vakhayev, Lema, 'Politicheskie fantazii v sovremennoi Chechnskoi respublike' in Dmitrii Furman (ed.), *Rossiia i Chechnia. Obschestva i gosudarstva*, Moscow: Sakharov Foundation, 1999, pp. 324–34.

Varavina, E. A. *et al.* (eds.), *Ot vekovoi otstalosti—k sotsializmu. Osushchest-vlenie leninskoi natsional'noý politiki v Checheno-Ingushetii (1917–1941 gg.). Sbornik dokumentov i materialov,* Grozny: Checheno-Ingushskoe Knizhnoe Izdatel'stvo, 1977.

Villari, Luigi, *Fire and Sword in the Caucasus,* London: T. Fisher Unwin, 1906.

Viola, Lynne, *Peasant Rebels under Stalin: Collectivisation and the Culture of Peasent Resistance,* Oxford University Press, 1996.

Voinovich, Vladimir, *The Life and Extraordinary Adventures of Private Ivan Chonkin,* transl. Richard Lourie, New York: Farrar, Straus and Giroux, 1977.

Volkonskii, N. A., F. fon Kliman and P. Bublitskii, 'Voina na vostochnom Kavkaze s 1824 po 1839 g. v sviazi s miuridizmom', *Kavkazkii Sbornik,* X (1886), pp. 1–224, XI (1887), pp. 1–185, XII (1888), pp. 1–216, XIII (1889), pp. 152–334, XIV (1890), pp. 1–211, XV (1894), pp. 506–76, XVI (1895), pp. 405–80, XVII (1896), pp. 323–409, XVIII (1897), pp. 288–351, XX (1899), pp. 97–141.

Volkova, V. A., A. S. Hajiev, V. N. Ganzurov, B. O. Kashkaev, I. K. Keri-mov, M. Kichev, A. M. Mahomedov and A. Efendiev (eds), *Bor'ba za ustanovlenie Sovetskoi vlasti v Dagestane, 1917–1921 gg. Sbornik dokumen-tov i materialov,* Moscow: Izdatel'stvo Akademii Nauk SSSR, 1958.

Welch, Claude Emerson, *Anatomy of Rebellion,* Albany: State University Press of New York, 1980.

Whittock, M., 'Ermolov: Proconsul of the Caucasus', *The Russian Review,* XVIII, 1 (January 1959), pp. 53–60.

Williams, Brian Glyn, 'Commemorating "The Deportation": The Role of Memorialization and Collective Memory in the 1994–96 Chechen War', *Memory and History,* 12, 1 (spring/summer 2000), pp. 101–34.

Wolf, Eric R., *Peasent Wars of the Twentieth Century,* New York: Harper and Row, 1969.

Yah"yaev, L. (ed.), *Belaia kniga. Iz istorii vyseleniia Chechentsev i Ingushei, 1944–1957 gg. Vospominaniia, arkhivnye materialy, fotodokumenty,* Groznyi and Alma Ata: n.p., 1991.

Yandarbiyev, Hamzat, *Prestuplenie Veka,* Groznyi: Kniga, 1992.

Yandarbiyev, Zelimkhan, *Chechnia—bitva za svobodu,* L'vov: 'Svoboda Narodiv' Press, 1996.

Yarichev, Umar, *Lavina vremeni. Stikhi,* Groznyi: n.p., 1990.

Yarmolinsky, Avrahm (ed.), *The Poems, Prose and Plays of Alexander Pushkin,* New York: The Modern Library, 1964.

Zaks, Anna Borisovna, *Tashev-Khadzhi. Spodvizhnik Shamilia,* Groznyi: Kniga, 1992.

Zelkina, Anna, 'Islam and Politics in the North Caucasus', *Religion, State and Society,* 21, 1 (1993), pp. 115–24.

———, *In Quest of God and Freedom: The Sufi Response to the Russian Advances in the North Caucasus (Chechenya and Daghestan),* London: Hurst, 2000.

———, 'The "Wahhabis" of the Northern Caucasus vis-à-vis State and Society: The Case of Daghestan' in Moshe Gammer (ed.), *The Caspian Region,* vol. II: *The Caucasus,* London: Routledge, 2004, pp. 146–78.

Zelkina, Anna, 'Some Aspects of the Teaching of Kunta Hâjjî. On the Basis of a Manuscript by 'Abd al-Salâm written in 1852 AD', *Journal of the History of Sufism,* Vol. 1, 2 (2000), special issue: 'The Qadiriyya Order', pp. 483–507.

Zemskov, V. N., 'Massovoe osvobozhdenie spetsposelentsev i ssyl'nykh (1954–1960 gg)', *Sotsiologicheskie Issledovaniia,* 1991, 1, pp. 5–26.

———, 'Spetsposelentsy. (Po dokumentam NKVD-MVD SSSR)', *Sotsiologicheskie Issledovaniia,* 1990, 2, pp. 3–17.

Zheleznov, B. L., *Pravovoi status Respubliki Tatarstan,* Kazan: Tatarskoe Knizhnoe Izdatel'stvo, 1996.

Zhivaia pamiat'. O zhertvakh stalinskikh repressii, Groznyi: Ministerstvo kul'tury ChIASSR i Checheno-Ingushskii gosudarstvennyi ob'edinennyi muzei, 1991.

Zisserman, Arnold, 'Otryvki iz moikh vospominanii', *Russkii Vestnik,* 1876, 3, pp. 50–105; 4, pp. 416–61; 12, pp. 479–555; 1877, 1, pp. 162–213; 2, pp. 529–78; 3, pp. 80–138; 6, pp. 504–59; 1878, 2, pp. 529–82; 3, pp. 20–52; 4, pp. 585–633; 6, pp. 722–88; 11, pp. 56–97; 1879, 2, pp. 685–734.

Zürrer, Werner, *Kaukasien 1918–1921. Der Kampf der Grossmächte um die Landbrücke zwischen Schwarzen und Kaspischen Meer,* Düsseldorf: Droste Verlag, 1978.

INDEX

243